Praise for
How to Have Impossible Conversations

"This is a self-help book on how to argue effectively, conciliate, gently persuade. The authors admit to getting it wrong in their own past conversations. One by one, I recognize the same mistakes in me. The world would be a better place if everyone read this book."

> —Richard Dawkins, author of *Science in the Soul* and
> *Outgrowing God*

"In a Free Republic there would be no 'impossible conversations,' which begs the question: are we truly free anymore? After reading, listening, and conversing with Peter and James, I am convinced that they are the Galileo's, I. Kant, and even William Tyndale of our time."

> —Glenn Beck

"I thought I knew all I needed to know about conversations and arguments. I was wrong. I just knew a lot about debates and rows. In their insightful and highly readable new book, Peter Boghossian and James Lindsay offer all kinds of ingenious pathways to constructive dialogue.

At a time when public discourse has degenerated into mud-slinging and when campuses favour every kind of diversity except viewpoint diversity, this is an invaluable contribution. I guarantee that reading it will make you more—much more—persuasive."

—Niall Ferguson, Milbank Family Senior Fellow,
The Hoover Institution, Stanford

"In these polarized times, people live inside social media echo chambers of their own extremism, growing ever more self-righteous. This smart, scientifically grounded book, teeming with social and emotional wisdom, teaches how to break that isolation and effectively converse with someone with very different opinions. It will make you more adept at challenging, even changing, someone's beliefs, biases, and sacred values. And it might even pave the way for making some of those changes yourself."

—Robert Sapolsky, John A. and Cynthia Fry Gunn Professor of
Neurology and of Neurosurgery, Stanford University

"Drs. Boghossian and Lindsay offer critical advice regarding how to talk about contentious issues in today's political climate. *How to Have Impossible Conversations* is a necessary guide to navigating disagreements—and building bridges—using approaches backed by evidence and science."

—Debra W. Soh, PhD, science columnist and political
commentator

"This fascinating book provides not only useful instruction on how to talk with someone who thinks differently, it also offers a powerful method of questioning and reducing confidence in unsubstantiated beliefs to help people think about what is true."

—Helen Pluckrose, Editor, *Areo Magazine*

"In the course of my work over the past quarter century I have been having impossible conversations with Holocaust deniers, creationists, anti-vaccination advocates, 9/11 Truthers, chemtrail conspiracy theorists, believers in astrology and ESP, proponents of alternative medicine, religious fundamentalists of many faiths, and dozens more people with whom I disagree vehemently. I've gotten pretty good at it but I had no idea what I was doing until I read *How to Have Impossible Conversations*, a sterling compendium of the most effective techniques of communication. I wish I'd had this important book at the start of my career as I would have saved myself many a fruitless dialogue. This book is the start of healing our contentious and divided age."

—Michael Shermer, Publisher, *Skeptic* magazine, Presidential Fellow Chapman University, author of *Why People Believe Weird Things*, *The Moral Arc*, and *Heavens on Earth*, and for 18 years a monthly columnist for *Scientific American*

"We live in a time when discussing controversial issues, even with good friends, is becoming almost impossible. Peter and James have written an indispensable road map to prevent us from heading off the cliff."

—Dave Rubin, *The Rubin Report*

"We have arrived at an impasse. It is everywhere, and feels permanent. As algorithms steer our attention, we are each locked within a warren of echo chambers. Each day, this digital water we swim in causes a deepening entrenchment of our beliefs, and a growing willingness to caricature our opponents. When forced into contact with the other, we are repelled, indignant. How could anyone be so stupid? And we are shocked to discover the one thing that unites us with them is that they feel exactly the same way in return! It is not hard to spot the danger in this dynamic. It undermines the most basic logic of democracy, and threatens to derange the west, if not the world. But Boghossian and Lindsay have drawn up a plan to bridge the divide. They have bottled an antidote: A how to guide for talking to the enemy. Each drawing on decades of experience having impossible conversations, the authors have written what may be the ultimate instruction manual for crossing enemy lines and living to tell the tale. And not a moment too soon."

—Bret Weinstein, PhD

"There are two ways to participate in civil conversations in our hyper-politicized age—build a time machine, or read this book."

—Marc Andreessen, General Partner, Andreessen Horowitz

How to Have
Impossible
Conversations

How to Have

Impossible

Conversations

A Very Practical Guide

PETER BOGHOSSIAN
& JAMES LINDSAY

hachette
BOOKS

New York

Hachette Go, an imprint of Hachette Books
Hachette Book Group
1290 Avenue of the Americas
New York, NY 10104
HachetteGo.com
Facebook.com/HachetteGo
Instagram.com/HachetteGo

Printed in the United States of America

Previously published by Da Capo Lifelong 2019
First Hachette Go edition 2020

Hachette Books is a division of Hachette Book Group, Inc.
The Hachette Go and Hachette Books name and logos are trademarks of Hachette Book Group, Inc.

The publisher is not responsible for websites (or their content) that are not owned by the publisher.

Print book interior design by Amy Quinn

Library of Congress Cataloging-in-Publication Data has been applied for.

ISBNs: 978-0-7382-8532-0 (trade paperback), 978-0-7382-8534-4 (e-book)

LSC-C

Printing 10, 2024

To our families

Contents

When Conversations Seem Impossible

THIS BOOK IS ABOUT HOW TO COMMUNICATE EFFECTIVELY WITH people who hold radically different beliefs. We live in a divided, polarized era, and we're not talking with each other. The repercussions of this are vast and deep, including the fear of speaking openly and honestly, an inability to solve shared problems, and lost friendships.

CONVERSING WITH AN ASSHOLE

Nearly two decades ago, one of this book's authors, Peter, was discussing affirmative action with a colleague (SDL), a white female who described herself as a liberal. As conversations about controversial topics tend to do, it quickly became heated. Then, as is par for the course in these situations, before long it went downhill, fast. Let's take a look back:

> SDL: *You keep denying that it [affirmative action] is fair.*
> Boghossian: *Yeah, that's because it's not. Who's it fair to?*
> SDL: *I told you already. Traditionally marginalized groups, like African Americans. They're coming from a deficit. They didn't have the same opportunities that you and I had.*
> Boghossian: *But why does that require manufacturing outcomes?*
> SDL: *You sound like a broken record. Because they're Americans, and they deserve better. You don't understand because you've never*

had those struggles. You've gone to good schools and never dealt with even a fraction of what they deal with on a daily basis.

Boghossian: *Let's say you're right. I don't think you are, but let's say you are. What evidence do you have that affirmative action is a way to remedy past injustices?*

SDL: *I don't have any evidence. It's the right thing to do because—*

Boghossian: *So you have no evidence. You have complete confidence in a belief for which you have no evidence.*

SDL: *You're not listening.*

Boghossian: *I am listening. I'm trying to figure out how you could believe so strongly in something with no evidence. Do you think African Americans are better off with Clarence Thomas? Do you think it was a good thing that he's a Supreme Court justice, or would African Americans be better off with a liberal white male?*

SDL: *You're [expletive] annoying. Seriously. I can't believe you're a teacher.*

Boghossian: *I'm sorry you feel that way. Maybe if you could better defend your beliefs you wouldn't be so annoyed with someone who's asking you softball questions.*

SDL: *What do you teach your students?*

Boghossian: *You're not my student. And don't get so upset.*

SDL: *You're an asshole. We're done.*

She was right. Peter wasn't listening; he was annoying; and he was being an asshole. In this brief exchange, he interrupted, used "but" in response to her statements (probably the least wrong thing he did), shifted topics, and didn't answer her questions. He was so focused on winning—and even intellectually embarrassing her—that he ruined the conversation and closed the door to productive future exchanges. SDL walked out on the conversation, but she should have walked away sooner.

Conversations between people who hold radically different beliefs about religion, politics, or values have always been challenging. In that sense, the conversation between Peter and SDL wasn't likely to go smoothly, but it didn't have to go that badly. There are good and bad ways to have conversations with people who hold radically different beliefs, and better approaches aren't just imaginable, they're achievable. Because our current cultural environment is deeply polarized, it's even harder than usual to converse productively across these divisions.

Even since Peter's conversation with SDL nearly twenty years ago, our conversational spaces have fractured, and people have far more difficulty conversing *with* people who hold strongly different views. The bickering and bad faith seem endless: liberals versus conservatives,[1] religious people versus atheists, Democrats versus Republicans (in the United States), this sect versus that, some identity group versus some—or every—other one, and the angry, reactionary, or radical fringes against the bewildered and exhausted center.

Across these divides and many others, people struggle to talk with each other. Sides have been chosen, with battle lines drawn. In this space, few people know how to talk to "the other side," and many consider those who believe differently to be an existential threat—that is, someone whose presence threatens everyone else's very existence. And it seems like there's neither a solution nor an escape. We don't even know how to cope with disagreements over family dinners, yet we find ourselves having heated arguments with acquaintances and on social media. Many people deal with this by hiding from contentious conversations. That's fine, and in certain circumstances it may even be the right thing to do. However, it's only an occasional solution. It's also vital to learn how to have these difficult—even seemingly *impossible*—conversations.

WHAT IS AN IMPOSSIBLE CONVERSATION?

When we say "impossible conversations," we mean conversations that feel futile because they take place across a seemingly unbridgeable gulf of disagreement in ideas, beliefs, morals, politics, or worldviews. We don't mean exchanges that occur in situations in which some people are absolutely unwilling to speak with you. Extreme examples where people are violent or threatening, or adamant in their refusal to talk or even to listen, are *not* what we mean by "impossible conversations." When someone refuses to speak with you, there's no conversation to be had. No book can teach you how to force someone to converse if they won't speak with you. These circumstances, however, are exceptionally rare. Most people will engage you most of the time on most topics.

Although productive discussions with people who hold radically different beliefs can be extremely difficult, they are only literally impossible in fringe cases. Usually, the more invested someone is in their beliefs, the more they want to speak about them. The difficulty in these cases isn't having someone speak to you; it's that a give-and-take seems hopeless because the person across from you fails to speak *with* you and instead speaks *at* you. In such cases, you're viewed as a receptacle to pour ideas into, or as an opponent to be debated and vanquished.

How to Have Impossible Conversations teaches you how to have conversations with anyone who's willing to speak with you, even though those people and those conversations *seem* impossible. Maybe someone's angry, or maybe your political differences seem so profound that a civil discussion feels impossible. But if someone's willing to talk with you, even if they're an extremist, die-hard believer, or intense partisan, this book will teach you how to effectively communicate with them.

Of course, it's easier to not engage in conversations with those who hold different views, but avoidance is not always possible. Someone might approach you; you might find yourself "trapped" with friends or family when religion or politics comes up; or you might find the topic too important to leave alone. When you find yourself in these situations, it's far better to know how to navigate than not. This book will empower you to handle such conversations, even when they become heated. It will give you options.

WHY HAVE IMPOSSIBLE CONVERSATIONS?

Ultimately, *How to Have Impossible Conversations* is about talking to people who hold different beliefs. What people believe matters, and what you believe matters. If you believe it's cold, you'll want to put on a jacket because you believe that it will make you warmer. So, too, with moral and political beliefs. If you believe foreign invaders are stealing our jobs and raping and murdering our citizens, you're more likely to vote for a strongman who'll promise to seal the borders and keep you safe (and if you believe your political opponents want open borders, you're even more likely to vote accordingly). If you believe fascists are everywhere and verging on a government takeover, you're more likely to sympathize with the pleas of those who advocate for violence by "punching Nazis." Beliefs matter because people act upon their beliefs—whether those beliefs are true or not (and it's far easier to be wrong than right).

Beliefs can also change, and there are good and bad ways to change them. Conversation is a good way. Force is a bad way, for all the obvious reasons—plus, it's downright ineffective. Despite what some people's frustration tells them, people never change their beliefs by being punched in the head by someone who hates them. In almost all cases, *the best* way to engage beliefs is through open conversation. This is because conversation is something done *with* someone (the *con-* in conversation stems from Latin roots meaning "with") and can be a gentle and effective intervention on their beliefs. Conversation is inherently collaborative, and it creates an opportunity for people to reconsider what they believe and thus potentially change how they act and vote. In fact, conversation offers *you* the opportunity to reconsider what *you* believe and reassess how *you* should act and vote.

WHAT CAN BE DONE?

Our response to this pervasive social dysfunction is to treat having impossible conversations as a skill to be mastered and a habit to be engaged. Don't be afraid to voice your opinion. Don't fear disagreement. Don't hesitate to ask questions. People are waking up and realizing that there *is* political capital to be gained, friendships to be had, insight to be gleaned, and intellectual integrity to be harnessed by meaningfully engaging others and even crossing moral aisles. You can be part of this renaissance. To join, you only need to know how to productively engage people in ways that are less likely to make them defensive and more likely to help them hold their beliefs less tenaciously. You can achieve this by using proven, evidence-based techniques like those found in this book.

Over the course of this book, we'll explain how to create productive dialogue out of what might otherwise have been dueling sermons. Demands for you to "listen and believe" can nearly always be replaced with you *listening, understanding, and then instilling doubt*. We know because we've had countless conversations with zealots, criminals, religious fanatics, and extremists of all stripes. Peter did his doctoral research in the Oregon State Prison System conversing with offenders about some of life's most difficult questions, and then built upon those techniques in thousands of hours of conversations with religious hardliners. James developed the ideas for his books and articles by engaging in extended conversations with people who hold radically different views about politics, morality, and religion. This book is the culmination of our extensive research and a lifetime of experience in conversing with people who profess to be unshakable in their beliefs.

In our highly polarized society—as we cope with the increasing demands of a revolutionary social media economy—impossible conversations are inevitable. The goal, then, should not be to hope you can avoid them, or to skulk in the shadows when confronted with different beliefs, but to seize the opportunity. Learn what you need to do to hear and be heard. Stand up. Speak up. But speak wisely. *How to Have Impossible Conversations* offers solutions to the problems of timidity, incivility, fear, and distrust that blight our conversational landscapes.

What to Expect and How to Use This Book

How to Have Impossible Conversations contains thirty-six techniques drawn from the best, most effective research on applied epistemology, hostage and professional negotiations, cult exiting, subdisciplines of psychology, and more. It has a simple format, organized by difficulty of application: fundamentals (Chapter 2), basics (Chapter 3), intermediate (Chapter 4), advanced (Chapter 5), expert (Chapter 6), and master (Chapter 7). Some techniques teach you to intervene in the cognitions of others, instill doubt, and help people to become more open to rethinking their beliefs. Other techniques are oriented toward truth-seeking. Some are just plain good advice. Their underlying commonality, regardless of your conversational goal, is that they all empower you to speak with people who have radically different political, moral, and social worldviews.

We've streamlined and simplified conversational questions and templates for you. There is no fluff. We've included exactly what you need to immediately have effective conversations across deep divides. And if you're interested in exploring the literature, extensive endnotes cite the relevant research. These, however, aren't necessary for success. You can be just as effective without reading the endnotes, but if you want to delve into more detailed explanations of why our techniques work, that's where to begin.

Many sections also include vignettes of actual conversations. From these, you'll see how to incorporate new skills and techniques into discussions, without it feeling unnatural or contrived, or like you're doing a hard sell. Some sections also contain brief stories from real-life mistakes we've made. From these, we hope to demonstrate how valuable it would have been if we had these techniques.

Our advice is to take your time with each chapter before moving on to the next. More advanced chapters build upon earlier chapters. Consequently, *we urge that you read this book sequentially and not skip ahead*. To make the best use of *How to Have Impossible Conversations,* have real face-to-face conversations in which you practice the techniques you're learning, chapter by chapter, *before* moving on to the next. This is especially true with Chapters 2 and 3, which you'll undoubtedly think you've already mastered; these chapters contain indispensable tools upon which the success of more advanced techniques, strategies, and approaches depend.

Finally, we believe we're entering an era of renewed interest in effective, across-the-aisle dialogue. People are sick of not being able to speak about controversial subjects and of having to constantly walk on eggshells when voicing their opinions. This book is for those who have had enough. Enough name-calling. Enough censuring. Enough animosity. It provides a comprehensive tool set that enables you to take charge of your conversations. You'll learn how to intervene in someone's thinking and help them change their own mind *and* how to mutually search for the truth. Even with hardliners and ideologues. Conversations that remain civil, empower you, and change even the staunchest of minds *are* possible—even across deep divides. Here are the tools to have them.

two

The Seven Fundamentals of Good Conversations

How to Converse with Anyone, from Strangers to Prison Inmates

#1—GOALS
Why are you engaged in this conversation?

#2—PARTNERSHIPS
Be partners, not adversaries

#3—RAPPORT
Develop and maintain a good connection

#4—LISTEN
Listen more, talk less

#5—SHOOT THE MESSENGER
Don't deliver your truth

#6—INTENTIONS
People have better intentions than you think

#7—WALK AWAY
Don't push your conversation partner beyond their comfort zone

You think that the heads of state only have serious conversations, but they actually often begin really with the weather or, "I really like your tie."

—Madeleine Albright

Everything is based upon fundamentals—everything. If you are able to execute a complex maneuver in ballet, for example, it is because you understand basic elements of the art. All expertise is built upon fundamentals.

Engaging in civil and effective conversations is a skill. It takes knowledge and practice, and you'll need to begin with fundamental principles. Later, when they become ingrained, you won't have to think about their use. They'll come naturally. But without them you can expect frequent upsets, derailed conversations, and strained relationships.

Most basic elements of civil discussion, especially over matters of substantive disagreement, come down to a single theme: making the other person in the conversation a partner, not an adversary. To accomplish this, you need to understand what you want from the conversation, make charitable assumptions about others' intentions, listen, and seek back-and-forth interaction (as opposed to delivering a message). Learning to listen is the first step in the give-and-take of effective conversations. You'll need to overcome the urge to say everything that's on your mind. Finally, you'll need to know when to end your conversation gracefully.

In all, this chapter teaches *seven fundamentals for good conversations*: identifying your goals; forming partnerships; developing rapport; listening to the other person in the conversation; shooting your own messenger (that is, *not* delivering your own truth); keeping in mind the other person's intentions, which are probably better than you assume; and knowing when to walk away.

Even if you master no more than these fundamentals, almost all of your conversations will improve dramatically—with everyone. Without them, any other skills you attempt to master will lack the necessary foundation and won't be nearly as effective. In what follows, therefore, we address the seven fundamentals in the most logical order.

#1—Goals

What's Your Purpose?
People enter into conversation for vastly different reasons. Often, people

just wish to talk and connect, but at other times more functional goals are at work. These include any of the following:

- Reaching mutual understanding (parties seek to understand each other's position, but not necessarily to reach agreement).
- Learning from each other (figuring out how other people arrived at their conclusions).
- Finding truth (collaboratively figuring out what's true or correcting mistaken beliefs).
- Intervening (attempting to change someone's beliefs or their methods of forming beliefs).
- Impressing (parties seek to impress a conversational partner or someone who might be watching).
- Yielding to coercion (feeling forced to speak with someone).

In each case, if you first identify your conversational goal(s), then your path will become easier. Ask yourself, "Why am I having this discussion? What are my goals? What do I want to get out of this?" Your answer might be any of the instances above, or you might just want to keep your conversation light, friendly, and agreeable.

You can have more than one goal, have no particular goal, or change your goals mid-conversation. These are all fine, but you must be clear to yourself about your goals when beginning a discussion.[1] Start by asking yourself whether you're more interested in finding the truth or helping someone reconsider what they believe. Maybe it's both, or maybe you're leaning more heavily toward one than the other. Once you know your goals, use the conversational techniques that best help you achieve them.

#2—PARTNERSHIPS

During the 1970s, Peter's mentor, Portland State University psychology professor Dr. Frank Wesley, investigated why some US prisoners of war (POWs) defected to North Korea during the Korean War. His research showed that virtually all of the defectors came from a single US training camp. As part of their training, they had been taught that the North Koreans were cruel, heartless barbarians who despised the United States and single-mindedly sought its destruction. But when those POWs were shown kindness by their captors, their initial indoctrination unraveled. They became far more likely to defect than those POWs who either hadn't been told anything about the North Koreans or had been given more neutral accounts of them.

Conversation Partners

The way to change minds, influence people, build relationships, and maintain friendships is through kindness, compassion, empathy, treating individuals with dignity and respect, and exercising these considerations in psychologically safe environments.[2] It comes naturally to all of us to respond favorably to someone who listens, shows kindness, treats us well, and appears respectful. A sure way to entrench people in their existing beliefs, cause disunity, and sow distrust is through adversarial relationships and threatening environments. It is easy to dislike someone who is mean-spirited, treats you poorly, doesn't listen, or disrespects you. You can doubtless recall examples from your own life.

Fortunately, it's fairly easy to create trusting, safe communicative environments and avoid conflict.[3] Here's how: View yourself as a *conversation partner*. That is, treat others as if you're working together to have a fruitful conversation—because you are. Seeing your conversations as partnerships is the single biggest step you can take to ensuring conversations stay civil and to building relationships instead of damaging them. Adopting this stance is also surprisingly easy.

From Winning to Understanding

Question: How do you switch from viewing people as opponents, moral degenerates, or even enemies to valued partners and collaborators?

Answer: Shift your goal from winning to understanding.

Make *understanding* your conversation partner's reasoning your (initial) goal.[4] Abandon adversarial thinking (conflict, strife, arguing, debating, ridicule, and the idea of winning), and adopt collaborative thinking (cooperation, partnership, listening, and learning).[5] Shift from, "This person is my opponent who needs to understand what I'm saying," to "This person is my partner in a conversation and I can learn from him—including learning exactly why he believes what he believes."

You may be saying to yourself, *I can talk to a lot of people like a partner, but I couldn't do that with a racist!* Yes, you can.[6] If the black musician Daryl Davis can have civil conversations with Klansmen and help them abandon the KKK (and he can: he has a closet full of their relinquished hoods to prove it), then *you* can talk to a racist, or to *anyone holding any belief system,* and discover why they believe what they believe.[7]

One key to realizing you can have seemingly impossible conversations is recognizing that discussions are natural learning environments for both people. Treating an individual as a partner in civil dialogue does not mean accepting their conclusions or buying into their reasoning.[8] (The mark of an educated mind, it has been said, is to understand a statement without having to accept it.[9]) It means thinking along with someone so that you understand not just what they believe but also *why* they believe it—in that process, maybe they'll come to understand your reasoning, or see that their reasoning is in error, or maybe you'll discover that you're harboring a false belief.[10] Conversational partnership isn't about agreement or disagreement, it's about civility, charity, and mutual understanding.[11]

At worst, you'll have to endure hearing something truly vile, in which case you will come away from the conversation with a better understanding of why people hold repugnant beliefs. More likely, you'll foster comfortable conversational environments, build relationships, better position yourself to understand and address similar arguments, and maybe even revise your own thinking.[12]

There's a catch, of course. You can't control someone else's behavior. You can only control your own. So, *you* have to be the one who initially attempts to understand your conversation partner's reasoning—even if they're unwilling to reciprocate. You'll also have to take an active role in establishing and maintaining the partnership dynamic and be ready to walk away if that becomes impossible. We'll say more on this in the chapters that follow.

Forming Partnerships

Here's how it works in practice, in a few easy points:

1. Make your goals of collaboration and understanding explicit.[13]

    Say, "I really want to understand what led you to those conclusions. I hope we can figure this out together."

2. Give your partner room to decline the conversational invitation, not answer your questions, or end the conversation at any time.

    Do not pressure someone to converse if they're uncomfortable participating.[14]

3. Ask yourself, *not your partner,* "How could someone believe that?"; and ask it in earnest, with curiosity instead of incredulity.

    As you try to figure out the answer, the likelihood increases that your conversation will stay on track and not turn nasty.

#3—RAPPORT

Anthony Magnabosco (AM) is a Street Epistemologist.[15] Street Epistemologists apply the famous Socratic method of questioning and other conversational tools to help people reconsider how they know what they think they know.[16]

Anthony met Kari (K) after she returned from a hike. In the conversation that follows, Anthony immediately establishes rapport. That is, he connects with her and helps her feel comfortable before conversing about her belief in God.[17]

AM: *Good morning! How are you? Would you happen to have five minutes to do a chat?*

K: *Sure, sure!*

AM: *Okay, thanks. Are you okay if I livestream and record it?*

K: *Okay. And what's it about?*

AM: *Excellent question . . .*

K: *[laughs]*

AM: *I have conversations with strangers for five minutes—*

K: *Okay . . .*

AM:—*to see what they believe and why.*

K: *[brightly] Okay!*

AM: *And it's fun.*

K: *Okay!*

AM: *Okay, thank you!*

K: *Should I take my sunglasses off?*

AM: *Whatever you prefer. Whatever you're more comfortable with.*

K: *Okay. [removes sunglasses]*

AM: *What is your first name?*

K: *Kari.*

AM: *I'm Anthony. [extends hand for a handshake]*

K: *Nice to meet you.*

AM: *Hi! Nice to meet you too! How do I spell that?*

K: *K-A-R-I.*

AM: *Okay . . . [writes down her name for his video notes] Do you hike here a lot?*

K: *Yes.*

AM: *Awesome! I've come here a couple times, but it's usually with my kids, so I can't go as fast as I want to.*

K: *Exactly! I usually come here with my kids.*

AM: *Yeah, yeah! They slow you down!*

K: *Yeah.*

AM: *Did you cruise through it pretty fast, or . . . ?*

K: *Actually, you know, this is the first time I came by myself, so it was fun to just go do something harder.*

AM: *Okay, well, good, good!*

This lasted approximately two minutes. In those two minutes, Anthony built enough rapport so that Kari felt comfortable talking with a stranger about her personal beliefs. He proceeded to speak with her about her belief in God.

Friendliness, Comfort, and Trust

Rapport is a kind of friendliness. When you've built rapport with your conversation partner you experience a closeness where you both feel comfortable, get along, mutually empathize, and work toward building trust. It is the most important element in having simple, friendly chats that avoid divisive issues and bring people together, and the same magic of friendliness it produces is indispensable for goal-directed conversations. If viewing conversations as partnerships does most of the work toward having great conversations, establishing and maintaining a friendly atmosphere improves the situation even further. The more individuals diverge in their stances, the more important it is to build and maintain rapport.[18] Moreover, "As this connection grows, the [person with whom you're speaking] is less likely to be defensive and more open to suggestion."[19]

To build rapport, ask sincere questions (that is, questions for which you'd like to find answers, as opposed to asking questions as a tactic). For strangers, movies, music, how they know mutual friends, and the like, are good topics for starting to build rapport. If you're already familiar with someone, then spend a little time catching up: how are their kids, parents, new house, and so forth? As a general rule, depending on the context, rapport building at the beginning of a conversation takes only a few minutes.[20]

If you already have rapport with someone, as you will with a friend, keeping your friendship should rank higher than winning an argument or scoring rhetorical points. Friends are more likely to listen and be more earnest in their consideration of your ideas. Far more importantly, however, they're your friends. Nurture and even cherish the rapport you have with them instead of threatening it. This does not mean you cannot disagree with your friends. To the contrary, disagreement can make a friendship stronger, but remember that you're friends first. Spend time enjoying the rapport-building stage before you jump into contentious issues. And don't forget to chat with them as friends and leave goal-directed conversation out of it to focus on the friendship!

Practices to Build Rapport

Here are some specifics for building rapport, whether with strangers or friends:

1. Build rapport immediately.

   Do not start the conversation with a substantive issue, especially if it is controversial.

2. If you do not know someone, here are a few obvious initial questions to begin the rapport-building process:

Hi. My name is X. How are you?

Nice to meet you, I'm X. What's your name?

This is my first time here. How did you find out about this place?

Immediately after those initial ice-breaking questions, you can ask rapport-building questions that explore people's motivations and interests:

Can you say more about why that's important to you?[21]

What got you interested in that?

How do you spend most of your free time? What are you passionate about? (Don't ask "What do you do?" as this rarely reveals someone's passions.[22])

What do you like to be called?[23]

Where'd you learn about that?[24]

3. Find common ground.

   There are countless things you and your conversation partner have in common.[25] Maybe you both practice jiu jitsu, like sushi, have tattoos, enjoy science fiction, are expecting parents, live in the same neighborhood, or feel passionately about some political issue. Be mindful of these commonalities if your conversation becomes heated.

One automatic commonality all but psychopaths have in common is an impulse for the good: you both want the best for yourselves, your friends, and your community. While you might diverge on what those outcomes would look like, living better lives is a foundational commonality.

4. Do not parallel talk.

Parallel talk is taking something someone says and using that to reference yourself or your experiences. For example, if someone tells you they just got back from Cuba, don't starting talking about the time *you* went to Cuba. Ask them about their experience in Cuba. Don't make their stories about your life. Parallel talk damages rapport.

5. Invest in the relationship, independent of your political views.

Friendships engender trust and openness, which act like bridges across divides. Remember the adage, "No one cares how much you know until they know how much you care." As we'll discuss in more detail in Chapter 3, this refers to how much you care about *them* and the things *they* care about, not about *your* political or moral commitments.

6. Engage in substantive conversation only if you're willing to make time.

Do not rush and do not "hit and run." If you can't substantively engage someone's ideas, leave it for a time when you can. It impairs rapport to force or speed through conversations.[26] If your time is limited, use the moments you have to build rapport or catch up.

7. Be ready to talk about something else.

You know that uncle who ruins your family get-togethers because he just can't leave his religion or politics alone? Don't be that person. If the conversation gets sticky, be ready to change the subject to something less serious. If the conversation has moved on from a contentious issue, don't be the one to bring it back up. Forcing issues destroys rapport.

8. Avoid call-outs, except for severe infractions.

Calling out someone means telling them, usually immediately, and in a harsh way that aims at inducing shame, that they have crossed a moral boundary. This is often followed with moral instruction, for example, "You should do this . . . " or "You shouldn't do that . . . " Calling someone out, especially midstream in their thought, damages rapport.

Find a more delicate and better-timed way to bring up your concerns. Chances are, your partner is doing the best she can to express her thoughts. Rather than calling out her offenses, try to make sense of what she is saying and appreciate her authenticity, however rough around the edges. Of course, if someone is deliberately rude or abusive, you should stand up for yourself, say something, and set clear boundaries—or end the conversation.

9. Be courteous.

Say "please" and "thank you." Also, say "I appreciate that" after someone offers a counterargument or disagrees with something you've said.[27]

#4—LISTEN

Think about listening in terms of your own experiences. Who would you rather come over for dinner, someone who knows "everything" and is convincing, or someone who is an attentive listener and engages you and makes you feel heard? If you are fortunate enough to have friends who are skilled listeners, then you already know who to invite for dinner. People find it deeply satisfying when they are heard, and the rewards you can reap by conscientiously and authentically listening are enormous.

If you do not listen, you cannot understand. And if you cannot understand, there is no conversation. Listening is more difficult than it seems, so it requires practice. Do what you can to make listening the center of your approach to conversation.

Best Practices to Improve Your Listening Skills

Here are some suggestions to immediately improve your listening:

1. "Go—" "No, you go."

   If you start to speak at the same time as someone else, don't continue speaking. Instead, say, "Go ahead." If they say, "No, you go," respond, "That's okay, you go," and then let them speak.

   Think about this like coming to a door at exactly the same moment as someone else. Don't dive through the door; rather, step back and motion them forward. If they do the same and motion you to step through, then the option of stepping back farther and gesturing for them to walk through is available. Similar to defensive driving, you can always yield your right-of-way, but assuming the right-of-way only works when you truly have it.

2. Look directly at someone and turn your body toward them.

   Nod to acknowledge when you understand. This cannot be an act. Listen authentically. Fully engage.

3. Unless your partner is searching for a word and you know it, do not finish their sentences.

   Listen. Do not jump in to speak before having heard and processed what they're saying. Listen.

   If at any point the conversation becomes tense, listen more, talk less, and don't rush to fill silence with words. Wait. It is difficult to have an adversarial relationship with someone who's an excellent listener.

4. Pause.

   Pauses are crucial moments when people reflect. Do not rush to fill them. Pauses may build trust and rapport while offering you a chance to understand your partner's reasoning.

   In Western cultures, people tend to be uncomfortable with even a moment of conversational silence (these are sometimes termed "lacunas"). Rather than a problem that needs to be solved, pauses should be viewed as opportunities; a moment of unbroken silence offers a "reflection event" for participants.

5. If you find yourself distracted by something in your immediate environment, either turn your back toward the distraction or explicitly identify what's distracting to you.

   This can form a common bond if your conversation partner also finds the same thing distracting. For example, if you're distracted by a heated conversation in the adjacent room, say, "They're really having an intense conversation. It's distracting me. Is it distracting you?"

6. If you're unclear about what someone means, place the burden of understanding upon yourself.

   At a pause point in the discussion, say, "I'm not sure I understand. Can you explain that?" Avoid saying, "That was unclear," or "That doesn't make sense," and especially, "You were unclear."

7. The moment you sense fear, frustration, anger, outrage, or disgust from your conversation partner, pay attention to the specific words she uses.

   Fear, frustration, and the others, are feelings. One of the best ways to sort out feelings, especially in strained conversations, is to listen and *acknowledge them* as soon as possible.

   Repeat specific feeling words, for example, "I hear that. I understand your frustration."[28] Acknowledgment through use of the same words can potentially direct the conversation away from conflict.[29] If nothing else, this demonstrates that you were listening.

8. If you start to fade or find yourself distracted when someone is talking to you, look them directly in the eyes and state, "I'm sorry. Can you please repeat that?"

   If you find yourself persistently distracted to the extent that it interferes with your listening, then it is likely time to end the conversation.

9. If you and your partner accidentally speak at the same time, and your partner continues while you remain silent and listen, when

you resume the conversation do not do so with the words that caused the interruption.

Let's say you're having a conversation and you interrupt each other. The last words you used were, "So he told me—". When you begin speaking again, do not start with, "So he told me." This makes it seem like you didn't listen to anything your partner just said. Instead, when you resume, acknowledge your partner's point with alternative wording and continue with their thread of the conversation. Alternatively, let go of what you were going to say and follow what your partner was saying.

10. Do not pull out your phone when you are having a conversation.

This is true even if you would like to search for more information on the topic.

11. Say, "I hear you," to acknowledge you're listening.

Mean it. "I hear you" is simple yet effective.

#5—Shoot the Messenger

Have you ever thought you made a convincing case for a position only to have someone promptly reject your conclusion? This frequently occurs because people deliver messages and the recipient rejects the act of delivery. Nobody likes to be lectured.

The research literature on effective conversations shows that delivering messages *does not work*.[30] This is because messengers don't speak across political and moral divides, or even converse—they deliver messages. Conversations are exchanges. Messages are information conveyed in one-way transactions. Messengers espouse beliefs and assume their audience will listen and ultimately embrace their conclusions.

Even when messages are not delivered across any sort of political or moral divide, they tend to be poorly received. In the 1940s, the psychologist Kurt Lewin and his students published a series of studies concerning an attempt to get housewives to incorporate sweetbreads (organ meats) into home-cooked meals to help with meat shortages during World War II.[31]

Some housewives were given a lecture about why incorporating sweet-breads was important for the war effort. Others were invited to self-generate reasons for their importance in group sessions similar to today's focus groups. Lewin observed that 37 percent of the members of the groups who self-generated reasons followed through and incorporated sweetbreads, and in the lectured groups, only 3 percent did so.[32]

There are many reasons why the self-generated groups had a much higher compliance with the desired behavior (one of which we return to in Chapter 6, Altercasting). Among these is that people tend to reject delivered messages and accept ideas they believe are their own.[33] If you've had a friend reject every idea you propose until days or weeks later when she happens upon one of them "for herself," then you have firsthand experience with this phenomenon.

When a messenger delivers undesirable news or facts that contradict the recipient's closely held beliefs, the hearer's temptation is to be angry with (or historically, to kill) the messenger for delivering the unwelcome information. (The original adage is "Don't shoot the messenger" for a reason.[34]) The easiest way to avoid this reaction is not to deliver uninvited messages.

Delivering Messages Does Not Work

Here are some suggestions for shifting from a message delivery service to a conversation:

1. Distinguish between delivering a message and authentic conversation.

    Delivering a message feels like teaching, whereas a conversation has give-and-take that rewards with learning. If you find yourself thinking, "If they only understood this point, they'd change their mind," you're delivering a message.

    Ask yourself, "Was I invited to share this, or am I just telling them?" If it's the latter, you're probably coming across as a messenger.

2. Approach *every* conversation with an awareness that your partner understands problems in a way that you don't currently comprehend.

   You'll be less likely to deliver messages if you're more focused on figuring out how someone knows what they know than if you presume to understand the reasoning behind someone's conclusions.

3. Don't meet their message delivery with your message delivery.

   That's not a conversation, but an invitation to debate. It's a message delivery service and a recipe for frustration and deepening someone's commitment to their beliefs. Remember: nobody likes to be lectured; in tense conversations, people care more about their message than about those it seems to contradict.

4. When you realize your partner is being a messenger, do *not* shoot the messenger.

   If you shoot the messenger in your partner, you will destroy rapport and may derail the conversation. *"Shooting messengers" should only be a self-inflicted act: take aim at your own messenger.*

   If your partner enters messenger mode, begin a listening and learning mode centering on asking questions. Questions can be an effective way to nudge the conversation back on track. They are also integral to intervention techniques described in later chapters.

5. Deliver your message only upon your partner's explicit request.

   Be succinct. Then return to a collaborative mind-set that's centered upon listening and learning. Thank them for listening and ask if they have a reply. Say, "Thank you for giving me the opportunity to say that. I appreciate it. Any thoughts you'd like to add?"

#6—INTENTIONS

The following discussion, between Socrates and Meno, is from a classical text of Greek philosophy, the dialogue *Meno* written by Plato in the fourth century BCE.

Socrates: *Do you think some men desire bad and others good? Doesn't everyone, in your opinion, desire good things?*

Meno: *No.*

Socrates: *And would you say that the others suppose bad things to be good, or do they still desire them although they recognize them as bad?*

Meno: *Both, I should say.*

Socrates: *What? Do you really think that anyone who recognizes bad things for what they are, nevertheless desires them?*

Meno: *Yes.*

Socrates: *Desires in what way? To possess them?*

Meno: *Of course.*

Socrates: *In the belief that bad things bring advantage to their possessor, or harm?*

Meno: *Some in the first belief, but some also in the second.*

Socrates: *And do you believe that those who suppose bad things bring advantage understand that they are bad?*

Meno: *No, that I can't really believe.*

Socrates: *Isn't it clear then that this class, who don't recognize bad things for what they are, don't desire bad but what they think is good, though in fact it is bad; those who through ignorance mistake bad things for good obviously desire the good?*

Meno: *For them I suppose that is true.*

Socrates: *Now as for those whom you speak of as desiring bad things in the belief that they do harm to their possessor, these presumably know that they will be injured by them?*

Meno: *They must.*

Socrates: *And don't they believe that whoever is injured is, in so far as he is injured, unhappy?*

Meno: *That too they must believe.*

Socrates: *And unfortunate?*

Meno: *Yes.*

Socrates: *Well, does anybody want to be unhappy and unfortunate?*

Meno: *I suppose not.*

Socrates: *Then if not, nobody desires what is bad, for what else is un-happiness but desiring bad things and getting them?*

Meno: *It looks as if you are right, Socrates, and nobody desires what is bad.*[35]

People Do Not Knowingly Desire Bad Things

In the *Meno,* Socrates said that people do not knowingly desire bad things. Individuals act, believe, and desire based upon the information they have. If they had different information, they'd derive different conclusions. For example, physicians used to treat patients with leeches because they thought diseases were caused by an excess of blood. They attached leeches to patients because they wanted to help them. They desired the good—to improve patients' health—but they didn't have information we have now, which is that excess blood is unrelated to disease. We all have an impulse for goodness. However, lacking a comprehensive picture contributes to the failure of arriving at correct conclusions.[36]

When you encounter a person with radically different beliefs, you might think they're ignorant, crazy, or malicious.[37] Resist this inclination and instead consider that they view issues from a different perspective or that they're acting upon what they think is the best available information. Chances are far better that they mean to help but aren't great at communicating than that they're actually ignorant, crazy, or malicious.

In a disagreement, people frequently assume their partners' intentions and motivations are worse than they are.[38] Many people, for example, assume conservatives are racist, liberals aren't patriotic, Republicans don't care about poor people, or Democrats are weak on national defense. They then go on to assume that these perceived shortcomings motivate beliefs and arguments. This is usually false.[39]

The intentions and motivations you assume in your conversation partner are likely worse than their actual intentions and motivations. For example, it is simply not the case that most Republicans don't care about poor people. Rather, they're likely operating under the assumptions that opportunity "trickles down" through job creation and that tough love helps motivate people to raise themselves out of poverty. Within this framework, cutting taxes on high-income earners stimulates opportunities that trickle down to those who are economically disadvantaged.[40] What matters isn't whether they are correct or incorrect; it's that their intention is to improve a bad situation, which is a far better motivation than many Democrats assume.[41]

Assuming your partner has malicious intentions stifles your conversation. It halts cooperation and undermines the possibility of using the conversation to arrive at truth. It may also make your words seem snarky and put people on the defensive (which will make it less likely they'll change their beliefs). Even more damaging to conversations is that making negative assumptions about your partner's intentions makes *you* less capable of listening.[42]

If you must make an assumption about your partner's intentions, make only one: their intentions are better than you think. People don't knowingly desire bad things, so assume your partner has good intentions.[43] (Internet trolls and psychopaths, covered in Chapter 7, are distinct exceptions.)

Here's how you can immediately apply this:

1. If your partner assumes you have bad intentions, do not waste time trying to convince her otherwise.

   Instead, switch the conversation from your intentions to your reasoning. Say, "I absolutely do not want to be wrong for one more instant than I have to be. If something is wrong with my reasoning, please let me know."[44]

2. If you start to assume your partner has bad intentions, switch to a frame of curiosity.

   Consider that they may know something you do not know. Explicitly ask about the issue. Say, "I'm having a hard time understanding where you're coming from. I assume you must know some things about this that I don't. Could you tell me more about where you're coming from on that so I can understand better?"

3. Admit frustration.

Say, "I'm feeling frustrated. I want to understand where you're coming from. I'm also unclear about your intention. Could you tell me, what is your intention?" This is an open-ended question that leaves room for interpretation. If they respond, "What do you mean, what's my intention?" reply, "What are your hopes for this conversation? What would you like to get out of it?"

Often people you find frustrating are just trying to help; equally often, they're doing so from the messenger stance. That's why they frustrate you.

4. "Do not feed the trolls."

In Internet-speak, trolls are people who have bad intentions and act maliciously. Trolls are toxic to conversations.[45] Let them waste their time. Stop playing their game. Block or mute their accounts.

You're under no obligation to engage someone whose goal is to irritate you. Never be bullied into having a conversation. Have a conversation because you want to, not because you are being harassed for not speaking to someone. Consent applies to *all* participants.

#7—Walk Away

For years, I (Peter) have been developing interventions to change a sports fan's team preference. For example, if someone likes the Dallas Cowboys, I have been trying to figure out what to say to convince them to like the New England Patriots. My success rate has been abysmal.

The following is an attempted intervention I had with an LA Lakers fan. My first goal was to instill doubt about whether or not he should be a Lakers fan, and my second goal was to convince him to be a Trail Blazers fan. "LA fan" was approximately twenty-eight years old. We met while waiting in line for a table at a popular LA restaurant.

Boghossian: *I just don't get it. The players on the team aren't even from LA. Right?*

LA fan: *Well, yeah.*

Boghossian: *Where are they from?*

LA fan: *[rattles off players and cities]*

Boghossian: *Okay. Got it. If they were from LA, then I could totally understand why you'd be a fan. Right? I mean, they'd be from here and there'd be kinship and familiarity and such, yeah?*

LA fan: *Well, yeah. But they're my team. This is my city. I love LA!*

Boghossian: *Who doesn't? Great place. But the team is filled with people who aren't from here.*

LA fan: *But they play for the city. They play for us. So when they win we win!*

Boghossian: *Would you feel more intensely about the Lakers if every team member was from LA?*

[pause]

LA fan: *What do you mean?*

Boghossian: *I mean if every single player on the team was born and raised in Los Angeles, would you feel more strongly? Would you be more connected to the team?*

[pause]

LA fan: *Maybe. Yeah. Maybe. I think so.*

Boghossian: *So shouldn't you be less enthusiastic and connected given that they're not from LA? I mean if you'd be more enthusiastic if they're from LA, then shouldn't you be less enthusiastic because they're not?*

[long pause]

At this point I should have ended the conversation on a light note. I should not have moved on to my second goal of changing his team preference. But I persisted and tried to guide him toward another team. (It is much easier to instill doubt than it is to nudge people toward a belief or to change their preference.) The consequence of this was that he doubled down on his Laker enthusiasm and the tenor of the conversation changed. He became defensive and less curious. We were having a fun, enjoyable chat that I made less enjoyable and less fun because I pushed the conversation to where he became defensive.

Exit, Stage Left

Know when to walk away, even when the conversation is going well.[46]

Putting pressure on your partner to continue a discussion beyond their comfort level shuts down listening, encourages defensiveness, and turns the conversation into a frustrated rehearsal of why one of you is correct and the other dense. Consequently, your conversation partner may double down on his views and the rapport between you will erode, possibly hurting your friendship.[47]

There may come a point when you've exhausted your options. Perhaps you have nothing left to say, you feel like you've been going around and around, or you're at an impasse. A common mistake is to attempt to "fix" or reset conversations and then continue. Don't. Instead, part amicably.

People need time to wrestle with doubt, incorporate new information, mull over challenges and different perspectives, and rethink their positions.[48] And so do you. Changing one's mind happens slowly and in a way that suits one's individual psychology and habits.[49] Over time, new beliefs and attitudes integrate with, or entirely replace, existing ones.[50] Forcing a conversation beyond someone's comfort zone denies you and your partner an opportunity to reflect while placing a strain on the relationship. Politely leaving a conversation when all parties are getting along can be an opportunity for those involved to reflect on issues.

Finally, try to end on a positive note. Sometimes even a simple "Thanks for chatting with me" is sufficient.

How to End a Conversation

Here are some suggestions for knowing when to end a conversation:

1. End the conversation if your primary emotion is frustration.

    If the discussion escalated to anger, you may need to walk away sooner than expected.[51]

2. Breathe.

    Literally. Breathe. When you initially feel yourself becoming frustrated, back off, slow down, don't feel pressured to fill pauses with speech—and breathe.[52] Take a deep breath.[53] If you do not calm down, then end the conversation and walk away.

3. If someone wants to end the conversation, politely thank them for speaking with you.

    Don't engage someone past their comfort threshold.

4. If you think you have caused your partner to doubt one of her beliefs, that is a good time to stop the conversation.

    Allow her to explore her doubt, and to wonder about it on her own terms. If she continues to express curiosity, state that this is a good opportunity for both of you to think about these issues. You can then part ways or change the subject, depending upon the context.

    Attempting to fill your partner's doubt and wonder with your beliefs is sometimes genuinely educational, but it can also be a form of evangelism. Don't evangelize. It is an unethical abuse of the vulnerability that accompanies doubt to use it in an attempt to sway your partner (except in exceptional circumstances of genuine expertise or if someone holds a fantastically implausible, antiscientific belief).

5. Thank your partner when you end the conversation.

    The more you do not want to thank someone for the conversation, the more important it is to thank them. (There are exceptions to this. For example, if someone was smearing or harassing you.) Reticence to thank your conversation partner suggests an emotional attachment to the topic or that you have some personal issue with them that's likely bled through into the discussion. Thanking someone for their time is a basic courtesy. Thanking someone will also help conversations end on an upbeat, friendly note.

Conclusion

You now have the fundamentals necessary for effective, civil conversations. We urge you to practice this material before attempting to apply the techniques in the next chapter. The greater your mastery of the content in this chapter, the more success you will have when applying more advanced techniques.

Notably, you do not need to seek out conversations. Opportunities present themselves in day-to-day interactions—with coworkers, checkout clerks, wait staff, roommates, friends, relatives, and so forth. Simply go about your day and wait until you are approached.

Every conversation is an opportunity to practice being a kinder, more effective communicator. Becoming a better listener and partner in conversations can only have a positive effect on your relationships. Start now.

three

Beginner Level: Nine Ways to Start Changing Minds

How to Intervene in Someone's Cognitions

#1—MODELING
Model the behavior you want to see in others

#2—WORDS
Define terms up front

#3—ASK QUESTIONS
Focus on a specific question

#4—ACKNOWLEDGE EXTREMISTS
Point out bad things people on your side do

#5—NAVIGATING SOCIAL MEDIA
Do not vent on social media

#6—DON'T BLAME, DO DISCUSS CONTRIBUTIONS
Shift from blame to contribution

#7—FOCUS ON EPISTEMOLOGY
Figure out how people know what they claim to know

#8—LEARN
Learn what makes someone close-minded

#9—WHAT NOT TO DO (REVERSE APPLICATIONS)
A list of fundamental and basic conversational mistakes

I read, I study, I examine, I listen, I reflect, and out of all of this I try to form an idea into which I put as much common sense as I can. I shall not speak much for fear of saying foolish things; I will risk still less for fear of doing them, for I am not disposed to abuse the confidence which they have deigned to show me. Such is the conduct which until now I have followed and will follow.

—Gilbert du Motier, Marquis de Lafayette, in a letter to his father-in-law, the Duc d'Ayan, December 4, 1776

Now that you have a grasp on the fundamentals of effective conversations, you're ready to expand your repertoire and include interventions. Interventions are ways to intervene or intercede in how someone forms their beliefs. The goal of an intervention is to help people become less confident about what they believe, which is where changing someone's mind begins. In other words, just by speaking with someone you'll be able to intercede in their cognitions and give them the gift of doubt.

As we explained in Chapter 2, you have little prospect of achieving that goal by delivering your own message accompanied by what strike you as compelling facts. That approach is likely to backfire and leave your conversation partner more entrenched in her beliefs than ever. The most effective techniques for giving the gift of doubt are subtler, and they'll lead you to more interesting conversations.

To get started, you'll learn the power of modeling the behaviors you want to see in others and of focusing upon exploring questions. You'll learn to avoid talking past your conversation partner, or getting bogged down in unproductive conversation, because of disagreements about the meanings of words. In this chapter, you'll also learn one of the most powerful and simple techniques for engaging someone who strongly disagrees not only with you but also with the side she thinks you represent: building camaraderie by demonstrating you're not an extremist.

These basic skills open conversations and shift them into learning mode. In particular, you'll focus on the importance of understanding how and why your conversation partner thinks and believes as she does. You can then use that understanding to help others—and yourself—become more humble about what they think they know. It's always worth remembering: to give others the gift of doubt, you need to possess it yourself.

Finally, this chapter should help you avoid a raft of common conversational errors. These common errors can quickly undermine both truth-seeking and intervention-based discussions. Fortunately, they're easily avoided.

#1—MODELING

In 2015, at a meeting with Muslim community leaders in Australia, Peter repeatedly asked their spokesperson if he believed women should be stoned to death for adultery. He couldn't receive a straight answer. The first response he received was a deflection, so he repeated the question:

Boghossian: *Should women be stoned to death for adultery?*

Community Leader: *Why not men? Why shouldn't men be stoned for adultery?*

[Peter repeated the question and was met with a long, convoluted story he couldn't follow.]

Boghossian: *Ask me that question.*

Community Leader: *What do you mean?*

Boghossian: *Would you please ask me, right now, if I believe women should be stoned to death for adultery.*

[pause]

Community Leader: *Do you believe women should be stoned to death for adultery?*

Boghossian: *No. Now, do you believe women should be stoned to death for adultery?*

[long pause]

Community Leader: *Yes.*

Model the behavior you want to see in your conversation partner. If you want her to answer a direct question, answer a direct question. If you want her to be patient and listen, be patient and listen.[1] If you want her to start screaming, start screaming.[2] If you want your partner to be open to changing her mind, be open to changing yours. If you want them to be civil, be civil. If you want them to give ground, give some of yours. If you want her to listen to you, listen to her *first*. This advice is easy to hear yet difficult to follow. But it's indispensable, especially when speaking to people with whom you disagree. It's also crucial to prevent conversations from becoming derailed.

A Common Fallacy: "Someone Knows It, So I Know It"

A philosopher and a psychologist, Robert A. Wilson and Frank Keil, have researched the phenomenon of ignorance of one's ignorance.[3] In a 1998 paper titled "The Shadows and Shallows of Explanation," they studied the well-known phenomenon of people who believe they understand how things work better than they actually do.[4] They discovered our tendency to believe we're more knowledgeable than we are because we believe in other people's expertise. Think about this like borrowing books from the great library of human knowledge and then never reading the books. We think we possess the information in the books because we have access to them, but we don't have the knowledge because we've never read the books, much less studied them in depth. Following this analogy, we'll call this fallacy the "Unread Library Effect."

The Unread Library Effect was revealed in an experiment by two researchers in 2001, Frank Keil (again) and Leonid Rozenblit; they called it "the illusion of explanatory depth" and referred to it as "the misunderstood limits of folk science."[5] They researched people's understanding of the inner workings of toilets. Subjects were asked to numerically rate how confident they were in their explanation of how a toilet works. The subjects were then asked to explain verbally how a toilet works, giving as much detail as possible. After attempting an explanation, they were asked to numerically rate their confidence again. This time, however, they admitted being far less confident. They realized their own reliance on borrowed knowledge and thus their own ignorance.[6]

In 2013, cognitive scientists Steven Sloman and Philip Fernbach, with behavioral scientist Todd Rogers and cognitive psychologist Craig Fox, performed an experiment showing that the Unread Library Effect also applies to political beliefs. That is, helping people understand they're relying upon borrowed knowledge leads them to introduce doubt for themselves and thus has a moderating effect on people's beliefs. By having participants explain policies in as much detail as possible, along with how those policies would be implemented and what impacts they might have, the researchers successfully nudged strong political views toward moderation.[7] Taking advantage of this phenomenon, then, confers at least two significant benefits in an intervention. First, it allows your conversational partner to do most of the talking, which affords you the opportunity to listen and prevents them from feeling as though you're trying to change their mind. Second, *they lead themselves* into doubt rather than feeling pressured by someone else.

Modeling ignorance is an effective way to help expose the Unread Library Effect because, as the name implies, the Unread Library Effect relies upon information about which your conversation partner is ignorant—even though she doesn't realize it. In essence, you want her to recognize the limits of her knowledge. Specifically, then, you should model behavior highlighting the limits of *your own* knowledge. This has three significant merits:

1. It creates an opportunity for *you* to overcome the Unread Library Effect, that is, thinking you know more about an issue than you do.
2. It contributes to a climate of making it okay to say "I don't know," and thus gives tacit permission to your partner to admit that *she* doesn't know.
3. It's a subtle but effective strategy for exposing the gap between your conversation partner's perceived knowledge and her actual knowledge.

Here are some examples of how you can apply this in conversations. You can say, "I don't know how the details of using mass deportations of illegal immigrants would play out. I think there are likely both pros and cons, and I really don't know which outweigh which. How would that policy be implemented? Who pays for it? How much would it cost? What does that look like in practice? Again, I don't know enough specifics to have a strong opinion, but I'm happy to listen to the details." When you do this, don't be shy. Explicitly invite explanations, ask for specifics, follow up with pointed questions that revolve around soliciting how someone knows the details, and continue to openly admit your own ignorance. In many conversations, the more ignorance you admit, the more readily your partner in the conversation will step in with an explanation to help you understand. And the more they attempt to explain, the more likely they are to realize the limits of their own knowledge.

In this example, if your partner is an expert in this aspect of immigration policy, you might be rewarded with a good lesson. Otherwise, you might lead her to expose the Unread Library Effect because you started by modeling ignorance. Should your conversation partner begin to question her expertise and discover the Unread Library Effect, let its effects percolate. Do not continue to pepper her with questions.

It's worth repeating that this strategy not only helps moderate strong views, it models openness, willingness to admit ignorance, and readiness to revise beliefs. Modeling intellectually honest ignorance is a virtue that seasoned conversation partners possess—and it is fairly easy to achieve.

Ways to Model Better Conversation

Here are a few ways you can use Modeling, expose the Unread Library Effect, and intervene in someone's beliefs.

1. Say "I don't know" when you don't know.

    Not knowing something isn't a badge of shame, it's a public display of honesty, humility, and sincerity. Commend people when they say, "I don't know."

2. If you ask someone a direct question and they obfuscate or refuse to answer, ask them to ask you the same question. (See the
   example of stoning women for adultery at the beginning of this
   section.)

   Give them a succinct answer (that is, model what you're seeking) and then immediately ask them the identical question.

3. Model the behavioral traits that are key to effective, successful
   conversations: listening, honesty (especially admitting ignorance),
   sincerity, curiosity, openness, fairness, charity (not assuming bad
   intentions), focusing on justifications for belief, humility, humor,
   give-and-take, and willingness to change your mind.

4. From admitting you don't know enough to hold a firm position on
   a topic, ask for explanations, in as much detail as possible, about
   your partner's beliefs.

   Remember, Sloman and Fernbach's research showed that attempting to explain complicated topics often reveals the Unread
   Library Effect and has the result of toning down views.[8] *The more
   details you can ask your partner to provide* (for example, "What
   branch of law enforcement conducts mass deportations?" "What
   departments' budgets does this come out of and how much does
   it cost?" "What are the laws currently regulating the deportation of
   immigrants?" "What are the best arguments against those laws?"
   "Where are deportees held?" "What might go wrong?"), *the stronger the effect.*

5. Expose your own Unread Library Effect.

   Pick political topics that are important to you and try to explain
   how they work in as much detail as possible. Be specific about impacts and implementation. For additional practice, try it with everyday objects like your coffee maker or scientific processes, like
   how the semiconductors in electronics work. These make good
   examples to practice with, unlike complicated political positions,
   because they're easily checked online.

6. Model clarity; avoid jargon.

Strive for clarity. And unless you're a quantum physicist, avoid using the word *quantum*.[9]

7. Do not model bad behavior.

Don't interrupt people or treat them rudely. If you want to be treated with kindness and civility, be kind and civil. Most poignantly, if you want your views to be treated charitably, treat your partner's views charitably.

#2—WORDS

In 2017, James Damore, the Google engineer who authored the famous "Google memo," was fired allegedly for "perpetuating gender stereotypes." At Google's request, Damore had provided feedback as to what he saw as a problem at the tech giant. He later commented on the sequence of events during a public event at Portland State University:

> I had been working at Google for about four years and I noticed that we had some inclusion problems on our team some people wouldn't go to our group lunches or speak up in our team meetings, so I went to a diversity and inclusion conference at Google. Unfortunately, rather than talk about how to . . . include everyone on the team it just talked about diversity and specifically racial and gender diversity at Google. . . . They said . . . the population has 50 percent women, Google has 20 percent women, therefore sexism. . . . They asked for feedback and . . . I had actually been doing biology in grad school before going to Google, and I knew a little bit about psychology and actually why . . . there may be fewer women interested in tech. . . . So I wrote this document and I . . . explained these factors we have to take into account if we want to change Google to make it more appealing to more women and how we can actually fix some of these workplace issues and remove gender from the discussion.[10]

Although this example illustrates the many problems at play in Google's culture (e.g., in asking for feedback, company management only wanted the type of feedback that comported with a particular narrative about diversity), one misunderstanding comes from Google's nonstandard use of the words *diversity* and *inclusion*. Damore, understandably, took "diversity and inclusion" to mean improving the participation of all team members when clearly that was not what management intended by these terms. As a result of speaking frankly, though politely, across this terminological misunderstanding, Damore was fired from Google.

The Meanings of Words

Though many arguments seem to be about matters of substance, they're often just disagreements about the meanings of words.[11] One clue you're caught in such a situation is that you want to appeal to a dictionary. (Appealing to a dictionary to adjudicate the meaning of words isn't very helpful because people use words in different ways and because meanings vary across contexts. For examples, think about *faith, woman,* and, as we've just seen, *diversity*.)

Someone might say, for instance, "I hate the government," when they mean they hate intrusive government, corruption, bureaucracy, concentrated political authority, or regulations that don't comport with their values. Someone else might claim they like the government when they really mean they want security, stability, social services, and infrastructure. If these two people have a conversation about "the government," there's a risk they'll argue even if they agree about almost every issue of policy. Such clashes are frustrating because they appear to be substantive but are really about the meanings of words. Frustration and miscommunication can be reduced by defining words and agreeing upon definitions up front.

Disagreements about definitions can easily derail *moral* conversations because words can signify profoundly different things to different people. (As Peter explained in *A Manual for Creating Atheists,* religious people and atheists have disagreements about the meaning of the word *faith*.[12] It's thus important to clarify the meaning of that word in particular before a conversation continues.)

In politics, liberals might see welfare programs as a moral responsibility of a developed state, whereas conservatives might see them as the government discouraging hard work by providing handouts. That is, liberals might interpret issues regarding welfare in terms of care and harm, and conservatives might think of the issues mainly in terms of fairness (more on this in Chapter 7).[13] In this case, the word *welfare* means the same thing functionally, but carries distinct moral connotations for different audiences.[14] Here, talking directly about undeserved government handouts or alleviating poverty can avoid the morally charged term *welfare*. And notice how easily this conversation could be derailed into a heated argument about fairness and who *deserves* what! If you can't agree upon the meaning of a word that's central to the conversation (*truth, woman, welfare*), then you can either move on to another issue or discontinue the conversation.[15]

How to Get on the Same Verbal Page

Here are some simple ways to clear up disagreements about the meanings of words before they derail your conversations.

1. Define words up front.

    Say, "What do you mean by [X]?" or "How is [X] defined?"

2. Try to understand the context in which a word is being used.

    Ask, "Do you use that word in the same way in other contexts too? What would be an example of that?" For example, "I'm trying to figure out how the word [X] is being used here. Is there an example of the word [X] being used in another context that has the same meaning?"

3. Go with their definitions.

    If you've asked your partner for a definition, and they provide it, accept their definition and move forward. If you cannot accept their definition of a term that's crucial to the conversation, then move on to another issue or end the conversation.

4. Be attentive to a word's moral implication.

    If a word has moral significance, your partner may have convinced themselves of the truth of their belief because they think that holding that belief makes them a better person.[16] That is, they've likely worked backward from believing the belief makes them a better person to then finding evidence for the belief. (Their moral mind is overriding their rational mind.) For example, moral reasoning often follows this pattern: Jon believes good people believe X. Jon believes he's a good person, so Jon believes he should believe X. Jon then looks for evidence to support X and tends to believe X as a result, while believing he believes X based on the evidence he has found.[17]

#3—Ask Questions

Take a lesson from Socrates: focus your conversation on a specific question as opposed to a general topic.

Socrates is most famous for his ability to shake people out of erroneous beliefs. He mostly did this not through careful argumentation but with thoughtful, targeted questioning. Below are examples of Socrates' questions, selected from various dialogues written by his disciple Plato:[18]

- What is it to be a man? What is it to be virtuous? (*Apology, Meno*)
- What is courage? (*Laches*)
- What is justice? (*Republic*)
- Why obey the law? (*Crito, Republic*)
- What's worth dying for? (*Apology, Crito*)
- When is punishment justified? (*Gorgias, Crito*)
- How important is personal responsibility? (*Gorgias, Republic, Laws*)
- What's the best life? (*Republic*)
- What obligations do we have toward others? (*Republic*)

In each case, Socrates formed his inquiry around a clear question. His conversations were manageable because they were focused. If the conversation strayed, or things became unclear, he came back to the original question. As with attempting to expose the Unread Library Effect, focus on questions, not topics.

Calibrated Questions

When your questions are *open-ended,* meaning questions that allow your partner to talk at length about her thoughts in her own words (not give single-word answers like "yes" and "no"), they invite conversations. Hostage negotiator Chris Voss terms certain open-ended questions "calibrated questions."[19] A calibrated question usually starts with *how* or *what.* How and what questions don't lend themselves to yes-and-no responses as do questions beginning with *can, is, are, does,* and *do.*[20] For example, ask, "How does this seem to you?" as opposed to "Does this look good?" When in doubt, start with *how* or *what.*

Questions from good physicians provide us with examples of calibrated questions. Rather than asking, "Do you feel pain?" which invites only a yes-or-no reply, a seasoned doctor might ask, "What can you tell me about any sensations you are experiencing, such as pain?"

Closed questions, those questions that lend themselves to one-word or very brief answers, especially yes or no, do not invite further discussion and can make conversation awkward. They're also often used by trial lawyers when attempting to corner witnesses during cross-examination. In that context, they can be devastating in extracting admissions from individuals required to answer. Though they are sometimes useful, they should be used with discretion. Do you want to be cross-examined when you're trying to have a conversation? Of course you don't! No one else does either. You might use closed questions when a conversation partner is not forthright, as in the earlier example of stoning women for adultery. In that case, a simple yes-or-no question had a useful role to play.

How to Ask Calibrated Questions in Any Conversation

1. Once you've selected a topic, narrow it down and clearly state it in question format.

   Say, "Just so that I'm clear, the question here is [X], yeah?" Listen to your partner's response and modify the question accordingly. If the question needs to be reformed, then restate the new formation, saying, "Okay, I think I got it now. So the question is [X], yes?" This is an example where a closed question is useful, but only after it has been set up.

If they still don't agree with your formulation of the question, say, "What do you think the question should be?" or "How would you phrase the question?" Notice that these are both calibrated questions.

2. If the conversation goes astray, bring it back to the original question.

Say, "We were discussing X, let's get back to that if it's okay," or "We started discussing X, but somewhere along the way we became sidetracked. Can we get back to X?"

Alternatively, if you don't want to revisit your initial question, don't. If your conversation strays to more interesting territory, and you'd like to pursue that, then try to articulate another question as you begin a new discussion.

3. Be authentic.

The best questions show you're sincerely interested in exploring answers as opposed to asking a question to achieve some goal.[21] People respect—and crave—authenticity and distrust gimmicks. If you are genuinely interested in your discussion question it will show.[22]

4. Do not disguise statements as questions and avoid leading questions that carry an agenda.

For example, "How do you think the Republicans came to be indifferent to the plight of poor people?" The question is considered "leading," even though it's superficially calibrated, because it *assumes* the other person's in agreement that the Republicans are callous about the poor. This is an inauthentic means of communicating that either pretends you aren't arguing when you are or pretends you don't have an agenda. This is likely to backfire if the person with whom you're speaking doesn't share your assumptions.

5. Ask calibrated "How . . . ?" and "What . . . ?" questions.

Calibrated questions are open-ended and give the conversation an opportunity to develop in the directions you hope they'll go. In general, avoid closed questions (like yes-or-no questions) unless you want to clarify, stop obfuscation, or seek confirmation that you have correctly understood your partner's thoughts.

#4—ACKNOWLEDGE EXTREMISTS

In the southern United States, there's a proverb that may have been adapted from sales: "Nobody cares how much you know until they know how much you care." It took James a lot longer than it should have—more than a decade—to sort out what that simple statement means.

On a superficial reading, the proverb seems to mean one of two things. It either seems to mean that people will only care about your knowledge if you're passionate (that is, if you care a lot about the subject) or if you care about the people you're talking with. Both have merit but are worthless for changing opinions. These two perspectives on the proverb are relevant in sales, but they're irrelevant in conversations taking place across a moral divide.

Passion makes you easy to hear, but it rarely convinces people they should listen. It often does the opposite, painting you as a zealot or the kind of person who is generally out of touch with reality. (Think of a street preacher.) Similarly, interpersonal trust is rarely sufficient to bridge a moral divide. Many of James's close friends harbor dramatically different religious and political views, and caring about them as people only gets them to be willing to hear him out. It almost never leads them to agree with his conclusions or the reasons he holds them.

When James realized how this proverb applies on a moral level, it dramatically changed the ways he could converse with people who hold different views. The key that unlocks the riddle of this Southern proverb is recognizing the proper object of the verb *care*. It isn't "care about the topic," and it isn't even "care about the people" (though this is an important component); it's *care about the right things,* as seen from your partner's perspective. It's about sharing values.[23]

The decoded moral proverb: to win your partner's trust across a moral divide, you must be able to demonstrate that you care about your partner and, especially, about the values your partner cares about. Even if your partner cannot see you as being on his moral team, for him to trust you he must be able to see you independently from his enemies' team. If you fail to do this, few will care what you have to say (or why you're saying it). Understanding this point is critical to having conversations that reach across a moral divide.

Building this kind of trust is challenging and takes time. Many of the tools and approaches in this book can help you learn how to prove yourself trustworthy where it counts, that is, to someone whose moral worldview doesn't match yours. On the other hand, there's at least one way to ensure you *won't* have this trust, and it is altogether too common. Unless you can distinguish yourself from the people "on your side" who your conversation partner considers the most frightening, you'll never gain their trust; they'll never care how much you know about topics near to their deepest concerns, like religion, morals, and politics.

Extremists Go Too Far

It almost always helps a political and moral conversation to find areas of moral agreement. There's one easy point of agreement available in almost every conversation: point out how extremists *on your side* go too far.

If your partner is on the other side of a political divide, she will not trust the extremists on your side, making an easy point of agreement if you express the same sentiment. Because of our polarized media environment, she also likely knows more about "your" extremists than about moderate expressions of beliefs on your side. The same is true about knowing good arguments for your positions (as do you about their side), especially given the ways the media adage "If it bleeds it leads" tends to amplify lunatics. In other words, your partner across a divide is likely to unfairly attach beliefs about extremists "on your side" *to you.* Extremism fosters tribalism, polarization, unwarranted skepticism, distrust, defensiveness, and (frustratingly) unfair caricatures of the other side's views.[24] Worse, extremism on one side drives people to reciprocate with extremism on an opposing side (think of neo-Nazis and antifa). You can turn this disadvantage to your advantage, however, by explicitly disavowing your side's extremists.

Acknowledging extremists creates an easy and immediate point of agreement across nearly any moral divide. It will help your conversation partner recognize that you, someone on "the other side," recognize outrageous problems on your side, do not support them, and are not a zealot. This acknowledgment will assist in diminishing moral gulfs because it separates you from your moral tribe while identifying important common ground with your partner.[25]

For example, did protesters for a cause you support turn violent and vandalize property? Did they try to squelch more moderate voices? Did they behave like screeching children and shout over people trying to voice an opinion? Did they create massive societal disruptions that inconvenienced innocent people? Do they resort to slurs? Disavow all such behavior, no matter who does it. Instead of placing yourself across the divide by attempting to excuse incidents like these, you'll immediately find yourself on the same side by agreeing to be against the extremists on your side. This, can be a basis for trust and a safe point of agreement from which deeper conversations can emerge.[26]

Disavowing Extremists

Always be ready to disavow extremism. Here are some easy ways you can do that:

1. Identify how "your side" goes too far.

    If you try to figure it out and can't, there's a good chance you're part of the problem and should moderate your views. The easiest way to find out what your side is doing wrong is to ask someone on the other side, listen, temporarily set aside your ego and social identity, and believe them.

2. Do not bring up extremists on "their side."

   This is for them to do, or not. Don't make your conversation transactional by assuming that because you made some step toward acknowledging extremists on your side that you're owed reciprocity.

3. *Never defend indefensible behavior.*

   Placing yourself on the political Left in a civil society is not sufficient license to defend riots, violence, or injuring police officers. Being on the political Right is not sufficient to justify defending racist displays or determinedly obstructionist politics that jeopardize national interests such as threatening default on our national debt. Take a stand against troublemakers on your side. Clearly state that extremists do not represent you, your views, or your values, and then, if appropriate, explain why. When the choice is before you, always stand with something bigger than "your side" by standing for civil society, productive dialogue, and compromise over extremism.[27]

4. Identify extremists as "fanatics," "zealots," and "radicals."

   Your partner is likely to agree. This also acts as a bridge toward realizing the proverb "Nobody cares how much you know until they know how much you care."

5. Treat their side charitably.

   Specifically, avoid characterizing their side as represented by their extremists (remember, Modeling, above).

   Characterizing your partner's side—or your partner—as an extremist is likely to defensively trigger him to characterize your side—or you—as one. At the very least, by talking about their side as though it is the fanatical or vile one, you are almost guaranteed to make them think about your side the same way.

6. Check yourself for extremism and keep it out of your conversations.

   Try to be cognizant of ways you've adopted extremist or essentializing views (like "Conservatives are fascists" or "Liberals are smug busybodies") and work to uproot those beliefs in yourself.

Find other ways to express your concerns more realistically and fairly.

#5—Navigating Social Media

We've made mistakes on social media. A lot of them. We've tweeted:

> "I've never understood how someone could be proud of being gay. How can one be proud of something one didn't work for?" (Boghossian)

> "Why is it that nearly every male who's a 3rd wave intersectional feminist is physically feeble & has terrible body habitus?" (Boghossian)

> "What's the likelihood that Social Justice Warrior activism is largely motivated by personality disorders within its thought leaders?" (Lindsay)

Attempting to ask provocative questions on social media and then expecting a civil discussion isn't just naïve, it's imbecilic—and we're saying that about ourselves here first. *Provocative* and *civil* are two words that don't mix in the social media landscape. In cases like these, not only did we not achieve the effect we were seeking—to make people think more deeply and challenge cherished assumptions—we did just the opposite. People thought we were jerks.

Avoid Combative Conversations on Social Media

Diverse bodies of literature demonstrate that the evidence-based conversational approaches and strategies in this book apply to face-to-face interactions. It is unclear how closely that translates to online environments. Absent solid evidence about how to have effective conversations across social media platforms, we strongly suggest discussing charged issues only if absolutely necessary (and we can't imagine what conditions would make it absolutely necessary) and only once solid evidence emerges for how to do so productively. Conversations on social media may have certain benefits (you may feel better when you vent) and offer certain advantages (like not having to react in real time[28]), but they otherwise put an already difficult discussion into "hard mode." One fact about having divisive conversations or sharing provocative material on social media seems evident, however: it damages relationships and contributes to our toxic social media environment.

As a species, we evolved to converse face-to-face. When looking at someone, it's usually easy to read tone, body language, and facial expressions.[29] Text-based communication removes these vital cues. The advantages supplied by removing these indicators are overridden by disadvantages in the form of loss of content depth. Many text-based statements can be interpreted in meaningfully different ways that mere tone of voice would have resolved. Sarcasm, for example, is notoriously more difficult to detect in text than when spoken, and efforts have even been made to introduce sarcastic punctuation marks.[30]

Additionally, when different words receive different stresses in spoken language, the meaning changes. For instance, by stressing different words in "I don't think that's fair," the sentence takes on different meanings. Using boldface type to indicate stress, "**I** don't think that's fair" means "I personally don't think that is fair (but someone else might)." On another hand, "I don't **think** that's fair" means "I'm not sure whether that is fair or not." This nuance is obvious in spoken language and has to be guessed at in written text. Assuming wrongly can knock conversations off course and start senseless, divisive arguments.

These issues make text-based communication challenging, even when private. Social media is mainly *public,* however, and conversations in public forums have different dynamics and rarely stay limited to two thoughtful participants (we'll return to this shortly). These factors make conversations on social media more difficult even than text-only communications that lack the rich "music" and "dance" of tone of voice and body language present in face-to-face conversations.[31]

Complicating matters further, each social media platform presents unique challenges due to its particular infrastructure. Twitter, for example, is limited to 280 characters per tweet and is almost totally public. As a rule, do not argue on Twitter. (And if you feel you absolutely must engage, then stop after two responses, as the medium does not lend itself to nuanced positions—you can add a third response to explain this rule and invite emailed or other private correspondences if you like.) Think of Twitter as being on stage and addressing a large audience in extremely short bursts. You wouldn't argue if someone in the peanut gallery heckled you.

Facebook is more structured around personal social connections than Twitter. That makes Facebook like a family party where anyone you've ever met might show up. How would you behave at such an event? Your grandmother or work colleagues might not want to witness a heated, mud-slinging argument about the morality of certain sexual fetishes with your old college friends. Each platform has an infrastructure that fosters and caters to a certain audience. If you cannot control yourself and absolutely must vent, then understand your audience.

Two final points on social media conversations. First, when people post something on social media, unless explicitly stated, they probably do not want their belief to be corrected. Usually their purpose is to have their view *confirmed*. If what they shared outraged them, they want others to be outraged similarly. If they're making a point they feel strongly enough about to post on their personal pages, chances are they are trying to tell others about it, not invite criticism (that is, they are being messengers). Reciprocally, if you disagree with a Facebook post you may experience cognitive dissonance—an uncomfortable feeling that occurs when incoming information doesn't match your worldview. Your own dissonance may entice you to correct someone's belief; you may even think you're doing them a favor by repairing their faulty reasoning. However, you're far more likely to start an argument that hurts the relationship and further entrenches their views.[32]

Second, many social media conversations happen in a digital *public* space. These venues present towering barriers and complexities. A good conversation can rapidly be spoiled by the addition of a provocative or belligerent third party—or twenty of them. More significantly, when people have a public conversation they put their pride on the line; consequently, we tend to cling even more tightly to our views in a public forum than in private.[33] Imagine how much more fiercely you'd argue for your position if you did it taking a stand in front of a crowd of people you wanted to impress than if you were discussing it in private, one-on-one. Because changing one's mind or "losing" an argument is perceived as humiliating, it's no surprise that many discussion threads go viciously awry.[34]

In contrast, the primary advantages of having conversations on social media are two—neither of which requires the use of a *public* social media space. These can be summarized by observing that digital textual communication, for all its weaknesses, is not limited by time or space. If you have an Internet connection, you can have a low-cost conversation in real time with someone else nearly anywhere on the globe within moments. And you can take as long as you want to reply if your conversation partner says something that you need to think over and/or if you need to take some time to calm down.[35] This gives an opportunity to control initial emotional responses that can derail in-person conversations. These are genuine advantages, but again, recognize the differences between public and private conversations and take anything that might be contentious private before beginning.

Best Practices for Engaging Conversation on Social Media

Here are some simple guidelines for engaging on social media:

1. Remember: when a post is "deleted" it still remains on servers (this is true for Facebook, Snapchat, and even your text messages).

   Before you post, remember that whatever you send will be saved for a long, long time.

2. Never post (or answer emails, or even enter online conversations) when you're angry.

   If someone's reply to you makes you "see red," that's a sure sign you should *not* reply to it until you've calmed down completely.

3. *You do not owe a response to anyone on social media because they've engaged you.*

   If you feel you *must* respond to a heated social media comment, then reach out to the person privately.[36] Most social media platforms allow private messaging. Alternatively, you can simply email or call the person and respectfully ask if they'd like to discuss their post. (Notice how this is formed as a question, not a command.)

4. Never argue on Twitter.

   The 280-character architecture of the platform is not conducive to nuance, and the platform is particularly susceptible to problems like dog-piling, in which many people gang up, often rudely, on someone perceived as guilty of an offense.

5. Avoid religion, politics, and most philosophy on your *personal* Facebook page.

   The unique social structure of the Facebook environment is not conducive to religious, political, and most philosophical arguments.[37] It's also prudent to minimize your engagement with religious and political posts on Facebook (as it is unfortunately structured to display your engagement publicly to your friends, which is similar to you posting the material yourself).

6. If you absolutely, positively cannot control yourself, set up an anonymous Twitter account and rage at the ether.

   Don't tag anyone (which is usually abusive), just start discharging your anger, in all caps if necessary.

#6—Don't Blame, Do Discuss Contributions

How did Donald Trump, a real estate mogul and reality TV star with no previous experience in politics, get elected to the office of US president in November 2016? It seems like everybody "knows," and everybody knows it was somebody else's fault. Immediately after the election, many people were quick to blame *somebody*—anybody—no matter what side of the political aisle. Hillary Clinton and her campaign were blamed, so were the Democrats, FBI Director James Comey, the Russians, Vladimir Putin, Bernie Sanders, the Republicans, the Progressive Left, the Fox-watching Right, the "mainstream media," purveyors of fake news, WikiLeaks and its founder Julian Assange, and the list goes on.

How did those blamed respond? Did they respond unsarcastically, "Yup, guilty"? No. They denied their culpability, often shifting it to someone else by asking "What about so-and-so?!" Many doubled down on the behaviors for which they were being blamed.[38] For example, a large portion of the Progressive Left still clings to the belief that it was pervasive sexism or racism that proved decisive in the election. Some blamed *entire* racial groups and genders (men, generally, and white women particularly) for Clinton's defeat.[39] Instead of reflecting upon the ways in which their brand of identity politics might have contributed to Trump's success,[40] they intensified their belief that ours is an extraordinarily sexist and racist society and blamed privileged identity groups for their complicity.[41] *Time* magazine, for example, published an opinion piece just after the election claiming the results were "the revenge of the white man."[42] It needs to be explicitly stated: overzealous identity politics of just this kind likely *contributed* to Trump's election. More significantly, none of this blame, no matter who directed it at whom, has helped create better, more productive and civil conversations between America's warring political tribes.

Blame ends goodwill, immediately puts those blamed on the defensive, hinders problem solving, and dissolves rapport.[43] People don't want to be blamed when bad things happen, especially when it isn't *all* their fault. Rather than openly discussing an issue, then, the blamed usually attempt to redirect the conversation, often by denying the accusation, diminishing its importance, or hurling back blame in retaliation. For example, it seems almost all cable news opinion today is rife with "whataboutery." That is, pundits and commentators deflect blame from their side by forcefully asking, "What about [some roughly similar thing from the other side]?" Discussions about radical Islam, for example, are often met with, "But what about the Crusades!"

The Harvard Negotiation Project noted that there is an effective alternative to introducing blame into conversations. Instead of blame, invite people to collaboratively look for *contributions*.[44] That is, work together *with* people to get a more comprehensive picture of what happened so you can move forward toward solutions that address all aspects of the problem. Contributions are made by everyone, and most problems have more than one contributor. Blame, however, is one-sided.[45]

Blame is something laid upon someone. For example, "You did this!" It's past tense and judgmental. Identifying contributions is a joint, interactive approach to understanding a broader picture of how a state of affairs came to be; the idea of contribution is about understanding and forward thinking. When we understand the constellation of factors that contributed to our circumstance, we're ideally situated to solve those problems going forward.[46]

Now let's return to President Trump's election as a good example of considering a problem from the perspective of contribution systems instead of blame. One question that can be asked within a contributory framework is, "What aspects of the Progressive Left's behavior may have contributed to Trump's success with some voters?" People on the political Right will give an outsider's perspective. People within the Progressive Left can engage the question self-reflectively (and ease political tensions by doing so). Notice that this neither blames the Progressive Left for Trump's election nor denies that it shares some responsibility. Contributions arise in systems where multiple entities play a part; shifting away from blame, and toward contributions, avoids arguments over who's "at fault." By asking parallel questions about other contributing factors, more of the complete picture can become visible without blaming anyone.

For example, mapping the contribution system that led to Trump's election almost immediately produces any number of interesting, collaborative, brainstorming-type conversations in which people from every political position can explore various contributions. How did right-wing media like Fox News and talk radio play a role? What role, if any, did Russians play in the election? What did the Democrats and Republicans each do right and wrong? How much of a role did Libertarians and Greens play and what was it? What about Bernie Sanders? These open-ended questions offer opportunities to map a complex contribution system that gave rise to our political reality. They invite conversation, whereas blame invites defensiveness, hostility, and incivility. Remember the power of Modeling: mapping out one's own contributions to a problem can naturally lead others to engage in the same. This "honey" method is much better than the "vinegar" we usually employ in the form of heated arguments and shifting blame.

Our moral divide is widened by partisanship, which includes being overtly partisan, even on our own side.[47] When conservatives blame liberals for problems, or vice versa, each scapegoats an outside group, thus further justifying their own values (and their distrust of opponents) to one another.[48] This increases partisanship and thus damages civility across the divide. Avoid this by shifting to contribution. In any situation, the contribution system that led to a problem will probably turn out to be complex.

How to Shift Away from Blame and Toward Contribution

Here are some easy ways to shift from blame to identifying contributions:

1. Use the word *contribution.*

   Say, "What factors contributed to [X]?" and "What's your opinion about what contributed to that?" (Notice these are calibrated questions.)

2. Avoid saying, "X caused Y," for example, "Right-wing media caused Republicans to vote for Trump."

   "X caused Y" statements are both very difficult to prove and a subtle form of attributing blame. Especially in complicated systems like politics and social dynamics, many factors may have contributed, and are *causative,* but are not *the* cause.

3. Don't say "both sides do it" when bad behavior is pointed out about your side.

   Stating "both sides do it" is a way to switch from contribution back to blame. It's defensive. If you're a conservative and a liberal says, "Conservatives tend to ignore facts to push an agenda," don't reply, "Well, yeah, both sides do it." Instead, acknowledge but don't deflect when your side has been criticized. Say, "Yeah, that's true. Conservatives sometimes do that." Leave it at that.

4. If you reach a point where you just cannot avoid introducing blame into the conversation, whether to blame the person with whom you're speaking or the political group with which they identify, ask your partner, "Because I feel strongly tempted to blame the Democrats for this problem, can you please help explain the logic the Democratic side uses to justify their actions?"[49]

If you have the courage to take it a step further, invite them to share their views on how they feel *your* side contributed. If you can see your side's contributions for what they are, it can help dissolve the urge to blame someone else.[50]

#7—Focus on Epistemology

Epistemology, *noun*

e·pis·te·mol·o·gy

ə͵pistəˈmäləjē/

The theory of knowledge, especially with regard to its methods, validity, and scope. Epistemology is the investigation of what distinguishes justified belief from opinion.

The following conversation took place in Columbia River Correctional Institution (CRCI) in Portland, Oregon.[51] CRCI is a pre-release facility, meaning that prison inmates serve the last part of their sentences there before going back into the community.

Peter was teaching a ten-week course designed to help inmates develop critical thinking and moral reasoning skills, and thus desist from criminal behavior. The conversation was based upon Socrates' question in *The Republic*: What is justice?

Boghossian: *What is justice?*

Inmate 6: *Standing up for what you believe in.*

Boghossian: *What if you believe weird stuff? Like one of those lunatics who wants to kill Americans? Or what if you're a pedophile?*

[A 20-second silence.]

Inmate 6: *I think if you can stand on your own two feet and not care what anyone else thinks about you, and you're willing to fight for it and die for it or whatever, that makes you a man. Whether it's right or not.*

Boghossian: *So being a man would mean to be resolute in your beliefs no matter what? What if you're in the military, like in Rwanda, and you're told to butcher all these people, and you have this skewed idea of loyalty. And you stand up for what you believe, for your country or tribe or whatever, and you just start butchering civilians? Hutus or Tutsis or whoever. Is that just? Does that make you a man?*

Inmate 5: *Yeah, good point. It happened in Nam [Vietnam].*

Inmate 4: *What are you saying? That justice isn't standing up for what you believe in?*

Boghossian: *I'm not saying; I'm asking. What is justice? [Inmate 6] said it's standing up for what you believe in. But is it really standing up for what you believe in? Don't you have to believe the right stuff, then stand up for that? No?*

Inmate 6: *Yeah, maybe. Maybe.*

In this dialogue, which took place near the end of Peter's study, inmates were helping each other question their epistemology. That is, they were asking each other how they knew what they thought they knew.

Claims to Knowledge

This book contains one esoteric term: *epistemology.* Epistemology is the study of knowledge. It's the effort to understand *how* we know what we think we know. The most common mistake in conversations is focusing on *what* people claim to know (beliefs and conclusions) as opposed to *how* they came to know it (their reasoning processes).

Let's delve into an example of applied epistemology. Fred claims abortion is murder. "Abortion is murder" is a conclusion. You may be tempted to argue or agree with Fred about his belief. Don't. Instead, ask yourself how he came to this belief. The way he came to the belief is known as his epistemology. The best way to figure out how he concluded that abortion is murder is simply to ask calibrated questions centering on how he knows what he thinks he knows: "Hey, Fred, how do you know abortion is murder?"[52] Then listen to his response. It couldn't be any easier.

Though Fred could offer any one of a number of responses, his reasons will almost always fall into a few categories:

- Personal experience and feelings (he feels it's true in his heart).
- Culture (it's true because "everyone" believes it).
- Definition (it's true or good or bad because of the way it's defined; for example, eating too much broccoli is bad by definition because too much of anything is bad).
- Religion (it's true because it's taught in his place of worship and/or in his holy book).
- Reason (it's true because it can be reasoned to).
- Evidence (it's true because there's sufficient evidence to warrant belief).

Here's how to understand the way your conversation partner comes to knowledge, that is, his epistemology. First, find out the broad category in which he grounds his epistemology. Second, drill down to learn specifics. (For the purposes of this section, this is all you need to do. In the following chapters, we'll discuss how to proceed once you have a clear understanding of how your partner claims to know what he thinks he knows.)

For example, maybe Fred believes abortion is murder because he thinks it's written in Matthew 1:23, "Behold, the virgin shall be with child, and bear a Son." Then his reasoning is religious. Or, in response to your query, "Hey, Fred, how do you know abortion is murder?" Fred says, "My mother almost had an abortion. I wouldn't be here if she did." Then his reasoning is based in personal experience. Or he could reply, "When you stop a heart from beating, that's called 'murder.'" This falls into the category of definition.

It's likely the case, however, that Fred's reason for holding the belief falls into several of the categories above. You'll need to ask more questions and delve deeper. Usually, but not always, beliefs are supported primarily by one category and buttressed by at least one other. Religious reasons, for example, are almost always primary if they are present; that is, if someone comes to a conclusion based on a religious belief, religion is the underlying reason why the belief is held (even though more thoughtful believers downplay the role religion, or even evidence, plays in justifying their beliefs and shift to reason).

A significant benefit of focusing on epistemology, as opposed to engaging conclusions, is that people have developed practiced responses to having their conclusions challenged. Often referred to as "talking points," these are rehearsed statements/messages given in response to frequently heard arguments. Focusing on epistemology helps people explain *how* they arrived at their conclusions, providing a fresh route around rehearsed messages.

Further, if you challenge someone's beliefs, then you're far more likely to evoke a defensive posture than if you question their reasoning that led them to their beliefs. Challenging beliefs risks your conversation partner becoming defensive and hunkering down.[53] Focusing on epistemology avoids many of these issues because people are less threatened by having their epistemology probed than having their beliefs challenged.[54]

Simple Ways to Discuss How People Know

Here are some simple ways you can focus on *how* your partner comes to knowledge rather than just on *what* he thinks he knows:

1. Make a brief, positive statement before probing someone's epistemology.

Say, "That's an interesting perspective. What leads you to con-clude that?" Or, "Okay, cool. I think I understand, but I'm not sure. How does that work?" (Notice how these are calibrated, inviting questions, "What leads . . . " and "How does . . . ," as opposed to commands, "Explain that to me," and noncalibrated questions, "Can you tell me . . . ".) These very brief, initial positive state-ments, which act as a type of micro rapport building, may help your conversation partner feel more comfortable and thus be more likely to share her thoughts.

2. Ask "outsider questions."

Outsider questions help people view their beliefs as someone unfamiliar with those beliefs would view them.[55] For example, Muslims view Pentecostal beliefs about speaking in tongues as bizarre; Pentecostals view the common Muslim belief about Mo-hammad flying to heaven on a winged horse (*Buraq*) as bizarre; Scientologists view both beliefs as bizarre; and Pentecostals and Muslims view the Scientologist belief that we have memories going back trillions of years as equally outlandish.[56] Outsider questions can help people view their beliefs from the perspective of an outsider.[57] Say, "Would every reasonable person draw the same conclusion?"[58] If the person says yes, follow up with, "I'm a sincere, reasonable person and I'm having trouble drawing the same conclusion. How do I get there?" or "How come there are so many divergent opinions? I mean, why is it that when two people look at the same evidence they come away with different conclu-sions? How does one figure out whose belief is true and whose is false?"

Here are more examples of outsider questions: "Many people who live in [place] believe [contradictory belief]. How would they think about this belief?" (Notice this is not personalized by say-ing "your belief." The words *you* and *your* evoke a defensive pos-ture.) "Many Catholics who live in Mexico City believe that the path to Heaven lies in staying in good standing with the church.

How would they think about salvation by faith alone?" Similarly, "If someone who believed that had been born in another region of the world, and raised there since birth, what would they likely believe?" These questions may help people examine their views from a different angle. They're also subtle ways that invite people to reflect on their epistemology.

3. Start your conversation in wonder.

Ask yourself, "How did my conversation partner arrive at this conclusion? What was their reasoning process? Why does someone believe that? What are someone's reasons for thinking that's a good idea? What would an external observer who has no opinion of the subject think? Is the person's belief supported by her reasons?" If you're genuinely wondering "How could someone come to believe that?" you're more likely to adopt a learning posture and less likely to become frustrated.[59]

4. If someone's reasoning makes no sense, there's a good chance they reason that way to justify a (moral) belief that cannot otherwise be justified.

Ask, "Do you use that reasoning process for anything else, or just X?" or "Can you please give me an example of some other issue where you use that same reasoning process?" For example, James recently encountered "If you want women to change their behavior to prevent rape (say, by drinking less in public), you're really saying 'make sure the rapist rapes the other girl.'" In this instance, politely ask if they use that reasoning for anything else, and if so, could they please provide you with their best example. (Asking for their best example saves time.) You may need to provide an example of the same reasoning in other contexts. Say, "Would you say the same thing about other forms of prudence? If people who change their behavior to prevent being mugged, like carrying their wallet in their front pocket or holding a purse close under the arm, how could you claim that those people are really saying 'make sure the mugger mugs someone else'?"

Alternatively, use examples in the form of questions and ask whether that reasoning makes sense when applied to other issues: "How is that reasoning different from, 'I'm not going to teach you how to make sure your parachute is secure because there are some people who don't know how to secure a parachute'?" Or, "How does that differ from, 'We're not going to tell anyone to wear their seat belt because there will always be people who don't wear their seat belt, and some who do and die anyway'?" Follow up by asking, "If it's not similar, how's the reasoning different?" The key is to get your partner to focus on reasoning.

5. Try to derive other conclusions from their reasoning process.

Here's an example. Beth's reasoning process:

The enemy puts antiaircraft guns in civilian living areas.
Blowing up the guns will cause civilian deaths.
Therefore, we shouldn't blow up the guns.

Beth's conclusion is: "Therefore, we shouldn't blow up the guns." Here's how another conclusion could be derived from the same premises:

The enemy puts antiaircraft guns in civilian living areas.
Blowing up the guns will cause civilian deaths.
Therefore, it's even more urgent that we take out the guns to prevent the combatants from expanding and doing this to more civilians when the problem becomes too big to ignore later.

#8—Learn

Peter has sometimes been blinded by his beliefs. When he was on tour in Australia, a Christian group flew in an apologist from Singapore to debate him about the genesis of the universe. The apologist was a decent and kind man. He was also someone with whom Peter had significant disagreements.

Peter argued that the only way to know how the universe was created was through science, and because neither one of them was a physicist they were both unqualified to render a judgment. The apologist argued that we could reason our way to the fact that the universe was created by a supernatural entity. That is, he claimed it was possible to deduce that God created the universe.

Peter was unwilling to seriously entertain his argument and was convinced in the truth of his position. Peter did not hear him out. He should have listened and learned, but he doubled down and paraded his ignorance as a virtue: "Look how humble I am because I'm saying I don't know—and neither do you!" Peter was an ideologue (see Chapter 7) masquerading in the cloak of humility.

Although claiming "Nobody can know the origin of the universe" might be a good debate strategy, it closed him off to the possibility that his belief could be incorrect. In other words, it closed him off from genuinely considering whether we can reason to knowledge about how the universe came into existence. He missed an opportunity.

Sometimes *we* are the ideologues. Sometimes we are unwilling to learn. This is a mistake we all make. The opportunity to learn is a conversational ace in the hole that will nearly always let you have a friendly, profitable conversation, no matter the topic. If you are unable to seek truth collaboratively, can't intervene in someone's thinking, and civility seems difficult, you can switch to a learning frame. Doing so will help you understand your conversation partner's thinking in all but the most extreme circumstances. Adopting a learning frame is a tool that creates a soft landing for almost any conversation, allowing you either to profit or to end the conversation positively.

Learn How People Think, Especially Dogmatists

Adopting a posture of learning from someone who holds different views makes them feel heard. Even someone whose mind cannot be changed—in fact, especially a person like this—wants to be heard. Once a person has been heard and feels understood, they're more likely to open up to more productive, two-way dialogue.[60] And if they don't open up, your time will be well compensated: *you'll* learn.

This is particularly true with dogmatists who tend to lay down their principles as incontrovertibly true. Nothing you say seems to reach them. What can you do in a conversation when attempting to engage someone who holds beliefs dogmatically? Learn from them. Learn *how* they think. Specifically, bring the conversation back to epistemology, that is, attempt to understand how they know what they think they know. If you can learn the process they used to lead them to their beliefs, then you'll be better positioned in future discussions and you'll have honed your skills as an epistemological detective.[61] You may even tap into their own Unread Library Effect or get them to begin to doubt the epistemology behind their beliefs.

Talking with a dogmatist isn't the only time you can benefit from adopting a learning frame of mind. It works in *any* conversation. Your partner is not you. Therefore, your partner will have a perspective different from yours. She'll have different assumptions, different experiences, and different information that you might not have. You can always learn more about what she knows and how she knows it and in the process you'll have better, more productive conversations.

Conversational Techniques to Shift into a Learning Frame

Here are a few easy-to-use conversational techniques:

1. Learn your conversation partner's epistemology.

    Ask a question designed to reveal how they know what they think they know. Say, "How do you know that?" or "How'd you arrive at that conclusion?"

2. Be explicit.

    Say, "I want to learn" and "What more can you tell me [about X] so I can learn where you're coming from?" (This only works if you're sincere. If not, it will come across as condescending.)

3. If civility is your primary goal, or if productive conversation is impossible, make learning your go-to.

If you just want to get through a family reunion, learning is your emergency exit that allows you to make *almost any* conversation civil.[62] Adopt a frame of mind in which you are engaging in a study of someone with radically different beliefs than yours and try to learn all you can about how they form their beliefs.

#9—WHAT **NOT** TO DO (REVERSE APPLICATIONS)

There are many ways *not* to have effective, civil conversations. Below is a partial list of how *not* to conduct yourself. That is, the behaviors listed will usually, if not always, make your conversations go awry.

Conversational Behaviors to Avoid

- Be discourteous or uncivil.
- Display anger.[63]
- Raise your voice and talk over someone.
- Intentionally be disrespectful.
- Ridicule and blame someone.
- Laugh *at* someone.
- Attack a position before understanding it.
- Display an unwillingness to hear your conversation partner's arguments.
- Adopt the least charitable interpretation of someone's words.
- Accuse someone of being stupid if they ask a question or say they don't understand.
- Punish people for making mistakes or asking for help, information, or feedback.[64]
- Lash out at someone for speculating.
- Attack a person who holds a belief rather than the belief. ("Only a moron could believe that.")
- View people as being "ignorant, incompetent, negative, or disruptive."[65]
- Be dishonest with yourself about what you believe.

- Pretend to know something you don't know.
- Fail to say "I don't know" if you don't know.
- Focus on the belief instead of how the belief is known. (That is, focus on conclusions and not epistemologies. For example, "The death penalty isn't murder, those people deserved it," as opposed to, "What are the reasons one would think the death penalty is justified?")
- Suggest that a person can't really know something because of the color of their skin or other immutable attribute.
- Don't change your mind when presented with new and compelling evidence.
- Obfuscate (especially when someone asks you a direct question).
- Deliver messages.
- Fail to acknowledge vulnerability.[66]
- Insist that the extremists on your side are acting rationally.
- Correct someone's grammar (it's annoying).
- Call someone out for a moral transgression in a way that interrupts, distracts from, or takes away from the flow or content of their message.
- Interrupt.
- Finish others' sentences for them.
- Bully someone into having a conversation.
- Let yourself be bullied into having a conversation.
- Look at your phone while having a discussion.[67]
- Name-drop.[68]
- Be negative and complain.[69]
- Brag.[70]
- Refuse to disengage until there is a burned bridge.

Conclusion

The most important skill described in this chapter is learning how to figure out how people know what they claim to know. The other techniques can be seen as a way to facilitate that understanding. If all else fails, switch to a learning mode. Be explicit. State that you're trying to figure out how they know X and ask for their help by using calibrated questions. If nothing else, you'll be given insight into *how* people think and reason. This understanding will be tremendously helpful as you apply advanced and expert intervention techniques.

Finally, the techniques in all these chapters are cumulative. You'll be most effective by gaining proficiency in earlier chapters before attempting more advanced techniques. This is particularly true with interventions, because attempting to instill doubt in someone's beliefs is complicated.

Practice. Practice. Practice.

four

Intermediate Level: Seven Ways to Improve Your Interventions

Effective Skills for Changing Minds (Including Your Own)

#1—LET FRIENDS BE WRONG

It's okay if someone disagrees with you, even about a cherished conclusion

#2—BUILD GOLDEN BRIDGES

Find ways for your conversation partner to avoid social embarrassment if they change their mind

#3—LANGUAGE

Avoid "you," switch to third person or collaborative language like "we" and "us"

#4—STUCK? REFRAME

Shift the conversation to keep it going smoothly or to get it back on track

#5—CHANGE YOUR MIND

Change your mind on the spot

#6—INTRODUCE SCALES

Use scales to gauge effective interventions, figure out how confident someone is in a belief, and put issues into perspective

#7—OUTSOURCING

Turn to outside information to answer the question, "How do you know that?"

I never considered a difference of opinion in politics, in religion, in philosophy, as cause for withdrawing from a friend.

—Thomas Jefferson to William Hamilton, April 22, 1800

Intervening upon someone's beliefs takes intermediate-level conversational skills. Successful interventions often require more discipline and finesse than you need to apply the fundamentals, yet these techniques are still easily accessible. The skills taught in this chapter should make your conversations more effective at changing minds, but their success depends, in part, on a firm, natural grasp of the material presented in Chapters 2 and 3. In other words, you will need to integrate this chapter's intermediate skills with everything that you've learned so far.

Some of the techniques that follow operate in the realm of emotions, and they may require you to overcome natural impulses to argue, defend, and correct. At the same time, some techniques operate outside the emotional realm and demand exercising intellectual judgment. You'll need to assess the discussion and adapt accordingly.

In this chapter, you'll learn intervention techniques, that is, strategies for intervening in someone's cognitions and helping them revise their beliefs. As already noted, some require the exercise of emotional restraint. You might, for example, need to prevent yourself from lashing out at someone because they hold a belief you find repugnant. Likewise, building Golden Bridges, so your conversation partner can safely change her mind, requires you to set aside frustration and self-righteousness and to squelch the impulse to gloat. Being willing and able to change your mind on the spot, when it is warranted, also means that you have to set aside your pride.

Some techniques in this chapter also require you to develop intellectual finesse. The simplest of these involves quantifying your progress in the form of introducing numerical scales. Numbers can be quite useful for clarifying sticking points, or even for helping people change their own beliefs, but they can also come across as artificial or manipulative. Applying them effectively therefore requires more conversational finesse than is needed for the basics.

Learning to reframe the conversation in real time, so it stays on track, requires a successful integration of listening and learning techniques—and a little savvy. Outsourcing also means recognizing certain facts as outside your expertise. You'll need to abandon the false pride that's involved in trying to hide your ignorance. Instead, you'll be asked to muster the self-confidence to admit what you don't know.

#1—LET FRIENDS BE WRONG

> Boghossian: *You know I think that's [the alleged resurrection of Jesus] silly, right?*
> Vischer: *[laughing] Yeah.*

Phil Vischer, the creator of *Veggie Tales,* is a close friend of Peter's. He's not "just a Christian"; he also writes television shows that attempt to recruit children into the Christian belief system. Even though Peter has spent much of his professional life helping people escape faith-based belief systems, Phil and Peter are friends.

Don't Make Friendships About Agreement

Good relationships will keep you healthy and happy, healthier and happier than *anything*—including being right.[1] They are also consistently rated as the most important element of a good life by those approaching death.[2] Healthy relationships are founded upon far more than being correct—or even upon agreement. Meaningful relationships hinge mostly around factors like dependability, kindness, honesty, virtue, empathy, good conversation, mutual caring and goodwill, authenticity, common interests, and valuing the relationship.

Most of these have little to do with political or religious opinions, which centuries of human history have proven can largely be set aside in the name of friendship or family.[3] Religious or political agreement may help develop an initial connection, but they're seldom sufficient for a deep relationship. Friendships based solely on religious or political agreement are rarely sustainable, at least until some deeper substance to the relationship is found. In fact, friendships with these bases can be the opposite of sustainable, as people with weak interpersonal ties often become more guarded and warier when small differences in opinion manifest themselves over time. In a relationship built only upon superficial moral markers like religious (e.g., Catholic) or political (e.g., libertarian) identity, small differences can threaten the only basis the relationship has. If you consider how cliquish many church communities can be, you'll appreciate this simple fact about human interaction.

Why throw away a friendship because of a disagreement, especially a political one?[4] If an accident happened, and you were sick and dying, would it really matter if the person caring for you and holding your hand supported a different political party?[5]

How should you handle the "problem" of not being in complete agreement? Simple: *let people be wrong.*[6] Especially if you're friends. Let your friend say something incorrect and let it go without indulging the urge to correct or argue. (You may both be partly wrong about a given belief, so the truth of "letting her be wrong" has a deeper and more important meaning— it would be foolish to damage a relationship because we merely *think,* but do not *know,* that the other person is harboring an incorrect view about reality.[7])

Often, correcting people's beliefs doesn't go well.[8] Many disagreements are waged against the foundation of the relationship and can diminish the quality of friendships or ruin more superficial relationships. The decision to criticize, as opposed to engage, someone's beliefs—especially moral beliefs—must be made recognizing the possible costs, especially when the disagreement arises over morally rooted concerns. Differences of opinion, even moral opinions, are not necessarily moral failings. People hold moral beliefs for a range of reasons, from culture to personal experience to ignorance. If someone reasons her way to a false moral view, this doesn't make her a bad person. It just means her reasoning was in error.[9]

However, if you choose to engage a friend about an issue upon which you have a substantive disagreement, it's an opportunity for you to develop a deeper relationship. There are better and worse ways to do this; the best, start with listening. Make sure you *really* understand your friend's point of view and how she arrived at her conclusions. (When you do, restate it back to her and ask if you've understood correctly.) Show that you care about the values behind your friend's beliefs. Don't fall into the trap of caring more about being right than having fulfilling relationships.[10] If you remain unpersuaded of this advice, then remember that the best chance you have at influencing someone of a different moral position is through friendship.[11] Friendship, as Aristotle wrote, is indispensable for having a good life.

How to Let Friends (and Others) Be Wrong

1a. Say, "I hear you," and let your friend speak without interruption.[12]

When a contentious issue arises, especially if it's a personal criticism, allow your friend to voice their concerns without condemnation, correction, rebuttal, defensiveness, or refutation. Offering a listening ear will likely relieve tension, give your friend an opportunity to share feelings, and engender trust.[13]

Saying "I hear you" is a powerful and easy way to let your friend know you're listening. It's also useful when you aren't sure what to say next.

1b. If you don't understand, put the lack of understanding on yourself.

Say, "I don't understand," as opposed to telling your friend she shouldn't feel a particular way, that her belief is mistaken, or that "You're not making sense." You don't have to agree with someone to acknowledge her views.[14]

2. If a friend has a belief that is a deal-breaker, then that's the belief about which you should strive to have a conversation.

Approach them *privately* and sincerely, and tell them you find the belief upsetting and would like to talk. It may be that the belief causes an irreconcilable divide in your relationship and ends the friendship. If it does, then it's better to have discussed it and parted ways than to harbor anger or resentment.[15] If you choose to challenge your friend's belief, make sure you're motivated out of a genuine concern for their well-being and not a desire to be right. Most importantly, be kind.

3. Remember the marriage counseling adage, "You can be right or you can be married."

Healthy, meaningful relationships are often unnecessarily ruined over a stubborn need to feel vindicated, be right, correct someone's behavior, or win an argument. Let friends be wrong.

#2—Build Golden Bridges

A Golden Bridge is a means by which your conversation partner can change his or her mind gracefully and avoid social embarrassment.[16] Golden Bridges are musts for successful conversations.[17]

The following statements are ways to build Golden Bridges: "Everyone makes mistakes"; "Expertise is the result of having made many mistakes and changed one's mind accordingly"; "We all just want the best for ourselves and each other and are doing what we can with what we think is true"; and "This is an extremely complicated issue and there's just so much confusion surrounding it." And, simply, "All good" and "No worries." These statements give your partner an escape route from embarrassment or perceived humiliation.[18] Moreover, if they think, based on your past interactions, that you'll respond with a Golden Bridge, they'll be more likely to change their minds. For example, if you're having a heated discussion with someone and you're proven correct, the opposite of a Golden Bridge is saying "I told you so" or "Un-freaking-believable it took you so long to figure that out." It is far better to say, "I can see where you were coming from, though."

Few people will admit, either to themselves or others, that they have a mistaken belief if they think humiliation will be the consequence.[19] This is most acute when someone has to admit being on the wrong side of a moral issue or when their sense of moral identity (that is, feeling like they are a good person) is at stake (see Chapters 7 and 8).[20] For example, people who believe vaccines are dangerous and shouldn't be administered to their children must admit to irresponsible and dangerous parenting. That's difficult. Building Golden Bridges takes pressure off someone and makes it easier to admit ignorance or revise a belief. Say, "Yeah, vaccinations causing autism was a reasonable thing to fear given that initial study that was published."

Golden Bridges are particularly important if someone believes they're knowledgeable about a specific issue, is deeply morally invested, or faces a challenge to their sense of personal, moral identity. Rather than admit error and revise their beliefs, they may be too proud, too anxious, or too fearful of embarrassment and instead continue defending a mistaken conclusion.[21]

How to Build Golden Bridges

1. Give your partner the same out you'd want.

   How would you want to get out of feeling stupid, incompetent, put on the spot, or having to admit being on the wrong side of an issue? If you've thought of specific words you'd want to hear, consider saying them if you think they would resonate.[22] Sometimes even a simple "Cool" is all the Golden Bridge you need.

2a. Do not put a toll on a Golden Bridge.

   Don't offer people a way to change their minds, but then penalize them when they walk across (when, that is, they do change their minds). Don't say, "It's about time!" or "I told you so!" or make a statement accusing them of being slow on the uptake. Just let them graciously pass across the bridge.[23]

2b. Do not shame people.

   Don't say things like, "You should have known that," "It's about time," or "I can't believe you didn't think of that." In particular, do not treat someone poorly because they *used* to think something you now find objectionable. Think of shaming someone as being like a live hand grenade. As the Harvard Negotiation Project notes, "There is no such thing as a diplomatic hand grenade."[24] Hand grenades damage or blow up bridges; they don't build them.

3. Build a Golden Bridge when you feel under attack.

If someone attacks you personally, recast the attack as being about the issue. Listen, but do not counterattack. Instead, translate it. If someone says, "I can't believe you could be so ignorant and not understand how guns kill so many children," reply, "The way my position on gun control is stated might lead someone to believe I don't care about children. I hear the concerns about children's welfare and safety. I really do. In fact, I share them. I want to get to a solution that keeps children safe as much as anyone. How could we solve that problem?"[25] (Note the calibrated question, Chapter 3.) This reframes the conversation (more on this later in the chapter) while building a Golden Bridge from the feelings of shame, guilt, and embarrassment that often follow from having become angry or personally attacked.

4. Build a Golden Bridge to escape anger.

If the conversation is heated, give yourselves an opportunity to cool down. Say, "These issues are really frustrating, I know. They get to me too." (Depending on the circumstance, you could also add, "This issue is played out. Let's talk about something else.") These are types of Golden Bridges that act as escape hatches and allow opportunities for people to mull over new information at their own pace, perhaps privately.[26]

5. Build Golden Bridges by explicitly agreeing.

If your conversation partner says, "I want everyone to pay their fair share of taxes and be held to the same laws as everybody else," stating, "I agree. We have more in common than we thought" is a type of Golden Bridge. It switches the conversation to a collaborative frame, which is helpful when seeking solutions to problems.[27]

6. Build Golden Bridges to alleviate pressure to get everything right or to know everything relevant to an issue.

Say, "No one is expected to know/understand everything; that's why we have experts we can appeal to." (This is a type of

Modeling, Chapter 3, and can open up Outsourcing, below.) This Golden Bridge is particularly useful when your partner thinks she may be mistaken.

7. Reference your own ignorance and reasons for doubt.

Say, "I used to believe [X], [Y], and [Z]. It turns out those beliefs were wrong. When I learned [A], [B], and [C], I changed my mind. Personally, that was enough to sway me." This may offer your partner an opportunity to "save face" because it lets them know there was a piece of information *you* didn't have but that you now have, and if they have it their belief may change.[28] In other words, the problem is not that they're stupid or evil, but that they're lacking a complete picture of the problem. Remember Socrates' adage from Chapter 2: people don't knowingly desire bad things.

For example, some former Christians left Christianity after learning that the Bible condones slavery. They may have believed the Bible was morally perfect until they encountered reasons for doubting that belief, such as the book of Exodus instructing fathers on how to sell their daughters into slavery.[29] A former Christian might tell a friend, "I used to believe the Bible was morally perfect until I found reasons to doubt it, like the part in Exodus 21 that instructs fathers on how to sell their daughters into slavery. After investigating, I found a lot of reasons like that to doubt the Bible's alleged moral perfection."[30]

A caution: Some people may interpret "I used to believe [X], [Y], and [Z]. It turns out those beliefs were wrong. When I learned [A], [B], and [C], I changed my mind" as a slight. It may come off as accusatory based upon context, tone of voice, and the personalities at play. Use this technique with discretion.

#3—LANGUAGE

The following passages from an article by Justin P. Borowsky demonstrate how hostage negotiators use language to achieve the goal of hostage safety. Borowsky emphasizes the skill—and the necessary perspective—required to create a perceived collaboration between the hostage taker and the negotiator. This sense of collaboration can dissuade a hostage taker from breaking off the negotiation. Specifically, note the use of the word *them* to imply a kind of teamwork:

> For example, in the following exchange the hostage taker threatens to kill the hostage after demanding a getaway vehicle. The negotiator responds by saying that he doesn't think the hostage taker wants to harm the hostage and that they should keep working together to develop some more ideas to present to "them" (the negotiator's boss).
>
> HOSTAGE TAKER: either that or I kill her **(Threat)**
>
> NEGOTIATOR: well you've told me time and time again that you don't want to hurt that girl I don't think you do
>
> HOSTAGE TAKER: but I will
>
> NEGOTIATOR: give me an alternate, give me something else that I can present to them[31]

As Borowsky explains, the negotiator in this case was able to form a relationship of "we-are-in-this-together" with the hostage taker, a sense that "they were working together against 'them' (the officer's superiors)."[32] The negotiator used specific language to shape perception in a way that ultimately produced a good outcome:[33]

> The creation of a "them" linguistically constructs the negotiator and the hostage taker as two people attempting to work together against another party. By creating this perceived alignment, the negotiator is placing him- or herself in a position to convince the hostage taker to surrender.[34]

Depersonalize: Say "That," not "You"

Avoid using "you." The word *you* often makes the conversation about people and can put your conversation partner on the defensive.[35] Say "that belief" or "that statement" as opposed to "your belief" or "your statement."

Don't try to take this to extremes. You shouldn't, and can't, eliminate the word *you* entirely from your conversational vocabulary. You may have to say, "I'm sorry, I didn't understand. Can you repeat that?" or "Can you explain that to me?" (Notice that these are formed in terms of questions, "Can you please . . ." as opposed to orders disguised as questions, as in "Explain that to me.") In these uses of "you," you're not subjecting the *person* to scrutiny.

Small and Effective Ways to Change Your Language

The application of this technique is quite simple:

1. Use collaborative language.

   We is a wonderful and effective collaborative word. As sociologists Weinstein and Deutschberger (1963) write, "'We' tends to be one of the most seductive of English words. Its appearance almost automatically heralds a relationship structured in terms of mutuality and interdependence" (p. 459). You can also often replace *you* with *we,* as in, "How do we know that?" and "Why don't we think about it more?"

   Us is another effective, collaborative word that can be used to great effect. "*Let's* [short for "let *us*"] figure out how to settle this impartially" and "How can *we* test that?"[36] When in doubt, stick with *we* and *us.*[37]

   If that's too difficult or awkward, then shift to neutral language, the third person, and *one.* For example, "How could one figure that out?" See #2, below.

2. Use neutral language.

   Avoid *you* and *your,* as in "you believe" and "your belief." Switch to neutral language like *that* and *one's.* For example, "that belief" and "one's belief."

3. Speak about ideas and beliefs, not the people who hold them.

Be especially careful with labeling people based on some (or just one) of their beliefs. "Bill believes health care should be free for everyone and paid for by taxes" is much more accurate, fair, and specific than "Bill is a socialist." "Maria disagrees" is likewise better than "Maria doesn't care if people die because they cannot afford health care."[38]

4. Switch from "I disagree" to "I'm skeptical."

Disagreeing may trigger an adversarial response, whereas "I'm skeptical" signals that you're open to be persuaded but you're not quite there yet.

#4—Stuck? Reframe

Reframing a conversation means putting it on different terms and changing perspectives so that there can be a different—hopefully more agreeable—take on the issue. Almost any question, topic, or conversation can be reframed.[39]

Here's an example. Peter and his wife were absolutely overwhelmed with work and life commitments. It also happened that their daughter had an unexpected day off from school. Here's a snippet of conversation, at a time when both were stressed and tired:

Boghossian: *I can take her with me to run errands.*
Wife: *That's an unappealing way to say that. It makes spending time with her seem like a chore or a duty.*
Boghossian: *Yeah.*
[pause]

Boghossian: *True.*
[pause]

Boghossian: *What should I say instead?*
Wife: *Who gets to spend time with her?*

Peter's wife was correct. Reframing from a "chore" or "duty" to opportunity would clearly help his daughter be more receptive to the idea of spending time with her father. More importantly, it helped Peter reframe his own view.

There are many ways to reframe. One straightforward way is to reorient your conversation partner from perceiving a situation as a negative to perceiving it—as Peter's wife did in the example—as a positive. Another way is to change the subject to underlying interests, feelings, or assumptions.[40] If you're trying to hash out a political topic, like gun control, reframe the conversation to underlying interests of safety, security, or rights and how best to balance those interests. You've thus reframed it from a politicized issue to a safety issue.

Though we'll return to moral and identity-based reframing in Chapter 7, appealing to common identities (called "superordinate identities") like "American," or even "human," is a helpful way to reframe.[41] You can reframe the conversation to commonalities simply by mentioning them. Say, "I don't know, as a parent, guns make me nervous for my kids. I know you're a good mom, and you have guns. How do you deal with that?" In this example, being a parent is an appeal to a superordinate identity. That is, it's a commonality both parties share. By putting the focus on a shared sense of identity (being good parents—and noting the positive identity affirmation), you can reframe a conversation while giving it a new context that might be less contentious.

Finally, reframing is not "spinning." It's an attempt to recast a question or sticking point in a different light. Reframing is also a way to view an issue from a perspective that facilitates more open dialogue and less negativity.

How to Reframe a Conversation When You Get Stuck

1. Reframe the conversation around commonalities.

   For example, in a debate over gun rights, it is probable that both you and your partner are ultimately concerned with the balances between safety and freedom. Reframe the question to the best ways a balance can be achieved—or what the underlying motivations are for best achieving that balance. Say, "Ultimately, we're both interested in safety and freedom for people, but don't see eye-to-eye on how to achieve those goals. Can we talk more directly about the ways we can achieve a balance?" Once commonalities and points of agreement are secure, you can return to your original question. This reframes the conversation from a debate about safety and liberty to a more collaborative discussion about how those two positives can be balanced despite their natural tension.

2. Reframe the question to be less contentious.[42]

Say, "I hear you. I wonder if we can get around our disagreement by looking at it another way. Maybe we're both just concerned about making sure we give the best opportunities to citizens. What do you think?" Reframing is particularly useful if people become frustrated.[43] In brief: translate what you're saying into terms that are more helpful, seek commonalities and underlying interests, and appeal to superordinate identities.

3. Figure out what you need to say for them to respond, "That's right."[44]

Reframe accordingly. Unlike a simple "Yes," which could mean different things in different contexts, "That's right" signals understanding of a position or embracing of an idea. Note that "That's right" is different from "You're right." When your partner says, "You're right," it "sticks" to you as opposed to their owning the conclusion.[45] Often the path to securing "That's right" is through reframing an issue that was perceived as negative to an issue that's now perceived as positive.

#5—Change Your Mind

When Peter was on tour in Australia, he had an intense conversation about the ethics of a government-owned radio station covering religious topics (e.g., the BBC covering an issue related to the Anglican Church). A young man offered the rather obvious argument that the reporting might be biased and said he wasn't sure if there were any safeguards that could prevent prejudice from leaking into the reporting. To both Peter's and the young man's surprise, a woman who was arguing on the other side of the topic said, "I really never thought about that before. I think that's right. Yeah. That's right." Both Peter and his conversation partner were taken aback, and a long pause ensued. Long pauses usually mean reflection and a potential for belief revision. They are, in these cases, a conversational success.

Change Your Mind on the Spot

At any point in the conversation, if you realize you've been harboring an incorrect belief, say, "I just realized my belief might be wrong. I've changed my mind." Because this almost never happens, when it does, your conversation partner will likely be completely taken aback.

There is, of course, a catch. You should *only* say this if you're sincere. "I've changed my mind" is therefore a type of invitation. It displays the virtues of revising beliefs and modeling, and thus becomes an invitation for others to do the same. It's also the ultimate rapport builder—it's almost impossible for someone to dislike you after you say this.

For example, assume you believe it's none of the government's business whether or not motorcyclists wear helmets. You believe it should be the rider's choice, because any accidents impact only the rider. Then your conversation partner tells you that most states would see a dramatic increase in their yearly taxpayer-funded Medicaid expenditures if helmet laws were repealed, meaning the decision not to wear a helmet impacts people other than the rider (taxpayers, not to mention her family, friends, coworkers, employers, and everyone else directly and indirectly affected by their lives).[46] Suppose further that this argument convinces you to rethink your stance on motorcycle helmet laws. Say so: "Wow, that may be right, I need to rethink my belief."

#6—INTRODUCE SCALES

Introducing scales (numbers) into your conversation can resolve places where the conversation got stuck, encourage new reflection and belief revision, and provide a means for you to track the success of your interventions.

"On a scale from 1 to 10 . . . "

Ask, "On a scale from 1 to 10, how confident are you that X [the belief] is true?" Beyond knowing how confident someone is that a belief is true, asking someone to assign a numerical value to their confidence does two things:

1. It tracks the effectiveness of your intervention.
2. It helps put issues into perspective.

We'll now unpack these items.

Track Your Effectiveness

As soon as you've settled on a discussion question (see Chapter 3, Ask Questions), ask, "On a scale from 1 to 10, how confident are you that X [the belief] is true?" (If they don't like that scale, suggest 1 to 100. If they refuse to assign a value to their confidence in a belief, then abandon this technique.) Immediately after the conversation, repeat the question and compare the pre- and post- numbers. For example, if before you engaged someone's belief they assigned a confidence value of 10 that "The federal government should crack down on states that have legalized marijuana" but after the conversation they self-report a 9, then they moved 10 percent. In other words, you now have a discrete metric that tracks your ability to intervene in someone's cognitions and instill doubt.

Introduce Perspective

You may have heard "American society is a patriarchy!" from the extreme end of the feminist spectrum. If you aren't a devotee of that brand of feminist thought, you might find this statement bizarre. Saying so, however, won't be met with "Yeah, you're right. It's an exaggeration. I'm trying to make a rhetorical point, but maybe I shouldn't express myself like that. Thanks." It will probably initiate a "No, it isn't!"/"Yes, it is!" argument instead. (The extent of patriarchy exhibited by a society is a matter of degree, but those degrees are bulldozed by the original statement.)

Instead, ask them to put the problem on a scale. Say, "I'm curious to understand how much of a patriarchy. Suppose Saudi Arabia is a 9 out of 10 in patriarchy. Where is the United States on the same scale?" If the United States is even just a 2 out of 10 in patriarchy, it isn't wholly wrong to say, "Americans live in a patriarchy," although it isn't totally correct either. Asking for a scale helps break away from all-or-nothing thinking, the "Yes, we do!"/"No, we don't!" mentality.[47]

Here's an example found on the other end of the political spectrum. If you're told "Our government is tyrannical!" ask, "How tyrannical? If Mao's regime in China was a 9 out of 10 in governmental tyranny, where's the United States right now?" Sure, the US government engages in some behaviors that appear—or in some cases are—tyrannical, but a binary "It is" or "It isn't" is not sufficiently nuanced.

How to Bring Numerical Scales into Your Interventions

1. Ask, "On a scale of 1 to 10, how confident are you that X is true?" at the beginning and end of the conversation.

   Compare these numbers to judge your effectiveness.

   If your partner says she's 9 or 10 confident a belief is true, you'll need the techniques found in Chapters 6 and 7. Moral beliefs in which people place unusually high degrees of confidence are often related to identity concerns. When someone self-reports a 9 or 10 confidence in a belief, it is even more important to figure out the epistemology that led them to their conclusion (Chapter 3, Focus on Epistemology).[48] Conversely, in rare instances when someone reports a 2 or 3, they have little to no confidence that a claim is true. In these instances, you can explore why their confidence is so low.

2. If you find yourself arguing with someone in a "Yes, it is!"/"No, it's not!" pattern, for example, "The United States is racist"/"No, it's not!" put it on a comparative scale.

Say, "How racist is the United States now as compared to the 1950s?" Scales add precision that can pin down, clarify, offer perspective, and get conversations back on track.[49]

3. Bring in scales that compare the importance of issues during sticking points.

   Asking someone whether or not they think racism is an important issue may elicit angry reactions and spark incredulity. However, asking, "On a scale from 1 to 10, how important is racism as compared to climate change? What number would racism be and what number would climate change be?" clarifies how intensely a belief is held and whether any disagreement is worth spending time on.

4. Use scales to help your partner reverse their thinking.

   Here's another way to phrase the scales question: "On a scale from 1 to 10, with 1 being no confidence and 10 being absolute confidence, how confident are you that belief is true?" Let's suppose they say "I'm at an 8." Rather than asking them, "Why not 6?" or even "What would it take to move you to 6?" immediately follow up by asking about a *higher* number. Say, "Just out of curiosity, why didn't you say 9?" Doing so will help them reveal their doubts.[50]

5. Here's how to use an even more advanced version of Introduce Scales: If they're above a 6 on a 1 to 10 scale, ask, "I'm 3 on that 1 to 10 scale that X is true. I'm not sure how I'd get to where you are, at a 9. I want to see what I'm missing. Would you help walk me through it?"[51]

   Used in this way, scales are an opportunity to have someone guide you step-by-step through their epistemology. This is effective because *they're* explaining the epistemological gap without you having to think on your feet and generate questions. That is, *they* are clarifying what you're missing, which may decrease their confidence and may even reveal their own ignorance in the process.[52] Better still, if their confidence in a belief is justified by the epistemological process that brought them to it, then *you* learned something and you can adjust or increase your confidence accordingly. Note: This technique combines Focus on Epistemology and the use of calibrated questions with Introduce Scales.

6. Keep a log of your conversations.

Note what lowers confidence levels and what does not. Refine. Discard. Repeat.

#7—OUTSOURCING

Most people have a stronger opinion on an issue than is warranted.[53] No one has expertise in more than a few areas, at most, but we often place disproportionately high confidence values in our beliefs.[54] One way to deal with this is to explore the Unread Library Effect (Chapter 3). Another is to engage in Outsourcing.

Outsourcing is a broad strategy for turning to outside information to answer the question "How do you know that?"[55] The goal is to help your conversation partner become curious enough to want to know how they can justify their knowledge claims, or to help *you* realize something you haven't had access to. You might, for example, have a disagreement with someone about income taxes. He hates them and you think they're a useful, necessary condition for membership in civilized society. After a few questions you ascertain why he finds them unduly burdensome: he thinks if someone makes more money, they'll bump up to the next tax bracket and thus have less disposable income. What's the best way to approach the fact that his understanding of a graduated income tax may be incorrect? You can't just say, "That belief is incorrect," because the conversation could devolve into a "Yes, it is"/"No, it's not" quagmire.

One way to address the dispute is to allow external information into the discussion. When dealing with taxes, it's not particularly difficult because there are readily available sources and experts who will all converge upon an identical answer. The difficult part is attempting to navigate more complex questions, especially moral questions. Before pulling out your phones and googling, first try to secure agreement on "Where could we go to find the answer?"[56]

This question might shift the conversation to "What sources/experts/ etc. should one trust and why?"[57] It might also reveal where your conversation partner is receiving their information, thus making it easier for you to understand their epistemology. If you can agree upon an external source, great. If not, attempts at Outsourcing will likely help you understand why they think a particular source is authoritative or offer you a new venue from which you could learn.[58] Finally, even the act of asking someone to consider what kind of expertise might be relevant can help people consider that they might not know as much as they think they know.[59]

Best Practices for Bringing Outside Information into Your Conversations

1. Use Outsourcing toward the end of a conversation.

    Say, "I'm not sure about that. If I could be shown reliable data, I'm open to changing my mind. Bring it back next time we talk. If it's persuasive enough to change my mind, I will." This one statement makes use of several techniques at once: Focus on Epistemology, Modeling, Learning, Build Golden Bridges, and Partnership. (Asking someone to provide evidence is not the same as interjecting your own evidence. See Chapter 5: *Do not offer evidence unless explicitly invited to do so*—even then, ask questions and make sure they genuinely want you to provide evidence. Presenting conflicting evidence may cause the backfire effect and further entrench your conversation partner in her beliefs.)

    Black musician Daryl Davis sometimes uses this technique— specifically, when he claims to know people's ideas are wrong— to de-convert members of the KKK.[60] Davis often meets with Klansmen and then sends them off seeking information that might support their claims, which he believes they cannot find, and capitalizes upon the doubt sown by their own research.[61]

2. If you're stuck mid-conversation, ask, "How would an independent, neutral observer figure out what source of information to trust?"[62]

You can also ask, "If we were to ask an expert who shares this opinion, who's an expert on the other side of the issue who makes the strongest case, who would that be?" Note also that this is a type of "outsider question" (Chapter 3).

3. Here are a few alternative ways to phrase Outsourcing (and disconfirmation, Chapter 5) questions:

   ❑ "What specific evidence could we find that might settle this?"[63]

   ❑ "What evidence should be sufficient to persuade an independent observer?"

   ❑ "What evidence is there that could persuade *every* reasonable person?"[64]

   ❑ "What's the best counterargument for why one should question conclusions drawn from that evidence?" Followed up by asking, "What's the best argument of two well-known experts and why are these arguments incorrect?"

4. Combine Outsourcing with building Golden Bridges.

   Say, "Let's set this aside for now and come back to it later when we have more information." (Notice the use of the team word *we* and the absence of the word *you*. See Language, above.) Don't press your partner to change her views. It's okay to let an issue rest, revisit it later, and build a Golden Bridge while doing so.[65] Combining Outsourcing with Golden Bridges can also defuse a tense situation. Doing so provides people with a shame-free way to analyze, verify, and assimilate the new information in their own time without feeling pressure to change their mind on the spot.

5. If, in an attempt at Outsourcing, you invite your partner to present evidence for her beliefs, and she responds, "There's no point in seeking evidence because there is no evidence that would change my mind," then her belief is not based on evidence.

   What it means to hold a belief based on evidence is, by definition, that one is open to the possibility that evidence might be discovered that would change one's mind. If no evidence would change one's mind, then one is not forming one's beliefs on the basis of evidence. Therefore, there's no point in Outsourcing. This is discussed in more detail in Chapter 5, Seek Disconfirmation.

6. Outsourcing only works with empirical questions.

Outsourcing only works with verifiable, testable propositions about the world or verifiable facts. It's not termed "moral outsourcing" because it does not work with moral questions, which are notoriously difficult to resolve.

Consequently, do not attempt moral outsourcing by appealing to "moral experts," for example, the Pope, your favorite theologian, your mother, a wise man you once knew, or a talk show host. If your partner does defer to her experts as a means to outsource moral questions, you have several options:

❑ Say, "I don't recognize X as a moral authority." (Be careful, however, as this might evoke a defensive posture. Your partner might infer that you have a moral deficiency because you don't recognize her expert.)

❑ Say, "The issue I have with that is that there are different people who profess to be moral experts and often these people have conflicting views. This gets us back to our original question of how can we figure this out."

❑ If your conversation is more thoughtful, say, "The problem with bringing moral experts into our conversation is that one has to already buy into the moral system before deferring to that person's authority. For example, we're not Scientologists, so neither one of us defers to L. Ron Hubbard's moral pronouncements."

7. Ask, "Whose expert opinion can I read to gather more information?"

Either (a) your partner won't have any relevant experts to name, at which point her underinformed state may become obvious to her; (b) she will name someone whose bias is well-known, at which point you can follow up by asking, "How is that source authoritative?" and "What are the best arguments against that position?"; or (c) she will name a genuine expert from whom you can learn.

8. Ask, "Who are the three best experts who disagree with that position?"

   This is a useful question for exposing the illusion of explanatory depth (Chapter 3).

9. If your conversation is stuck, say, "We seem to be stuck. How about we only use statements/information/evidence both sides would agree upon?"

CONCLUSION

In Plato's dialogue *Gorgias,* Socrates says that it's better to be refuted than to refute. What he means by this is that it's better to stop believing something false than it is to attempt helping someone stop believing something false. This is exactly what happens in some interventions—you attempt to intervene in someone's cognitions and you end up intervening in your own and revising your beliefs. This is the highest form of intervention, and when it happens don't run from it, embrace it. You were just afforded an opportunity to stop believing something that was false.

Not everyone, however, will view exposure of a false belief as an opportunity. Most will resist and cling to their beliefs. Many people will become upset. Some may even lash out *at you.* In these instances, building Golden Bridges and using cooperative language are crucial. Exercising your judgment is also crucial, as sometimes you should just listen to your friends, let them be wrong, and move on.

In the course of your conversation, if you do realize you're incorrect, say so. "I've changed my mind" is an incredibly powerful and empowering phrase. It's the perfect modeling behavior, has the potential to deepen your friendships, and if you're talking to someone you don't like, it's guaranteed to catch them off guard and reset the relationship.

Five Advanced Skills for Contentious Conversations

How to Rethink Your Conversational Habits

#1—Keep Rapoport's Rules
Re-express, list points of agreement, mention what you learned, only then rebut

#2—Avoid Facts
Do not bring facts into a conversation

#3—Seek Disconfirmation
How could that belief be incorrect?

#4—Yes, and . . .
Eliminate the word *but* from your spoken vocabulary

#5—Dealing with Anger
Know thyself

> *Bore, n.: A person who talks when you wish him to listen.*
>
> —*Ambrose Bierce*

The following pages will teach you *five tools and techniques to successfully navigate contentious conversations*. First, you'll learn how to employ Rapoport's Rules for disagreement. These require not only that you *really listen* but also that you restate your conversation partner's position as well as, or better than, she did *before* you openly disagree. You'll then learn the counterintuitive skills of avoiding facts and focusing upon disconfirmation rather than confirmation. (That is, focusing on the conditions under which a belief could be false rather than what evidence might hold that makes it true.[1])

We also advise eliminating the word *but* from your spoken vocabulary. This is more challenging than it sounds. The natural tendency to half-heartedly acknowledge your partner by saying "Yes, but . . . " when you disagree is hard to break. Finally, we give specific advice on the problem of anger, which derails many conversations. You'll learn important facts about anger, frustration, and offense. You'll learn how to discipline your angry impulses and the best responses when your conversation partner becomes angry.

Dealing with negative emotions, especially anger, requires identifying triggers *before* they come up in conversation. It also requires listening and managing your emotions in real time. If this is impossible during a tense discussion, you'll need to discipline yourself to walk away.

The skills in this chapter are classified as advanced because they require you to change some conversational habits. They also require you to control your emotions (to an even greater degree than the intermediate skills introduced in Chapter 4). Both of these are difficult, yet they're crucial for having effective discussions across political and moral divides. These advanced skills will initially seem counterintuitive, because they run counter to the way we're naturally prone to engage people. Nonetheless, they can be learned and practiced, and eventually they'll feel natural, just like any other skill.

Finally, the techniques described in this chapter may backfire if you make a mistake. Take things slowly. We recommend becoming comfortable and effective with the intermediate-level approaches from earlier chapters before attempting to integrate advanced skills into your repertoire.

#1—KEEP RAPOPORT'S RULES

In this brief dialogue, Anthony Magnabosco (AM), the Street Epistemologist whose dialogue we showcased in Chapter 2, is conversing with a stranger, Kari (K). They're discussing faith, belief, and God:

> AM: *If it wasn't the god that helped you through that difficult time and it really was yourself, how could you figure it out?*
>
> K: *I think that's where faith comes in.*
>
> AM: *Faith would help you figure out that it wasn't the god?*
>
> K: *No, I think faith is where you believe that that was truly working in your life.*
>
> AM: *I'm gonna rephrase this, and if this isn't what you're saying, let me know. I don't want to misrepresent your position, but are you saying that the way that you're so certain that it was the god that helped you get out of that situation, the reason why you can say that you know it, is because you have faith that it happened?*
>
> K: *I have faith in something above and beyond that's more powerful than me. I have a belief.*[2]

Before Criticizing . . .

The Russian-born American game theorist Anatol Rapoport had a list of rules for offering disagreement or criticism in conversations.[3] These rules are now known as Rapoport's Rules, and they have been described by American philosopher Daniel C. Dennett as "the best antidote [for the] tendency to caricature one's opponent."[4] Dennett neatly summarizes Rapoport's Rules in his book *Intuition Pumps and Other Tools for Thinking.* If your goal is to engage someone successfully, take these steps in this order:

1. Attempt to re-express your target's position so clearly, vividly, and fairly that your target says, "Thanks, I wish I'd thought of putting it that way."

2. List any points of agreement (especially if they are not matters of general or widespread agreement).

3. Mention anything you have learned from your target.

4. And only then are you permitted to say so much as a word of rebuttal or criticism.[5]

Adhering to Rapoport's Rules can be difficult, especially in a heated discussion, but it will *significantly* advance the civility and effectiveness of your conversations.

First, if you hold yourself to Rule 1, your conversation partner will know you've made a sincere attempt to understand their position.

Second, by keeping to Rule 2, you'll demonstrate shared commonalities. This is especially important if you're across political, religious, or moral aisles, because it helps maintain common ground and a collaborative framework. Rule 2 also makes points of agreement explicit, so that if the conversation gets stuck or heated you can return to them as a way of advancing the conversation through rapport building.

Third, Rule 3 models and helps foster an attitude of mutual learning and respect. If you've gleaned anything from your partner, pointing it out might encourage them to do the same. In the educational and corrections literature this is termed "pro-social modeling."[6] Pro-social modeling means demonstrating the behavior you want others to emulate; in the case of Rapoport's Rules, you're trying to model mutual respect and openness. Even if there's no reciprocity, Rule 3 will help maintain a semblance of collaboration while showing your partner you value their input.

Rapoport's Rules are an amalgam of various skills, strategies, and themes presented in Chapters 1 through 3 (Modeling, Listen, Shoot the Messenger, Learn, etc.). When used in conjunction with other approaches, they help make conversations effective, engaging, and productive. The rules are also a safeguard against carelessness and thoughtlessness, because they force you to understand a position before criticizing, challenging, or refuting. They are, ultimately, a prophylactic against incivility.

#2—Avoid Facts

Christian fundamentalist and Biblical Creationist Ken Ham is responsible for the Ark Encounter, a 510-foot (155-meters) full-size Noah's ark in Grant County, Kentucky. Ham is the perfect example of someone who cannot be swayed by facts. He believes the Genesis flood narrative literally and incorrigibly.

In a public debate with science popularizer Bill Nye in February 2014, both Ham and Nye were asked what would change their minds about creationism and evolution. Nye said, "Evidence," and Ham said, "Nothing." Ham has explicitly stated that there's no evidence that would cause him to revise his beliefs.[7]

Ham is not missing a piece of evidence that would cause him to change his mind; rather, he cannot be swayed by evidence, including rigorous peer-reviewed scientific studies.[8] For him, the issue is settled. Ham believes his belief cannot be disconfirmed (see Seek Disconfirmation, page 104). None of Nye's many, many facts presented during the debate (and since) has had any impact on changing Ham's mind. To engage someone like Ham, you have to avoid facts.

This certainly does not mean that you should disregard evidence or encourage others to do so. It *does* mean that introducing facts into a conversation is likely to backfire unless done at the correct moment and with great care.

Bad Facts, Bad!

The most difficult thing to accept for people who work hard at forming their beliefs on the basis of evidence is that not everyone forms their beliefs in that way. The mistake made by people who form their beliefs on the evidence is thinking that if the person with whom they're speaking just had a certain piece of evidence then they wouldn't believe what they do. Many people believe what and how they do precisely because they do not formulate their beliefs on the basis of evidence—*not* because they're lacking evidence. The same goes for forming beliefs based upon reasoned arguments.

Few people form their beliefs on the basis of rigorous consideration of reasoned arguments. Complicating matters, most people believe they *do* have evidence supporting their beliefs (Ken Ham makes a career out of tricking himself into believing this) because they consider only those points that support what they already believe.

Most of us do not do a good job of forming our beliefs on the basis of evidence (because we tend to focus on confirming what we believe rather than disconfirming what we believe). This isn't merely a problem of having limited access to evidence. We tend to form beliefs on the basis of cherry-picked selective evidence that supports what we already believe or what we want to believe.[9] Virtually everyone formulates most of their beliefs first and then subsequently looks for supporting evidence and convincing arguments that back them up.[10]

Creationism is the perfect example. The evidence for evolution is absolutely overwhelming and scientifically uncontroversial, yet 34 percent of Americans reject evolution entirely and only 33 percent of Americans "express the belief that humans and other living things evolved *solely* due to natural processes."[11] With few exceptions, this isn't because they've not been exposed to the evidence for evolution or have not heard the relevant arguments. It's for a variety of other non-evidence-based factors, like morality (thinking that if they believe, or pretend to believe, in creationism they're morally good people) or social factors (everyone in their local community believes it, or pretends to believe it, and their need to fit in is greater than their need to seek out what's true).[12] In all these cases, their moral and social minds are overriding their rational minds.[13]

Offering evidence—facts—almost never facilitates belief revision for any belief with moral, social, or identity-level salience. (Recall that the backfire effect occurs when one becomes increasingly certain of the truth of one's beliefs when presented with conflicting evidence. See Chapter 2, notes 34 and 47. The backfire effect redoubles a believer's commitment to her beliefs, increases your frustration, and often results in a wasted conversational opportunity. *Facts are the main culprit in eliciting the backfire effect.*[14]) There are many psychological and social reasons why evidence fails to persuade, but chief among them is that people care deeply about being "good." That implies, in agreement with the evidence, that feedback they receive from peers and other people whose esteem they value goes much further than facts in influencing what they believe.[15]

Vaccine deniers, for example, are most concerned about being good parents, and their erroneous beliefs about vaccines are based upon a network of other beliefs—like that "natural" means good and "artificial" means bad—that leads them to conclude withholding vaccines is crucial to good parenting. (What if their child is vaccinated and something goes wrong? How could they live with themselves having made that choice? Worse, what if they're wrong, and they've been withholding potentially life-saving medical care from their children?) Consequently, presenting someone with facts will almost never do what almost everyone thinks it will do, change minds.

First, Do No Harm

One reason you shouldn't introduce facts or evidence is to avoid giving your conversation partner a reason to defend her positions. This is especially true if she'll look foolish and "lose" by doing so (debates are, obviously, another matter, but most conversations aren't debates and shouldn't be treated as if they are). This is also true if one has invested a lot of time, energy, and money into a belief and participates in a community that supports that belief (religion, fantasy-based martial arts, the reputation of one's alma mater).

If your goal is to help your partner change her mind, which it probably is if you're willing to enter debate mode and introduce facts, evidence, and careful arguments, then your attempt to talk her *out of* certain beliefs is more likely to talk her *into* them. Introducing facts gives her a reason to defend her beliefs against those facts. She'll then seek out arguments to dismiss your facts and selectively choose facts of her own to bolster her position.

Introducing facts with the intention of changing someone's mind, except under the extraordinarily rare circumstance when there's no moral, social, or identity concern (discussed further in Chapter 7), gives your conversation partner a reason to become more entrenched in her beliefs. It also helps her develop and rehearse defenses against challenges to those beliefs, which can lead to believing her erroneous beliefs are based on solid evidence and sound reasoning.

So, What Should You Do?

If you shouldn't offer evidence, what should you do? There are competing answers to this question, and they can all be effective.

1. Ask questions that expose problems and contradictions. For example, if Sam believes the soul weighs seven pounds, ask, "Do you think four-pound babies have seven-pound souls?"[16]
2. Focus on epistemology. Once you have a thorough understanding of why someone believes what they do, you can offer targeted questions that sever the link between their conclusion (the soul weighs seven pounds) and how they claim to know their conclusion ("A German scientist weighed bodies when people died and found they lost seven pounds").
3. Combine these two approaches with disconfirming questions (see Seek Disconfirmation, page 104). That is, ask what evidence would cause them to change their mind both about the soul's weight and the reliability of how they know it has weight. Say, "What if that experiment couldn't be replicated, would you change your mind?"

There is one time, and one time only, to bring up facts in your conversation: when your partner explicitly makes the request. Even then, double-check. Avoid offering facts unless you're certain of their accuracy and invite your partner to check them independently.

If facts do enter the conversation, model intellectual humility by expressing your reservations. Say, "I could be wrong about this, but it's my understanding that X" (Chapter 3, Modeling). People may ask for facts not out of curiosity but to initiate debate or to attempt to expose your ignorance (to win the debate they're attempting to start). This trap can be partially avoided by stating, "I could be wrong about this," or "To the best of my knowledge."

How to Navigate Facts in Your Conversations

1. Do not introduce facts into your conversations.

   Do not turn conversations into debates by giving your conversation partner a reason to defend her beliefs. This is especially true if your goal is to instill doubt.

2. If you cannot control yourself and feel compelled to introduce facts into the conversation, ask disconfirming questions about facts. When introducing facts, it is nearly always better to do so via questions than with statements because questions invite answers while statements may encourage arguments.

   Ask, "What facts or evidence would change your mind?" You'll then know what facts you should introduce, but more importantly, you'll understand how someone is conceptualizing the issue. You might ask someone who believes the soul enters the body at the moment of conception (a belief from which arguments about abortion and stem cell research arise) what evidence would change that belief. If she responds, "Some proof that the soul doesn't enter the body at the moment of conception," you might ask about the facts defining identical twins, who under religious traditions ostensibly have two souls but who are, at the moment of conception, just one ovum fertilized by one sperm.[17] You could follow up your statement about identical twins by asking if the evidence you provided changed her belief.

   If you can provide the facts she seeks, do so with caution. If you cannot, say, "I don't have that information. I can get back to you after I look into it."

3. If invited to introduce facts, double-check and make sure that's what your conversation partner wants.

   If so, then before doing so say, "I may be wrong about this. It's my understanding that . . . " This models humility and shows that your belief can be disconfirmed.

#3—Seek Disconfirmation

disconfirm, *verb*
/ˌdɪskənˈfərm/
Etymons: DIS- *prefix*, CONFIRM *v.*
Etymology: < DIS- *prefix* + CONFIRM *v.*
To show that (a statement, hypothesis, etc.) is not or may not be true; to disprove, invalidate.

disconfirmation, *noun*
/ˌdɪsˌkɑnfərˈmeɪʃən/
Etymology: < DIS- *prefix* + CONFIRMATION *n.*, after DISCONFIRM *v.*
The process or result of disconfirming a hypothesis, etc.; an instance of this.[18]

I (Peter) had the following conversation with one of my father's friends, DB. DB was economically and socially conservative, lived in a fifty-five-plus retirement community in Las Vegas, and was in his early sixties. The following conversation begins *in media res*:

> DB: *There's just no question that the media is biased against Trump. I don't understand if you won't admit it or you don't believe it.*
> Boghossian: *Neither, really. I'm just trying to figure out the best example of this. What's your best example?*
> DB: *I told you already, the entire Russian malarkey. It's all horseshit. All of it. They [the liberal media establishment] are absolutely out to get him.*
> *[he spoke for a few minutes about why various allegations against Trump were false]*
>
> Boghossian: *Okay, so what would it take to change your mind? I mean, what evidence could you be provided with that would convince you he colluded with the Russians before the election?*

DB: *I just explained why it's all false.*

Boghossian: *I mean hypothetically. What evidence would persuade you? What would you find persuasive? I'm not saying I can provide that evidence; I'm just trying to figure out what it would be.*

DB: *Well, there is no evidence because it's all bullshit.*

Boghossian: *Okay, well, maybe I'm not doing a good job explaining myself. Let's try this. If WikiLeaks exposed emails from someone high up in Trump's camp that detailed collusion, would you believe it then?*

DB: *No. I'd believe they'd be faked.*

Boghossian: *What if they were corroborated, somehow, by other emails from other leaked sources?*

DB: *I told you, they'd be faked.*

Boghossian: *What if Putin came out on Russian TV and told the world he collaborated with Trump before the election? Would you believe then?*

[a brief pause]

DB: *No. He'd just be doing that to ruin the reputation of the United States. Like—*

Boghossian: *Sorry for interrupting. What if Trump admitted it under oath? Would you believe then?*

[long pause]

DB: *I dunno.*

Under What Conditions Could the Belief Be False?

The single most effective technique to instill doubt and help people change their minds is to ask, "Under what conditions could [insert belief] be wrong?"[19] This is called disconfirmation.[20]

If, hypothetically or in principle, a belief is disconfirmable, that means it can be *dis*-confirmed; in other words, there are conditions under which it could be false. If a belief is *not* disconfirmable, then there are no conditions under which it could be false. It is thus an absolute, immutable truth.[21] For example, the statement "There is intelligent life on other planets" is disconfirmable because, to paraphrase Carl Sagan, we could be the first. Someone has to be the first.[22]

It is generally accepted that truths of logic and mathematics are not disconfirmable. For example, there are no conditions under which 7 + 5 does not equal 12. Similarly, certain statements are true by definition. For example, "A bachelor is an unmarried man" is not disconfirmable because "bachelor" is defined as "an unmarried man." There are no conditions under which a bachelor is not an unmarried man, just as there are no conditions under which 7 + 5 does not equal 12.

If your conversation partner recognizes conditions under which his belief *could* be false, that belief is disconfirmable.[23] When he thinks there are *no conditions* under which his belief could be false, his belief is not disconfirmable and he regards that belief as an absolute, immutable truth. People who hold beliefs that cannot (in their minds) be disconfirmed, such as "Cloning humans is morally wrong," "Abortion is morally justifiable," and "Homosexuals should not be allowed to adopt children," think they believe timeless, unconditional truths.

We often try to change someone's mind by endeavoring to teach something (usually by presenting evidence) or attempting to persuade someone to adopt an alternative belief. That is, we deliver a message (Chapter 2, Shoot the Messenger). This is a mistake. If your goal is to help your partner revise her beliefs, *the* easiest and fastest way to do this is by asking disconfirming questions.[24]

Aliens Hijacked the Beer Truck

You're driving down the road with a friend and there's a beer truck in front of your car. Your friend says, "That truck is filled with beer!" You respond, "How do you know that?" and he replies, "Because it has 'BEER' written on the side, the driver has on a delivery uniform, and it's in the middle of the day."

Here's a heresy: "How do you know that?" is a powerful question for helping people think, but *it's not the best question. The best question is, "How could that belief be wrong?"* Here's why: "How do you know that?" doesn't "work" the way people want it to. If you're driving down the road with your friend, and you see what appears to be a beer truck, he exclaims, "That truck is filled with beer!" and you respond, "How do you know that?" He'll either look at you like you're a fool or he'll state obvious reasons, like "It has the word BEER written on the side, duh." So "How do you know that?" outlined his epistemology, but it did nothing to change his beliefs. Remember, people are prone to seek out confirming evidence for their beliefs while being blind to contradictory evidence, so they're usually able to articulate (the selective) evidence they use to support their beliefs. This epistemological blind spot often has to be intervened upon directly to induce doubt.[25] (A related phenomenon applies with more complicated problems, like moral, political, or economic issues.)

Similarly, providing a counterexample also does little and may even entrench them in their belief. If you say, "Maybe the driver hijacked the truck," a reasonable response would be, "Oh please. Given that there's no evidence that she hijacked the truck why should I take that seriously?" Both by asking, "How do you know that?" and by offering counterexamples, any reasons they provide will be used to further convince themselves their existing belief is true. You have, in a very real sense, further entrenched them in their beliefs. In such a case, you've conducted a reverse intervention. Instead of sowing doubt, you've increased their confidence that their beliefs are true.

Seasoned interventionists know better. While asking people how they know what they think they know is important, their go-to is to *ask disconfirming questions*. That is, those adept at intervening in people's cognitions ask some variation of "Under what conditions could that belief be false?" In this example, an open-ended disconfirming question is, "How could the belief that the truck is filled with beer be incorrect? That is, under what conditions could that belief be false?"[26] Imagine your friend has four possible responses:

1. "My belief can't be wrong."
2. "My belief could be wrong if aliens hijacked the truck, tossed out the beer, and loaded it with ray guns." (wildly implausible)
3. "It could be wrong if the driver already delivered all the beer and was on her way back to refill the truck." (plausible)
4. "I don't know."

For (1) if he says, "My belief can't be wrong," then his belief cannot be disconfirmed. There is no evidence that could change his mind. Note: By "*his* belief cannot be disconfirmed" we do not mean "*the* belief cannot be disconfirmed." It is his state of belief that is being commented upon.

Although (2) is wildly implausible, your friend did provide a condition under which his belief could be false. Therefore, his belief can be disconfirmed, although he has set the bar unreasonably high.

Obviously, (3) is far more plausible than (2). On (3) his belief can be disconfirmed.

If he said he doesn't know (4), then his belief could or could not be disconfirmed. You'd need to engage him further to make this determination. For the purpose of this section we won't detail this response because further questioning will resolve the category into which his belief falls.

Thus, there are three general categories of disconfirmable belief:

1. Not disconfirmable.
2. Disconfirmable, but only under wildly implausible conditions.
3. Disconfirmable.[27]

Let's take a look at the relevant conversational strategies to pursue in each case.

1. Beliefs Are Not Disconfirmable: "I Can't Be Wrong!"

When someone makes a knowledge claim, that means they're professing to know something. Whether or not a belief is disconfirmable is a type of knowledge claim. To say a belief cannot be disconfirmed, that is, there are no conditions under which it could be shown to be false, amounts to claiming absolute knowledge over the relevant domain of reality. If Emily claims that "There is intelligent life elsewhere in the universe" is not disconfirmable, even hypothetically, then Emily is claiming to know—with absolute certainty—specific conditions about the universe.

This is crucial and worth restating: If someone states their belief is not disconfirmable, they're claiming to be *absolutely positive* about an aspect of reality where the belief operates. Specifically, they're claiming to know that it's impossible for certain states of affairs to exist. In this example, Emily is claiming to know there is other intelligent life in the universe. Her belief is epistemologically sealed and cannot be revised. Philosophers refer to this as "epistemic closure" or "doxastic closure," depending on the context.

What's a productive way to engage a conversation partner who says her belief cannot be disconfirmed? Here's how you should *not* deal with it: by bringing up counterevidence (remember the section immediately above this, "Avoid Facts"). Think back to the conversation about President Trump at the beginning of this section. Bringing up counterevidence or facts would have given DB an opportunity to dig in his heels and argue that Peter tried to convince him that Trump may have colluded with the Russians. Here's how you should deal with a conversation partner who professes a non-disconfirmable belief: in the form of a question, present a possible state of affairs or a reason—but not evidence—for how the belief could be in error. In our beer truck example, you might ask, "What if the beer truck is leaving its last delivery where it dropped off the remainder of the beer?" Offering a condition under which a belief could be false may be an effective tool to shift a belief that is not disconfirmable to one that is.

If repeated disconfirming questions fail ("What if the truck had a flat tire and is coming back from the mechanic? Or what if its cooling system broke, and it's going to the repair shop?"), you might want to reconsider your conversational goals. It might be that they hold the belief with unshakable confidence and it really is not disconfirmable (to them). There may be little point to having a discussion about the conditions under which a belief could be false if someone explicitly and emphatically tells you there are *absolutely no* conditions under which that belief could be false, and they discount any possible conditions that you raise.[28] The way to figure out whether the belief really is disconfirmable is simply to present possible disconfirmability questions/conditions and to gauge their reactions.

Typically, conversations like this can only get somewhere by shifting away from epistemology, that is, how someone knows what they think they know, to identity and morality questions (covered in more detail in Chapters 7) such as, "What personal qualities would lead someone to endorse this view? What about someone who disagrees?" (identity), "What would it mean to you if you abandoned that view? What would that look like?" (identity and morality), and "Why would or wouldn't someone be a bad person if they didn't hold that belief?" (morality). Notice the shift from disconfirming questions to calibrated "What does it mean?" questions.

This shift is significant because the majority of beliefs that are not disconfirmable are held because they relate to an individual's sense of what it means to be a good person. (The beer truck example, while helping explain the idea of disconfirmation, is not realistic. Virtually nobody has beliefs about the contents of a beer truck that cannot be disconfirmed, because whether or not it's filled with beer has no direct *moral* relevance to anyone's life.) Daniel Dennett calls the underlying belief that holding a certain belief makes them a better person "belief in belief."[29] The underlying belief (that they should believe X because good people believe X, and thus that abandoning X would make them a worse person) is actually preventing them from seeing and acknowledging reasonable disconfirmation criteria.

These conversations, then, seem like they're playing out at the level of hypotheticals ("What if life appeared on Mars in addition to Earth?") or facts ("Mars is too far from the Sun to support life") but are really about what it means for someone to be a good (good people don't revise *that* belief) or bad (bad people don't hold *that* belief) person (here, e.g., that belief might be "God created life uniquely on Earth, and this is a core belief in my religion, which good people believe").

Consequently, someone is unlikely to revise what they believe not because there are no conditions under which they could imagine their belief being false but because revising that belief would mean their (moral) identity has been compromised.[30] In other words, changing someone's mind is sometimes not an intellectual or epistemological issue but a moral one. (This is yet another reason why bringing facts into a discussion very rarely helps someone revise their beliefs.) Refusing to earnestly entertain disconfirming questions allows people to feel morally righteous for guarding their beliefs.[31] Consider the case of someone who opposes needle exchange programs. For her to change her mind, she would have to wrestle with having opposed a cause that could have alleviated much unnecessary suffering.

2. Disconfirmable but Under Wildly Implausible Conditions: "The Bones of Christ!"

When asking disconfirming questions, you'll sometimes encounter people who will say something so wildly implausible as to cause you to become perplexed.[32] If you find yourself thinking, "How could someone possibly believe that? That's just bizarre. That's the most outlandish condition. Why would someone even say that, much less think it?" then you're in this realm. Before proceeding with the conversation it's a good time to evaluate the discussion and your goals. Your partner may also be mentally unstable, in which case it might be better to walk away. When in doubt, exit.

Examples of wildly implausible disconfirmation conditions held by otherwise sane people abound in the field of theology. When asking the disconfirming question, "Under what conditions would you revise your belief that Jesus was resurrected?" a wildly implausible response would be "Show me the bones of Christ."[33] The idea behind this is that if you presented a bag that contained the bones of Christ they'd no longer believe Jesus was the Son of God because he could not have ascended to heaven. However, anyone who would offer this response is well aware that there's no possible way to provide the bones of Christ for reasons that have nothing to do with the supernatural. More importantly, if you or anyone else did present bones and claim they were Christ's bones, they'd certainly deny that claim.[34]

What's interesting about this example is that your conversation partner would do *everything* in their power to prove the bones were not Christ's bones. They'd deftly utilize any and every tool at their disposal. They'd know how to have the bones examined (take them to experts at a major university), what would constitute a sufficient rebuttal ("These could be anyone's bones!"), and how to pursue additional stages of inquiry into their authenticity. This hypothetical example speaks to something significant: people who hold wildly implausible disconfirmation conditions don't have any trouble understanding disconfirmation, epistemology, or how to access the tools of science when it comes to certain claims.

There's still more to learn from this. Suppose the bag really did contain the bones of Christ. Let's also assume there was an overwhelming scientific consensus that this was the case. Even after exhausting every rebuttal in their arsenal, it is unlikely that people who offered this disconfirmation statement would revise their belief in the resurrection, perhaps citing the lack of absolute certainty that comes with every scientific finding. We don't make this claim recklessly or to be insulting: millions of Christians do exactly the same thing with regard to their beliefs about the historicity of Noah's ark as found in Genesis 6–9, despite the impossibility of a global flood and other details of the story.[35] Wildly implausible disconfirmation conditions are almost always given not because of epistemological but because of moral reasons.

When wildly implausible disconfirmation conditions are offered, the person's belief may appear disconfirmable, but it is actually not. That's because it's not really operating on the level of facts and evidence; rather, it's morally motivated. The issue you must now address is *not* the belief or even how the person arrived at the belief; it's the belief that they should (or should not) hold that particular belief. It's their "belief in belief."

In most cases, people offering wildly implausible disconfirmation conditions know their belief is not objectively disconfirmable, but they're offering the response to make themselves appear—either to themselves, you, or onlookers—fair, reasonable, and open-minded. It is difficult and frustrating to engage people who provide wildly implausible disconfirmation responses. This is because they often know (on some level) that the confidence they have in their beliefs is not warranted on the basis of the evidence, but they feel the moral need to continue to hold the belief. Not only are they insincere in this regard, but to maintain a cherished belief they need to find some way to compensate for the difference between their confidence and the (objective) lack of evidence.

This compensation could come in the form of moral overreaction (claiming to be offended or indignant, or smearing you as, for example, a sinner, heretic, infidel, bigot, or racist for asking the disconfirming question), cheating with their epistemology (importing a way to artificially justify their confidence, such as appealing to faith; claiming to possess secret, revealed, or hidden knowledge; or inventing an entirely new tailor-made epistemology that favors their preferred conclusions), or social manipulation (threatening to ostracize you or to drive a wedge in your community or family).[36]

Complicating matters even further, it's possible your conversation partner has received some sort of training that's taught them rehearsed defenses to questions, such as apologetics training in Christianity or indoctrination associated with some forms of political/ideological activism. So how do you use disconfirming questions to engage someone whose beliefs are disconfirmable but only under wildly implausible conditions?

One way is by asking *why* her disconfirmation conditions are exactly what they are. Ask her to explain, in as much depth as possible, why different criteria could not possibly work. For example, if your partner's disconfirmation condition for her belief in Bigfoot is that every animal in the entire region is captured and examined and found not to be Bigfoot, ask, "I'm having trouble understanding. How did you go about setting your bar for doubt so high? I'm wondering why some simpler problem, like why after all this time a dead Bigfoot has never been found, isn't good enough to cast doubt?" (If you've introduced scales, Chapter 4, and they're a 10, ask, "Why isn't this good enough to lower the confidence of that belief to 9.9?") The goal here is to get them talking—and wondering—about more reasonable disconfirmation criteria. One way to do this is to ask, "Why do you think your standard for disconfirmation for this is so much higher than for other things?"

If talking about more reasonable disconfirmation criteria doesn't spark curiosity or doubt, ask your partner to ask you what your disconfirmation criteria would be if you were exploring the same belief (Chapter 3, Modeling). Say, "Could you please ask me what I think would disconfirm belief in Bigfoot? Then, if you want, give me your opinion." (NB: The TV show *Finding Bigfoot,* on Animal Planet, has been running for nine seasons. If the intrepid and relentless seekers haven't found Bigfoot yet, it's unclear what would constitute disconfirmation criteria for hardcore Bigfoot enthusiasts.)

If none of these avenues leads anywhere, switch gears and ask directly about morals, values, or identity concerns lurking beneath the surface. Ask, "What value does believing in Bigfoot provide over not believing in Bigfoot?" (This question seems odd with Bigfoot, but strange beliefs often rest upon underlying hopes, values, or identity concerns. For example, many people believe in ghosts because if ghosts exist then there is a way to go on existing after death. Even belief in Bigfoot could be a proxy for the need to feel like there's more out there than we know.) Or, returning to our previous example, "How would someone be a better or worse person if they accepted reasonable evidence that Christ did not resurrect and changed their beliefs away from Christianity?" If they find this question too charged, then switch to Islam, Hinduism, or Scientology (in other words, to outsider questions, Chapter 3). For example, "How would someone be a better or worse person if they accepted reasonable evidence denying the truth of basic tenets of Hinduism and then changed their beliefs?"

When you ask questions about the relationship of deeper issues and disconfirmation, or when you switch to different beliefs (from Christianity to Hinduism in the example above), you're less likely to evoke a defense posture and more likely to encounter a nonrehearsed response. Moreover, your interlocutor might even know kind, loving, decent people who don't share the same belief. This line of questioning makes it possible for disconfirming questions to become effective by helping people reflect more deeply upon the conditions that anchor beliefs that are disconfirmable under wildly implausible conditions.

3. Beliefs Are Disconfirmable: "Here's What It Would Take . . . "

If someone's beliefs are disconfirmable, and they can provide reasonable conditions under which they'd change their mind, then all that's left is to figure out if those conditions hold or how likely they are to hold. Before you begin, however, clarify exactly what it would take for someone to change their mind.

Suppose your conversation partner asserts the Iranian nuclear program is for peaceful purposes; specifically, it's to provide, as Iranian president Hassan Rouhani has repeatedly asserted, an economic safeguard against a collapse in oil prices.[37] Ask, "What would it take for you to change your mind? What evidence could I provide you, even hypothetically, that would cause you to revise that belief?" If she responds, "If a high-level Iranian official admitted it's not entirely for peaceful purposes," then qualify with follow-up questions: "How high is 'high-level'?" and "Who else's word, besides the president's, would you accept? Someone on the Guardian Council? More than one person on the Guardian Council? How many high-level Iranian officials?" Unless you clarify *exactly* what conditions would have to be met, it's possible you'll disagree about whether or not the conditions were sufficient.

Once you and your partner agree about exactly what it would take to change her mind, direct the conversation toward how you could figure out if the source or the information is valid (Chapter 4, Outsourcing). To get the process started, defer to your partner's advice as to where you should turn.[38] Say, "Well, I read X about that in Y, and if it's true, would that be good enough?" If she says, "Yes, it is," follow up with, "Great, so have you changed your mind?" If she says, "No, it's not enough" or "That's a bogus news source!" then you can recenter the conversation on how to go about finding the necessary information. If you know nothing about Iran and can't even locate it on a map, then switch the conversation to learning mode and ask questions that may lead your partner to expose her own Unread Library Effect.

When a belief can be disconfirmed, it's vital *not* to adopt the messenger role. Do not deliver facts or, even more importantly, your gospel. Doing so jeopardizes the disconfirmation process because your conversation partner loses the ability to reflect on her beliefs and convince herself of what's true—which is *far* more effective at helping people revise their beliefs than you telling her what's true. If the circumstances are such that your partner has opened up and become more vulnerable, do not abuse that vulnerability to deliver your message. In doing so, you're not truly attempting to impart doubt and help them become more humble about their beliefs so much as attempting to have someone adopt *your* beliefs. This approach, common in religious evangelizing and high-pressure sales, is ethically vulgar.[39]

Adding Disconfirming Questions to Your Conversations

1. Once you have a discussion question (Chapter 3, Ask Questions), ask your conversation partner how confident they are in their belief (Chapter 4, Introduce Scales).

    (a) If they respond "10," their belief is not disconfirmable, but make sure by asking, "I just want to make sure I'm clear. There's *no* evidence, even hypothetically, that you could encounter that would make you change your mind? Is that right?" If they say yes, then you have the following options: shift to a learning frame by asking a few more disconfirmation questions to learn about their belief, ask why they believe that and attempt to figure out their epistemology, switch the conversation to morality and identity, conduct an intervention on "Whether or not good people should be willing to revise their beliefs," or walk away.

    (b) If they respond "9 on a 1-to-10," their belief is disconfirmable. Immediately ask either, "Okay, you said 9 rather than 10, but, I'm curious, why didn't you say 10?" or "What could you learn that would adjust your confidence to 8 or even 7?"[40]

    (c) If they respond somewhere in the middle range, including 9, you can either ask what would lower their confidence, as in (b) above, or you can ask the nonintuitive question,

"Why isn't your confidence [a higher number]?" As will be discussed in Chapter 6 (Altercasting), this helps your partner think about the reasons they *doubt* their belief rather than reasons they already believe. It places the focus on disconfirmation rather than confirmation.

(d) If their belief can be disconfirmed but only under wildly implausible conditions, then you need to make a choice about whether to remain in the conversation. If you choose to continue, do so by asking disconfirming and outsider questions. Finally, if you're comfortable, voice your honest concern about their sincerity if you suspect they're insincere. In these instances, we prefer to altercast (Chapter 6, Altercasting) someone as rational and reframe the conversation around what rational people should believe.

2. If you wish to pursue a conversation with someone who holds a belief that is not disconfirmable, then ask the following questions, with brief follow-ups, in this sequence:

Epistemological questions
"Then the belief is not held on the basis of evidence, right?"
"Are you as closed to revising other beliefs or just this one? What makes this particular belief unique?"
"What are some examples of other beliefs you're not willing to change?"

Moral questions
"How is it a virtue not to revise this belief?"
"Would you be a good person if you didn't hold this belief?"
"Who are some examples of people who don't hold that belief who are good people?"

Transitioning from epistemology to morality offers you a glimpse of why someone *really* holds a particular view. In other words, virtually all non-disconfirmable beliefs are held because of moral reasons but appear to be held because of epistemological reasons.

Note that these questions help you talk about beliefs without directly addressing the specific belief, which might put your conversation partner on the defensive. This will likely be the beginning of a rewarding conversation because you'll be given a glimpse into psychological, moral, and epistemological mechanisms that trap people into fixed views of reality.

3. After you've tried and failed to use disconfirmation questions with someone who's a 10 on the belief scale and not open to revising their belief, use this conversational template:

    (a) "Think back ten years ago." (If they're younger decrease the number of years, e.g., if they're eighteen, change it to five years.)

    (b) Ask, "Ten years ago, not about this subject, but about whatever, have any of your beliefs changed? I mean, are all of your beliefs identical now to what they were ten years ago?"

    (c1) If they state that all of their beliefs are identical to what they were ten years ago, then go back to fifteen or even twenty years and re-ask the question.

    (c2) If they say one or more of their beliefs has changed, state: "Ten years ago you believed something you don't believe now. Wouldn't it be safe to say that ten years from now you'll look back at this time in your life and say the same thing? I mean, in ten years you'll realize that the you ten years before believed things that are untrue, yeah?" (NB: The word *untrue* is gentler than *false*. In general, use *untrue* as it's less likely to evoke a defensive posture. However, if the situation calls for being more forceful use *false*.)

    (d1) If they acknowledge that ten years from now they'll look back and understand they had false beliefs, then turn attention to the belief in question. Ask, "How do you know this particular belief won't be one of those beliefs you'll later come to view as false?" Framed this way, this question allows you a candid glimpse into their epistemology. Note also that this is a calibrated question.

(d2) If they state that they've always had *exactly* the same beliefs for as long as they can remember, then they're either being dishonest with you or with themselves, or suffering from an extreme form of doxastic closure. That is, their belief life is closed and not subject to revision. In this rare case, you'll need to evaluate whether to continue the conversation.

After this sequence they should be primed and more receptive to further disconfirming questions. Finally, do not make this easy-to-use technique your go-to, or you will not become proficient at asking disconfirming questions.

4—Yes, and . . .

Let's peek into the world of comedic improvisation:

In the context of improvisation for the stage, where there is no script to guide the direction of a scene, Yes, And goes like this: One actor offers an idea onstage and other actors affirm and build onto that idea with something of their own.

Someone might say, for instance, "Wow, I've never seen so many stars in the sky."

The actor sharing the scene has only one responsibility at that point: to agree with this and add something new to it. So that could be something like, "I know. Things look so different up here on the moon."

That simple statement affirms what the first actor offered and added another idea (i.e., they're far away from the city—so far that they are actually on the moon). In turn, this affirmation gives the first actor some information to build on and opens up a great many possibilities for this scene.

If the second actor had negated the first actor's offering with something like, "I can't see a single star . . . it's broad daylight," the budding scene would have stopped in its tracks and left the first actor to scramble to find a response that could bring the scene back to speed in a way that an audience would find interesting. In our experience, audiences want to see something cool build onstage; they're not really interested in watching actors squabble over the essential facts of a scene—that's boring as hell.[41]

Good Riddance, "But"

Eliminate the word "but" from your *spoken* vocabulary. Switch to "and." When stringing together ideas, do so with the word "and" whenever possible.

Researchers from the Harvard Negotiation Project call this habit adopting the "and stance," and it's also a popular technique in improvisational comedy ("improv").[42] "Yes, and . . . " is a way to organize points by linking them with the word "and." By adding "Yes, and . . . " you can acknowledge that your conversation partner's opinion *and* your opinion can be simultaneously valid, even when there's an apparent conflict.[43]

The word *but* is likely to evoke a defensive posture, especially when you and your partner are at odds. *But* places a conversational bump in the discussion by hindering the flow of ideas. *But* also negates superficial acknowledgment. Replying with, "Yeah, but . . . " isn't an authentic way to acknowledge your partner. It's more a way to challenge what your partner just said, and you've primed them to reject whatever you have to say afterward.[44]

Compare:

"**Yes, and** how should we deal with the children of illegal immigrants?"

to

"**Yes, but** how should we deal with the children of illegal immigrants?"

If you don't begin with "yes" you can still eliminate "but" by switching to "and". Compare:

> **"That's a great idea, and** what about felons who want to purchase guns?"

to

> **"That's a great idea, but** what about felons who want to purchase guns?"

If you completely disagree and do not want to begin with "yes," then use the word "interesting" and follow with "and." For example:

> **"Interesting, and** what about lost tax revenue on sales of illegal marijuana?"

and

> **"Interesting, and** how should we deal with burning flags on public property?"

(Note that these are "calibrated" *how* and *what* questions that don't lend themselves to yes-and-no responses.[45])

Pause to notice the flow in these but-versus-and sentences. In each example, the first sentence acknowledges someone's position without shutting them down. This is at the core of "yes, and-ing," and it's remarkably effective. "Yes, but . . . " gives the appearance that what you say next is an objection. It asks your partner to defend his view, whereas "yes, and" invites him to explain more about his beliefs, facilitating almost every aspect of a productive conversation. (Hint: Combine Rapoport's Rules with "yes, and . . . ". This reinforces acknowledgment *and* demonstrates listening and learning stances. Say, "Yes, I hear that you're saying X and see what you mean, *and* I'm left wondering what your thoughts are about felons who want to purchase guns.") The key is "to present your views as an addition to, rather than a direct contradiction of, your opponent's views," notes Harvard Negotiation Project cofounder William Ury.[46]

Finally, a note on the word "interesting." Saying you find something interesting doesn't mean you agree. "Interesting" is a fuzzy word that just means you find what they said to be of note. If you strenuously disagree, switch to "interesting, and . . . " or use the "and stance" to respectfully disagree before continuing to your point. Ury offers this example: "I can see why you feel strongly about this, and I respect that. Let me tell you, however, how it looks from my angle."[47] Replacing the "however" in the second sentence with an invitation, such as "if you don't mind," can make this approach go even more smoothly.

Getting to And

Bye, "but":

1. Remove "but" from your conversational vocabulary.

   Say, "Yes, and . . . " instead of "Yes, but . . . " or "No, but . . . ". If you disagree with someone's statement, say, "Interesting, and . . . " Or "I hear you, and . . . "

   Adopting this habit is surprisingly difficult. Practice.

2. If your view *and* your partner's view can both be true, say so.

   String together multiple "ands" in the same or consecutive sentences.[48] Say, "If I'm hearing you right, you're saying X **and** I'm saying Y. **And** when I see things from your perspective, I see why X is true, **and** when I see them from my perspective, I see why Y is true." For example, "I see why eliminating the capital gains tax might be bad in terms of deficits **and** I also can see why it might be good in terms of increasing employment."

#5—Dealing with Anger

Psychologist Paul Ekman, who has pioneered emotions research since the 1970s, notes simply, "Anger calls forth anger."[49] That is, anger often occurs in accelerating cycles both within an individual and between people. These cycles tend to ensure that conversations involving at least one angry partner escalate. In the wake of lost tempers are not just ruined conversations but also damaged relationships, burned bridges, terminated friendships, and even physical danger.[50]

Some conversations—and some people—will frustrate you, anger you, or even fill you with rage. If a discussion is upsetting to the point that you cannot act like an adult, walk away. *When in doubt, exit.* As the entertainer Groucho Marx once quipped, "Speak when you're angry—and you'll make the best speech you'll ever regret."[51]

Stepping away from or overcoming anger requires recognizing anger in yourself and your conversation partners—and the earlier you recognize it the better. Fortunately, there are options for effectively dealing with anger. Understanding how anger operates is particularly important when conversing across divides.

Anger often arises from either frustration or offense. In the case of frustration, we become angry with interference standing between us and what we intend. Maybe you want to change your partner's mind or get her to hear and understand your point (or merely to care about it), yet it isn't happening. A moral tripwire is pulled, and before you understand what's going on tempers flare. When we believe interference or offenses are deliberate, these impacts are stronger.[52] (Note that this should be a reminder to assume, charitably, that your partner has good intentions.)

This seems obvious but is difficult to bear in mind during a heated conversation.

Ekman writes, "Anger tells us that something needs to change. If we are to bring about that change most effectively, we need to know the source of our anger."[53] In these cases, *you* need to alter course and not press the issue. And yes, it *must be you* who changes even if your partner is angry—or dreadfully wrong—because you cannot control other people; you can only control yourself. If your partner becomes upset, it may be because you're pushing too hard, not showing her you're listening, or using charged language, or it may have nothing to do with you. Nonetheless, once anger creeps into the conversation something has already gone badly wrong.

Four Facts About Anger

Here are four facts about anger:

1. Anger blinds you and derails conversations.[54] You've heard of "blind rage," but even modest anger makes you the victim of your own nervous system. Emotions, especially anger, limit what knowledge, beliefs, and information you can access and process.[55] Consequently, it's difficult to remain civil when you're angry.

2. Anger seeks its own justification.[56] Think of anger as being a strong cognitive bias that pushes you to confirm your anger is justified. Anger leads you to misinterpret information that might cause you to feel anything other than angry. This effect is particularly poisonous because it leads you to assume your partner has bad intentions or is immoral.[57] "You're just saying that to make me upset!" is an example of such an assumption.

3. All emotions, including anger, carry with them what is known as a refractory period. During a refractory period, your nervous system and temporary emotional biases severely impact your information processing. There's nothing you can do except wait it out.[58] The more intense the emotion, the longer this effect may last, ranging anywhere from a few seconds to minutes or hours.[59]

4. By understanding how anger works and committing yourself to avoiding it, you can minimize its impacts on your conversations and in your life.

From these four facts, certain do's and don'ts follow.

Don't Do This

Don't meet anger with anger. If your partner starts to become angry, do not reciprocate. Do not lose your temper. This is even more important if you're attacked personally—do not attack back. If someone insults you, do not insult them in return. Doing so only escalates the situation.

Don't blame (remember Chapter 3, Don't Blame, Do Discuss Contributions). Particularly in a tense conversation, do not lay judgment on or blame your partner. Do not say, "I am just trying to have a civil conversation with you, and you're getting angry." This blames your partner for taking the conversation off track and is the opposite of building a Golden Bridge.

Don't make negative assumptions about your partner's intentions or motivations, or the source of her anger. You don't know what is making her angry unless she explicitly tells you (and, as many married people will affirm, even then you may not know it). She may be angry at you, at something you said, at the topic in general, at herself or her own reactions, or something entirely separate from you or your conversation.[60]

Most importantly, **don't** remain in a conversation if you feel unsafe. Walk away. If necessary, make up a pretext and walk far away.[61]

Do This During Your Conversation

Do monitor yourself and your partner for signs of anger. Recognize frustration, offense, or anger, and act *before* it grows. You don't have many choices when it comes to mastering your anger. You can either de-escalate or walk away.[62] You may need literally only a few minutes to overcome the refractory period, calm down, and be able to engage the topic in a more productive and civil way. Or not.

Ways to calm down include changing the subject, reframing the conversation, assuming charitable intentions and focusing on them (some people report repeating to themselves, "He's trying to help. He's trying to help. He's trying to help . . . " to be a kind of emotional salve), becoming interested about why your partner is acting this way (i.e., Focus on Epistemology), or combining these suggestions by becoming curious about why the conversation is making *you* angry and what you can do to help it de-escalate.

Do pause. When you sense yourself or your partner becoming angry, pause and say nothing. Let the silence work for a few moments (and even a few seconds will feel very long and very tense). The goal of pausing in the heat of the moment, as Ury notes, is "to disconnect the automatic link between emotion and action."[63] The trick, in the words of Ury and FBI hostage negotiator Voss: "Slow it down."[64]

Do listen. When your conversation partner is getting angry, the single best thing you can do in most circumstances is to stop whatever else you're doing and *listen*. It's very difficult to remain angry with someone who is patiently and earnestly listening, and if you break the cycle of frustrating dialogue early by switching to listening and learning, you can halt a great deal of your partner's mounting anger before it starts. It's also useful to acknowledge your partner's perspective, which can help reduce their frustration. Seize upon *any* point of agreement and focus upon that, rather than disagreement, at least until tempers cool. Remember, hearing someone out, even acknowledging their perspective, is not the same as agreeing.[65]

Do acknowledge and apologize for your share of anger that comes up. Say, "I'm sorry." An apology can be disarming, especially to aggressive or assertive people. Once someone is angry, both their aggression and assertiveness are going to be greater than usual, so don't underestimate the power of a quick apology for *any* share of the contribution you can own.[66] Start your next statement explicitly with "I'm sorry," and say again as you ease the conversation away from anger and hostility.[67]

Do walk away if necessary.

Do This Before Your Conversation

Do learn to recognize mounting anger so you can deal with it as soon as possible.

To catch anger early and redirect it before it becomes a conversational liability, it helps to recognize anger signals and early warning signs. The following may sound hokey, but it's effective: In a safe, private space (not in the midst of a conversation), as vividly as possible, remember a time when you were angry. Visualize the scene clearly until you start to feel the beginnings of anger, and take inventory about how you feel. Maybe you feel tense, or your breathing changes. Your brow may furrow, and your teeth may clench. You may even start to feel hot or stirred to act. Let those feelings grow for about thirty seconds, then relax and reflect. If you can identify these feelings and sensations in yourself as they occur, it will be easier to identify rising anger and to act accordingly.[68]

Your goal is to learn to identify the earliest feelings that arise along your path to anger. Once you can reliably identify those feelings, you can start to detect them when they arise in other contexts, like in challenging conversations. The sooner you can realize you're becoming upset, the sooner you can act to stop it.

Do remember and respect the emotional refractory period. Combine an awareness of your sensations of anger with an understanding of emotional refractory periods. As soon as you feel anger, acknowledge it, and then remind yourself that you may not be able to change immediately. Until the refractory period ends you are a prisoner of your own neurobiology, and until your neurobiology and psychological state return to normal, your ability to engage effectively in difficult conversations is compromised. This skews discussions toward incivility.[69]

Do identify your anger triggers ahead of time. Ekman offers a tip for keeping anger out of conversations: before you get into conversations that might make you angry, work to identify your anger triggers and defuse them ahead of time.[70] If certain topics make you angry—including moral triggers like racism, rape, blasphemy, desecrating a flag, and so on—acknowledge that tendency before it seduces you into bringing anger into an otherwise civil conversation.

Identify words you know are likely to upset you and find routes around those triggers. Remember that your partner is probably trying the best he can to express his ideas. He may be using language you find offensive for no other reason than because he doesn't understand or have other tools available. You may be doing the same. Remembering this can help you learn to let go of minor offenses.[71]

If you discover certain moral triggers that are so sensitive you simply cannot find a way to prevent them from making you outraged, learn what they are—then take action. You may need help from a trusted friend or counselor to overcome a particular trigger. In the meantime, it may be best to avoid having conversations about those topics. If your trigger emerges in conversation, consider acknowledging it. Say, "I don't understand why, but that topic always makes me upset. Because I want to have a good, unstressful conversation, let's talk about something else."

You cannot predict which triggers might come up in conversations, safeguard yourself from them perfectly, or prevent other people from speaking their minds, so you retain some responsibility to defuse or disengage emotional triggers. If you do not feel yourself capable of doing either, refrain from initiating conversations about topics you find upsetting or with people you find frustrating.

A Special Note About Acknowledging Anger

Pointing out anger is often interpreted by someone who's angry as an accusation, which can beget more anger.[72] Perhaps this is another way anger seeks to justify itself, or perhaps it's because we tend to feel a bit embarrassed about becoming angry.[73] One easy way around this is to label anger "frustration."

Do not say, "You're getting angry about this, so maybe we should change the subject." Instead, name the dynamic and try to describe it.[74] Say, "Our disagreement seems pretty deep on this, and I get how it's frustrating. Maybe we should set this aside for now." Notice the phrasing here is both open-ended and collaborative (the word "we"), is not overtly emotional ("seems" rather than "feels"), and acts as an invitation (Chapter 4, Language).[75]

When angry, you're more likely to make bad assumptions about your partner's intentions, say things you'll later wish you hadn't, seek to verbally hurt your partner, yell, or misconstrue your partner's words.[76] You're also less likely to apologize on the spot, back down, change your mind, or hear your partner out. In fact, when you're angry, you aren't likely to hear what your partner is actually saying, and your angry reactions can make you angrier.[77]

Finally, learning to see the situation from your conversation partner's perspective is essential and "one of the most important skills a negotiator can possess," according to former Harvard Law Professor Roger Fisher and his collaborators. In *Getting to Yes: Negotiating Agreement Without Giving In,* they write, "If you want to influence them, you also need to understand empathetically the power of their point of view and feel the emotional force with which they believe in it. It is not enough to study them like beetles under a microscope; you need to know what it feels like to be a beetle."[78]

Best Practices for Dealing with Anger

1. Bite your tongue.[79]

   Do not counterattack.[80] As much as you want to lash out, do not. Lashing out provokes and escalates and your goal should be to *de*-escalate.[81]

   No matter what someone says—insults you, calls you names, swears at you—do not reciprocate. If someone calls you stupid, calling them stupid in return only worsens the situation. *Do not counterattack.*

2. *Never* respond to emails or comments on social media while angry, offended, or outraged.

   Wait. Cool down.[82] (You're also not under any obligation to respond to social media posts. The amount of your attention you owe anyone who insulted you on social media is zero.)

3. Listen. Listen. Listen.[83]

   If conversations become tense, listen. When you're finished listening, listen more. Then ask clarifying questions. Then listen. Only then respond.[84]

4. Do not deny a tense situation.

   In some contexts, you may need to acknowledge tension and negative feelings like stress or anxiety.[85] Denying frustration does not make it go away.

5. Avoid the word *anger*.

   Saying someone is angry when they're upset can sound accusatory.[86] Instead, consider acknowledging the conversation as frustrating and naming it *frustration*.

6. Slow down.

> When you slow the entire process down, you're simultaneously calming it down.[87]

7. Immediately after a tense moment make an empathy statement.[88]

> This is an opportunity to form a deeper connection. Say: "It's hard," "That must be absolutely infuriating," "I hear you," and "That really frustrates me, too."

8. Make safety a priority.

> Do not endure angry rants. Walk away.[89]

CONCLUSION

With these tools and techniques you should now be able to engage in conversations involving contentious topics, such as religion, politics, and other issues with strong moral resonance. Once you've achieved proficiency, the techniques in this chapter will enable you to get around many conversational difficulties while nudging firmly held beliefs toward reasonable doubt.

Reaching this point in the book marks a certain milestone as well. In Chapters 2 and 3 you were introduced to the fundamentals, and in Chapters 4 and 5 you learned how to deal with more difficult conversations—ones where everything isn't necessarily going smoothly. Now, we're turning the page to expert and master-level techniques.

Six Expert Skills to Engage the Close-Minded

Breaking Through Conversational Barriers

#1—SYNTHESIS
Recruit your partner to help refine and synthesize your positions

#2—HELP VENT STEAM
Talk through emotional roadblocks

#3—ALTERCASTING
Cast your partner in a role that helps her think and behave differently

#4—HOSTAGE NEGOTIATIONS
Apply cutting-edge research on hostage negotiations

#5—PROBE THE LIMITS
Engage someone who professes a belief that can't be lived

#6—COUNTER-INTERVENTION STRATEGIES
What should you do if someone is attempting to intervene in your beliefs?

Being ignorant is not so much a shame, as being unwilling to learn.

    —Benjamin Franklin

This chapter focuses broadly on the theme of conversing with someone who is closed or rigid in their thinking. Note that these are expert-level skills. *We strongly suggest readers have a proficiency with techniques from the previous chapters before attempting to integrate those that follow.* This reflects our advice at each stage throughout this book, but it is especially important when developing skills at an expert level. We follow with *six expert skills to help you break through conversational barriers.*

First, you'll learn Synthesis. Synthesis is a type of philosophical exchange used by professional philosophers. You and your partner agree to help one another understand what each of you is not understanding and then refine your position. It requires courage and curiosity.

Second, you'll learn to help someone vent in a strategic way. Best used with friends and people with whom you're intimate, allowing venting is an act of patience that requires you to integrate techniques from previous chapters (listening, learning, letting your partner be wrong, dealing with anger, building Golden Bridges, and so on). You might hear things you'd rather not, but with sufficient patience venting will likely remove barriers to effective communication.

Third, you'll learn how to help your partner consider alternative beliefs by altercasting, also called "facilitated brainstorming." By altercasting, you help your conversation partners talk themselves into new ideas and behaviors by casting them in a particular role that they then live up to. Sometimes used in high-pressure sales and as a persuasive technique, Altercasting is considered ethically murky, and we'll address possible ethical issues.

Fourth, we distill cutting-edge research on hostage negotiations. This section advises you on how to apply principles to improve the chance of success with close-minded conversation partners.

Fifth, we show how to have conversations with people who hold beliefs they couldn't possibly act upon. We'll guide you, step-by-step, in exactly what you should say if you find yourself in such a situation.

Finally, we cover counter-intervention strategies and techniques. What should you do if someone tries techniques from *How to Have Impossible*

Conversations on you? We lay out a range of options from "Go with It!" to (subtly or not so subtly) thwarting the intervention.

#1—SYNTHESIS

Synthesis is keeping Rapoport's Rules plus seeking disconfirmation. Synthesizing means modifying your beliefs by using your partner's beliefs and disconfirmation statements. The goal is to clarify and strengthen your position and get closer to having true beliefs, not to produce agreement. Synthesis involves collaboratively arriving at a better understanding of the topic and developing a more refined, nuanced view. This technique is best used when you're both below 8 on the belief scale or when you each are taking up a position that might not match your actual beliefs "for the sake of argument." For instance, you and your partner might both agree to take up different perspectives on a topic and argue for them so you can better understand various perspectives, even if those aren't *your* perspectives. The goal is better understanding. At least one of you—and preferably both—needs to be not wedded to your beliefs. In fact, a useful and interesting way to engage in Synthesis is to assume the *opposite* side of the argument from your own inclinations and argue for it to the best of your ability.[1]

Unless either of you has specific expertise or the topic is straightforward—and sometimes even then—differences of opinion can be used as a leveraging tool to arrive at truth. Philosophers broadly refer to this as a "dialectic," that is, a kind of give-and-take verbal engagement that can help refine beliefs.[2] This process can also be viewed as an attempt at constructive, controlled disagreement: take your views and leverage the views of your partner to arrive at a more refined, informed, and nuanced position while offering her a chance to do the same.[3]

Achieving Synthesis in Five "Easy" Steps

Synthesis is difficult but straightforward. Here are five basic steps:

1. *Present* an idea. This can be done by invitation or by advancing your idea. (For the remainder of the steps, we'll assume you advanced an idea.)
2. *Invite and listen* to counterarguments.
3. *Employ* those counterarguments to generate specific ways to *disconfirm* your belief (Chapter 5, Seek Disconfirmation). That is, make intentional use of your partner's difference of opinion, focus on your position's weaknesses, and explore ways to falsify *your* ideas.
4. *Use* the instances of (possible) disconfirmation to refine your original position. Modify your stance by incorporating counterarguments.
5. *Repeat*. Begin with your new, refined position and run through another iteration.[4]

The first step, advancing an idea, is the easiest: state an idea you'd like to refine, or invite your partner to do the same. You'll get the most out of this process by advancing an idea you suspect is strongly influenced by your identity, morals, faith, or partisanship (for example, if you're a staunch liberal or conservative and your beliefs tend to cluster around party positions). Choosing a moral belief makes the conversation more difficult but also provides the most benefit because moral beliefs almost always entail epistemological blind spots that a Synthesis can help reveal.[5]

The second step—inviting counterarguments—is the most difficult. Since you're requesting a different perspective to challenge your belief, expect that belief to be potentially undermined. This can be difficult because it might make you feel intellectually inadequate, and it might even challenge your political identity.[6] If you're invested in being right, prepare yourself emotionally and mentally for challenges, especially if your best attempts at Synthesis come up short.[7]

To get the most out of Synthesis, you'll want your partner to expose at least one clear flaw in your reasoning *and* the ways in which your moral biases may have led you to commit that error. Say, "If I understand, this view is incorrect because of [X]. Are my conservative/liberal/etc. lenses unduly influencing me to make this mistake?" Remember Rapoport's number one rule: don't proceed past the second step until you can re-express exactly your partner's criticism of your idea and, ideally, ways in which she believes partisan bias may be misleading you. Make sure she confirms that you fully understood her criticisms before proceeding.

The third step, employing counterarguments to disconfirm your belief, is engaged collaboratively. Invite your partner to help you formulate clear ways in which your belief could be wrong. Ideally, these should be specific examples, and it should be clear why it's the case that if these conditions are met your belief is in error. For example, you might argue that all "pork barrel spending" represents a corruption of government and should therefore be illegal, and your partner might point out ways in which the trading of special interests among lawmakers can be positive-sum for all constituents while fostering collaborative relationships between legislators.

The fourth step—using disconfirmation to refine your original position—takes what you learned in the previous step and uses that to refine your original stance.

Finally, repeat. Use your newly refined position and begin the process again. Of course, depending on the criticisms levied the first time, and upon the degree of belief refinement, your conversation partner might not immediately be able to provide more useful feedback. It might work best to set the conversation aside after an iteration or offer to go through the same process with one of her beliefs.

You can use Synthesis on almost any disparate views that aren't logical contradictions (that is, something that violates the laws of logic, like someone claiming squares are circles) or disagreements about basic facts (in which case, Outsourcing, from Chapter 4, is the relevant tool). If it's even possible that one or both of you are wrong about your beliefs, there is room for Synthesis. For example, even atheism and belief in God can be synthesized by modifying one's understanding of the word *God*.[8]

How to Converse Like Philosophers

Synthesis relies heavily on having secure frames of learning and collaboration and a willingness to revise your beliefs. Synthesis is not possible if your partner cannot generate disconfirmation conditions. Being successful requires approaching ideas like Socrates: weigh disconfirmation conditions on their merits and don't be wedded to being right.[9]

To synthesize, work through the five steps that we set out earlier, which will seem increasingly natural as you develop this skill:

1. Present an idea.
2. Invite and listen to counterarguments.

    Ask your partner in the conversation to help you understand what she thinks you're missing. Say, "What am I missing? Is my reasoning flawed or am I missing a piece of information?" Remind yourself that you are not your beliefs.[10]

3. Formulate disconfirmation conditions.
4. Use the instances of (possible) disconfirmation to refine your original position.

    Modify your stance by incorporating counterarguments. Explicitly restate your new position.

5. Repeat.

    Begin with your refined position and run through another iteration. If the conversation has run its course or you need time to think, thank your partner and end the process.

#2—Help Vent Steam

Talk It Through

Sometimes, friends need to vent. You can encourage a friend to get everything off his mind while you listen, focus on understanding, build Golden Bridges, let him be wrong, not take issue with his statements, not interrupt, and continue to listen. Why? Sometimes people just need someone to listen while they rant. When he's finished speaking, use what are termed "conversation deepeners" (go deeper into an idea) and "conversation extenders" (keep the conversation moving forward). Say, "Tell me more," as an invitation to go deeper and extend the discussion.[11] And continue to listen.

Venting is best used with friends who cannot substantively engage in discussion because their feelings are too intense or their emotions obstructively leak into the conversation.[12] You'll usually have a feel for when venting can be helpful a few minutes after you've settled into a discussion question. Some cues are when friends make repeatedly harsh judgments, mischaracterizations, and accusations; assign blame; deliver overly assertive attempts at problem solving; or show visible discomfort or irritation.[13] These behaviors can signal feelings that need to be brought into the open.[14] (They may also be signals that a conversation isn't possible and your friend just needs someone to listen to her, or, alternatively, depending on your relationship, they may be a cue for you to exit the conversation.) Begin by using the following calibrated question: "How has this situation made you feel?"

Then pause and listen. Do not argue, contradict, rebut, or challenge. Just listen. When allowing someone to vent, *it's impossible to listen too much*. Once she's said everything she feels like saying, use a conversation deepener/extender, saying, "I want to hear more." If she explicitly says, "That's all," then respond, "Are you sure?" and listen. Only then should you ask questions—and those questions should focus on a deeper understanding of her concerns.

If you've used conversation deepeners and conversation extenders and you're *positive* your friend has nothing more to say, immediately transition to the first three of Rapoport's Rules. Clearly re-express what she said and ask if that's correct (Rule 1). Then listen. If your restatement is accurate, then list points of agreement (or sympathy) (Rule 2). Finally, mention what you've learned (Rule 3). Do *not* use Rule 4, rebuttal or criticism. After you've allowed someone to vent, there is no rebuttal or criticism. You can think about venting as an extended and more developed version of rapport building (Chapter 2, Rapport). Pausing to let your partner dictate the next direction for the conversation is often the best course of action.

If you're giving your friend an opportunity to draw out emotional or ideological feelings, she may become angry or frustrated. Be prepared to deal with anger as it arises, or walk away if necessary. (If this technique sounds like the therapeutic process engaged in by clinical psychologists and professional counselors, that's because it's closely related. Note: *If you are not a professional counselor, do not try to play one.* It will damage the conversation, your relationship, and possibly someone's well-being. Just be a caring, empathetic, and patient listener.)

Your friend might open up and talk through some barriers (which may potentially expose her Unread Library Effect or identity-level reasons behind her beliefs). Or she might not. The goals of this technique are to let your friend feel heard, talk past distress and defenses, and understand exactly what is causing distress. It's to give her feelings space. You may or may not be able to address her concerns, but you should have a crystal-clear idea of what they are so you're positioned to know how to help.

How to Help Someone Vent

Allowing your friend to vent should deepen your friendship. *If you're not comfortable listening to someone vent and dealing with anger, then do not attempt this technique.*

1a. To begin, say, "Tell me more" and "How's that make you feel?"

Then listen. Listen. Listen.

1b. Acknowledge your friend's feelings by repeating specific emotional words back to her.
   If she uses the words "frustrated" or "outrageous," *you* should use them. Say, "Yeah, that's *incredibly* frustrating," "Yeah, that *is* outrageous!" Make the conversation a space where she feels safe by being a sympathetic listener.[15]

1c. Each time she finishes talking, pause for a few seconds before saying anything.

Do not rush to fill conversational pauses. Let the silence, which may be uncomfortable, do much of the work.

1d. When your friend is finished venting, listen more.

1e. Use conversation deepeners and conversation extenders. Say, "Tell me more" and "How does that work?"

2. Gently encourage your friend to *describe,* not just express, her feelings.

Help your friend express the same ideas in a less defensive way by *describing* her feelings as carefully as possible, while adding nuance.[16] Encourage her to differentiate between *mad, angry,* and *frustrated* or to unpack the contents of a word like *upset.* Let *her* identify the words for her feelings and avoid naming them when she is venting.

3. Conclude your interaction with a sincere offer to help.

Say, "How can I help now or in the future? What can I do?"[17] Once you know what you can do to help, if possible, help. Follow up and let her know what you've done.

4. When your friend has finished venting, leave it.

Do not attempt to force a conversation that led your partner to become distressed. If it's important, come back to it after you've both had a chance to think things over.

#3—ALTERCASTING

Altercasting is a persuasion technique introduced in 1963 by sociologists Eugene Weinstein and Paul Deutschberger. Here's an example of its application in nursing:

Suppose for a moment, that a coronary patient, contrary to instructions, is found out of bed. The nurse now has three basic lines of action she might take in order to induce the patient to return to bed: (a) She may use the imperative: "Get back in bed"; (b) She may appeal to authority: "The Doctor says . . . "; or (c) She may altercast the patient:

"A person with your physical condition . . . " In the third instance she has communicated to the patient that he is a sick person and one of the obligations attached to that position is to remain in bed.[18]

In this example, the nurse established the role of a patient with a certain physical condition and the implicit expectations that come with it. The logic of her altercasting could be reduced to these three statements:

- People with these physical conditions should be in bed.
- You have these physical conditions.
- Therefore, you should be in bed.

Here are some more examples . . .

Peter was at his daughter's elementary school listening to her teachers' presentations on what they'd be studying in the coming school year. One of her teachers was fixated on how bad gentrification is, and she was going to have her students read material decrying its ills. At the end of her lecture, Peter approached her and said, "Thank you for telling us that. You strike me as a fair person, one who's interested in critical thinking and teaching different perspectives on issues. Will you be teaching other perspectives on gentrification as well?" She responded, "Yes. Absolutely. There's a book that offers another side of the issue that kids can read."

It's worth noting that she said nothing about fairness, critical thinking, or different perspectives in her lecture. Peter altercasted her in that role because he wanted her to teach different sides of gentrification (and other issues, for that matter).

Here's another quick example. If you say to someone who's texting, "Wow, you're a really fast texter," you've altercasted them as a fast texter. They'll then embrace that role and want to text more quickly.

Assigning a Role

Altercasting is a powerful yet controversial technique that can be used to influence behavioral changes.[19] The person is cast into an *alter*nate role from which it is easier for them to be influenced. The method is to assign someone a (socially) relevant role—as with helping her to visualize herself as a moral person, a careful thinker, or a civil communicator—and then to encourage self-generation of solutions or behaviors within that role. The technique uses a self-internalized, manufactured pressure to conform with a role, and it may lead the individual to persuade herself to act or think in certain ways.

The ethics of Altercasting can be murky for the obvious reason that it's potentially manipulative. Further, individuals can also be cast in a negative light and thus be induced to live up (or perhaps down) to negative casting.[20] For example, you could easily altercast someone as lazy or close-minded. Moreover, if you altercast in the wrong way, it might backfire because the duties of the role you've cast someone in might not be the duties they think they have to perform. For example, maybe you altercast someone in the role of "social justice teacher," but to them that means indoctrinating their students into a certain set of values you don't share.

These ethical concerns can be sidestepped by limiting Altercasting to two conversational techniques:

1. Take their favorite solution off the table.
2. Altercast conversational virtues like civility, fairness, and open-mindedness.

These techniques should present no ethical quandaries, while still proving effective for instilling doubt, removing your conversation partner's go-to solution(s), and having civil conversations.

Take Their Favorite Solution Off the Table

Suppose you're having a conversation about illegal immigration and your conversation partner strongly favors deportation as the solution. Suppose further that you disagree, and she doesn't want to discuss other options. Say, "I hear you. I'm curious as to your opinion. Let's say you're a senator in an immigration committee and you have the task of coming up with a solution to our immigration problem. You're there because you're a good problem solver, and your opinion is important to the committee. Now, just suppose you know the Senate absolutely will not accept deportation as an option. Your job is to come up with the best solution you can that doesn't rely upon deportation except in extreme and uncontroversial cases, like for murderers. What might you recommend if you had to, and if you couldn't recommend deportation? And why?"

There's a lot going on here. You acknowledged your partner's view ("I hear you"), asked for her opinion ("I'm curious as to your opinion"), and used calibrated questions. Then you altercasted your conversation partner as a person who is a good problem solver, knowledgeable, and important enough to come up with solutions ("you're a good problem solver, and your opinion is important to the committee"). Then you constrained the situation so that her preferred solution is not available ("just suppose you know the Senate absolutely will not accept deportation as an option") and asked her to brainstorm other possibilities ("your job is to come up with the best solution you can that doesn't rely upon deportation").[21] You altercasted her into a role in which she either has to do her best to think about the problem in a new way or reject the (positive) role in which you cast her.

If your partner goes along with the thought experiment, it might result in her self-generating more moderate solutions to the problem of illegal immigration than a proposal like mass deportations. After altercasting, she might be more likely to change her mind than by argument or even reasoned discussion. She is, after all, generating preferred solutions herself as opposed to you telling her why she's wrong (delivering messages).

If she does not go along with the role you cast, or if she cannot go along with it (some people simply cannot entertain hypotheticals, especially if they deal with cherished beliefs), then we recommend that you abandon Altercasting and fall back on techniques that are easier to use. As your partner brings up various ideas, you can engage with those ideas as conversation questions. You could, for example, use the questions to help expose her Unread Library Effect, or you could let them be a launch pad for Synthesis (see above).

To summarize this method of Altercasting:

1. Acknowledge your partner's view.
2. Cast your partner as a smart, creative problem solver in a particular, relevant role.
3. Construct the scenario so as to remove her preferred solution.
4. Have her brainstorm alternative solutions.

Altercast Conversational Virtues

You can also altercast conversational virtues. For example, you can altercast civility: cast your partner into the role of someone who values and is good at having civil conversations. Altercasting can be used "cold," especially on strangers, to inject the basic RNA of civil conversations directly into someone, almost like spreading a better-conversations virus to inoculate against incivility.

Here's the formula for altercasting civility:

1. Establish rapport.
2. Altercast your partner as someone who knows how to have productive, civil dialogue.

     Say, "You strike me as the kind of person who's civil. Someone who's good at having conversations." (This could be someone who is fair or open-minded as well, for other examples of conversational virtues.)
3. Engage her in conversation.

This casts your conversation partner into a role of civil communicator that she then works to live up to.

Alternatively, if used before the conversation becomes too heated, this technique can be used like a life preserver. If things start to become tense, acknowledge that tension and use it as a segue to altercast them as someone who stays calm. Say, "Okay, I feel tense. I'm a bit stuck. Can you help me? If you don't mind my asking, because you seem good at keeping your cool, how do you keep your cool when talking about something like this?" If done effectively, and your timing is right, this can help the conversation stay civil.

How to Create the Conversational Partner You Want to Have

1. Acknowledge, then altercast.

    Say, "I hear you about [X]." Then altercast your partner into a knowledgeable, creative role regarding the question you're discussing, but one in which his preferred solution is not on the table. Have *your partner* brainstorm alternative solutions.

2. Altercast your partner into the role of better conversationalist.

    Say, "You're good at having civil conversations." Or, simply, "You're good at keeping your cool."

3. If someone rejects the alternative role you cast for them, abandon the technique and move to other techniques in this book.

4. Recognize that someone is altercasting *on you* if they attempt to cast you into a role.

    You can then go with it, refuse, acknowledge what's happening, or altercast back on them.

#4—Hostage Negotiations

Hopefully, your seemingly impossible conversations will never be hostage negotiations. These take place in frightening circumstances, usually marked by extreme emotions and threats of imminent, violent homicide. Fortunately, however, there are established bodies of work from which professional hostage negotiators—whose goal is to end a situation peacefully—draw.[22] We've condensed and summarized this vast body of literature into six techniques that negotiators use to accomplish this objective. Let's jump directly into their application.

How Your Conversations Can Benefit from Hostage Negotiation Techniques

In previous chapters, we've covered many techniques and strategies used by hostage negotiators, such as listening (Chapter 2), rapport building

(Chapter 2), language and "that's right" (Chapter 4), calibrated questions (Chapter 5), and variations of Rapoport's first two rules (Chapter 5). There remain, however, a few select techniques and methods you can use in your most difficult interactions:

1. Use "minimal encouragers."[23]

   Examples of minimal encouragers are, "Yeah," "I see," and "Okay." Minimal encouragers are an effortless way to let your conversation partner know you're listening. We recommend minimal encouragers during particularly tense moments.

2. Mirroring.[24]

   When mirroring, you repeat the last few words of what someone said. For example, if someone exclaims, "I am just so sick and tired of these people pushing everyone around and trying to get their way," you say, "Get their way?"

   McMains and Mullins provide the following example: "A trapped armed robber in a bank might say, 'I have to get out of here with the money. It's for my kid. It's not for me.' A good mirroring response would be 'For your kid?' To which the robber might say, 'Yeah, He's got a fever and an infection and we don't have money for the pills he's supposed to take. He needs the money for the pills.'"

   On the same page they continue by giving an example of a poor mirroring response: "You expect me to believe that it's not for you?"[25] You can generally avoid such mistakes by repeating only the last two to three words, phrasing them as questions, and then letting the person talk while you *listen*. The goal of this application is to keep the person talking and volunteering more information that may become useful later in the conversation.

   Note: While mirroring signals that you're paying attention, do not overuse it. We prefer to mirror no more than four or five times in a seven-minute conversation.

3. Emotional labeling.[26]

   When you emotionally label someone's feeling, you give it a name. This is similar to helping someone vent, as described above, but more emphasis is placed on *you* labeling someone's feeling as opposed to coming up with a description together. Mc-Mains and Mullins write: "Emotional labeling can be used any time the subject expresses strong feelings that need to be defused. It can be used to communicate a deep understanding or to check on the negotiator's understanding of the problem. It is particularly effective with normal people who are in crisis, inadequate, borderline, dependent, suicidal, or angry people who need to be defused."[27]

McMains and Mullins offer the following example: "A subject who was angry about her husband's wanting to leave her for another woman said, 'I have the two adulterous SOBs in here and I am going to make them pay. Nobody should get away with hurting other people this way. They are going to know what it's like.'" The authors suggest that a good reply, using emotional labeling would be, "You sound pretty hurt about being left. It doesn't seem fair." As McMains and Mullins add, this "recognizes feelings without judging them."[28]

Be careful when emotionally labeling. Peter has found this technique particularly useful if one has a proven capacity for empathy and less useful if one mislabels another's feelings (for example, if you mislabel fear as anger). It often goes badly when one repeatedly mislabels those feelings. In the latter case, the risk is that your conversation partner will think you just don't understand.

4. Allow the person to save face.[29]

That is, build a Golden Bridge.

This is more something to be aware of as opposed to a specific technique. People are less likely to change their minds, particularly in front of those they view as important, if they think they'll lose face. Consequently, you should consider ways to allow your conversation partner to save face gracefully. This may include stating how difficult it was for you to change your mind about the issue or saying, "This is just such a difficult and complicated problem it's just so easy to not get it exactly correct."

5. Deal with small issues first.[30]

Try to create a "climate of success" by dealing with and resolving small issues first, then, "break down the big problems into a number of smaller problems that are each easier to handle."[31] For example, with the issue of assisted suicide, or death with dignity, you can first clarify the role of the physician in end-of-life choices. Once that's been separated from the role of the state, you have two separate but related issues and can focus on one at a time. It's helpful to combine this with Ask Questions, and home in on specific questions ("What should the role of the physician be?") as opposed to general topics ("assisted suicide" or "death with dignity").

6. "Use specific examples or case histories rather than statistical information."[32]

The former "remains more vivid in the mind and has a greater influence on behavior than isolated 'facts.'"[33] (Remember Chapter 5, Avoid Facts.)

#5—PROBE THE LIMITS

"At this point, if a straight white male told me 2 + 2 = 4, I wouldn't believe him."

This comment was made by a female colleague of Peter's at Portland State University. It offers a window into our society's current polarization of opinions and balkanization of trust. When you just read it, you likely wondered, "How can somebody have a productive, civil conversation following a statement like *that*?" Surely, with an individual so entrenched and unreasonable, worthwhile conversation must be impossible.

Not so. As we've emphasized throughout this book, productive and civil conversations are nearly always possible, and there is almost always a way to profit from them.

Unmasking Disingenuous Statements

Use the following experimental technique if someone professes a belief that's almost impossible—or frankly impossible—to live by.[34] For example, "If a straight white male told me 2 + 2 = 4, I wouldn't believe him." By probing the limits of a belief, you can reveal that the individual does not live according to the professed belief. Because humans are attuned to belief consistency, when you unmask an *in*consistency it can lead one to reconsider the absurd belief. The purpose is to help them understand that they do not actually hold the belief they claim to hold. (This is sometimes referred to as "verbal behavior." Someone says certain things, but what they say doesn't correspond to what they believe. It would be like someone saying, "I hate ice cream," while eating a big bowl of ice cream and seeming to enjoy it.)

When you encounter an impossible belief, use the following chronological Unmasking Formula:

1. Apply Rapoport's first rule: "Attempt to re-express your target's position so clearly, vividly, and fairly that your target says, 'Thanks, I wish I'd thought of putting it that way.'"[35]
2. Explicitly confirm that you've understood their belief correctly (implicitly giving them an opportunity to back down).
2a. Optional: If you possess a characteristic that they have targeted, begin by politely requesting permission to ask questions so that you may learn. If you're a straight white male, say, "I am not trying to convince you of anything. I'm curious and would like to ask some questions to learn more."
2b. Optional: In this preliminary stage, consider asking questions that ascertain how long the belief was held and attempt to figure out its origin. "Have you always held this belief or is it relatively new?" or "How did you come to this conclusion? Do a lot of other people believe this too?" This may be helpful in figuring out the nature of communal support, if any, for the belief. Once this is clear, you can understand the social support systems that help prop up the belief, which may give you a better idea of targeted questions you can ask.

3. Try to understand the limits of their belief in practice. Ask if the belief holds in other (more extreme) contexts. "If you went to the emergency room and the doctor happened to be a straight white male, would you believe him if he told you that you need an *immediate* emergency surgery to save your life?" or "If you walked into a dark room and wanted to see, would you inquire into the gender and race of the electrician who installed the lights or would you just flip the light switch?" In the case of the surgeon, follow up with, "If every other surgeon was occupied, would you let a straight white male surgeon operate on you?"

4. After this has been accomplished, ask, "Is there *any* circumstance that might lead you to act inconsistently with the belief?" and have them generate examples.

4a. If they say "No," then gently continue with examples similar to number 3. "Would you fly on a plane with a straight white male pilot? What if you knew for a fact the aircraft was developed or built by straight white men?"

   If the person says they would not fly on the plane with a straight white male pilot, ask about how that belief can be maintained in practice and request details. (This might expose the Unread Library Effect.) Ask, "How do you figure out the pilot's race when you book tickets?"

4b. If they say "Yes," then state, "What would that circumstance be?" and "Can you give me examples of other things you believe but don't act upon? What makes this special?"

5. By this stage you've either demonstrated it's impossible to sincerely hold and act upon the belief or not.

5a. If it's impossible to act upon, follow up by asking how one can tell when to act upon the belief and when to make an exception. (Now you're back to talking about epistemology.) Ask, "Okay, so if I'm hearing you right, sometimes it makes sense to listen to a straight white doctor, but other times you believe there are good reasons not to trust their opinion at all. How can we determine which time is which?"

5b. If you've *not* demonstrated that the belief is impossible, then they're either lying or delusional, or you were mistaken and they actually do live in accordance with their belief.

6—Counter-Intervention Strategies

If you think someone is attempting to intervene in your cognitive process/ beliefs with the express purpose of instilling doubt, you have three options:

1. Go with it.
2. Refuse to play.
3. Use counter-interventions.

We *highly* recommend option 1.

Go with It!

If someone tries to intervene in *your* cognitions, one option is to let them. Just go with it. By going with it and allowing their intervention to proceed, you're almost guaranteed to learn something. Ideally, you'll learn that your confidence in a belief was less justified than you thought, and you'll then (hopefully) hold the belief less tenaciously. You might even change your mind and hone your skill of imparting the gift of doubt. The person who's conducting the intervention might have techniques you should incorporate into your own repertoire, and you can learn what mistakes she is making and avoid them, or even develop an understanding of how *you* feel when *you* examine your beliefs. If you go with it, you'll learn something regardless of the outcome.

Stonewalling Socrates

Here's a secret: interventions only work if your partner engages you. It doesn't really matter what they say. They just need to say *something*. In Peter's doctoral dissertation, he describes how he tried to help prison inmates desist from crime by teaching them critical thinking and moral reasoning skills.[36] His fear was that inmates would remain silent, not that they'd become upset, that they wouldn't like him, or even that they'd find the discussions boring. If someone doesn't respond to you, then there's no intervention because there's no way to sow doubt—there's nothing to intervene in because there's nothing to work with.

If someone tries to perform an epistemological or belief intervention on you, you can *guarantee* it will fail by simply not participating. The best way to do this is to avoid saying anything. The next best way is to provide only closed-ended responses to their questions, like "Yeah" or "Not really."

Counter-Intervention Techniques

Counter-intervention strategies can be used when someone is attempting to perform an intervention on you. Apply these when remaining silent and walking away aren't options, *and* you've decided not to go with it. These counter-intervention techniques can also be used if you find yourself in high-pressure interrogations where you feel you have no avenue for escape. Deflecting and countering, then, may be your sole option. Every one of these techniques can be effective. *And every one is dishonest.* For that reason, we don't encourage their use.

Before beginning, the operating assumption is that you know someone is attempting to perform a belief/epistemological intervention on you. Telltale signs of this are if you're asked, "How confident you are in that belief?" (Chapter 4, Introduce Scales) or "What evidence could you be provided that would change your mind?" (Chapter 5, Seek Disconfirmation). If you hear these phrases there's a good chance someone is using the techniques from this book or from Peter's earlier book, *A Manual for Creating Atheists*.[37]

Here, then, are six effective counter-intervention strategies:

1. When you're asked how confident you are in a belief, either offer a much lower number or the polar opposite number. If you're asked, "How confident are you that the federal minimum wage should be increased?" and you're 9 on a 1 to 10 scale in confidence, either respond, "I think I'm a 6" or simply state, "2."

i. In the former case, this will make the intervention more difficult (if they even see a need to proceed, as 6 is already doubtful). It will also give them access to fewer techniques.

ii. In the latter case, there's no intervention because you don't believe what you profess to believe.

2. Offer the illusion of success. Early into the intervention, claim you've changed your mind. This is best done after an extended pause followed by an exclamation of wonder, like, " . . . wow, yeah. Wow."

3. State that you have doubts about your doubt.[38] That is, lead them to conduct an intervention on your doubt about your doubt and not on your belief. Borrowing from our previous example, if you're 9 confident (on the 1 to 10 confidence scale) that the federal minimum wage should be increased, your interlocutor will want to instill doubt and decrease your confidence to any lower number.

Instead, either ask her to help you see what you're missing so that you can get to 10, which is a kind of reverse altercasting, or state, "I have doubts about the federal minimum wage being raised, but I'm not sure that they are justified. Do you think my uncertainty about my doubt is justified?" If you're asked why you want to get to 10, state, "I'd like to fully explore the benefits of X [a higher federal minimum wage]."

4. If your belief is strongly held, state the actual confidence in your belief (on the belief scale) and add that you'd rather not hold that belief. Say, "I firmly believe the federal minimum wage should be raised, and I wish I didn't think that." (A stronger version of this is to say, "I firmly believe X, but I also think it is morally wrong to believe X.") This taps into the opposite of Daniel Dennett's belief in belief (noted in Chapters 3 and 5). Instead of people holding a belief because they think they should hold that belief, you claim to hold a belief and wish you could stop believing.

This negates many techniques in Chapters 6 and 7 that center upon morality, while putting the interventionist in uncharted territory. Of course, the interventionist may try to intervene upon your beliefs even more diligently to help you achieve your wish, but she will have to do so with far fewer tools at her disposal.

5. If someone is peppering you with rapid-fire questions (this is almost always a sign that they're a novice), say "Ah" or "Um" and count backward in your head from five. For example, "Why didn't you tell me before, huh?" You should reply, "Um . . . ," and think "Five Mississippi, four Mississippi, three Mississippi, two Mississippi, one Mississippi." This will effectively nullify the technique.[39]

6. Use questions to execute a direct intervention reversal. After they ask you a question such as, "How confident are you in your belief?" that reveals they're attempting an intervention, rather than answering, ask them a question about their question. Say, "If you don't mind, why are you asking me this question?"

   After they reply something to the effect of, "I'm trying to listen and learn" (Chapters 2 and 3), ask directly, "Are you trying to intervene upon my beliefs to change them?" Begin to ask them what their goals are, even, "On a scale from 1 to 10, how confident are you that my beliefs should be the ones to change? How do you know that your beliefs shouldn't be the ones to change?" The goal will be to reverse the intervention by making the discussion shift to questions about beliefs they hold that led them to attempt an intervention with you.

There are numerous other techniques for derailing or reversing interventions that are unorthodox, easy to see through depending on your proficiency, even more ethically suspect than those discussed so far, and *not* recommended. For example, you could do any of the following:

- Intentionally damage rapport.
- Invent your own epistemology (claim your cat guides you to the truth).

- Change the meanings of everyday words and alternate between different meanings (this is called equivocation and is frequently done in discussions of religion with the word *faith*).
- Offer wildly implausible disconfirmation conditions and claim that because they can't be satisfied you're even more confident you possess the truth ("If I were provided with the criminal history of every refugee, I'd change my mind, but since you've not been able to do that I'm even more confident in my immigration stance" or "If I were shown the bones of Christ, I'd change my mind as to the divinity of Jesus").
- Profess a type of relativism by claiming that statements are just true for you (e.g., "It's just true for me that everyone should own a gun").[40]
- Claim to change your beliefs several times over the course of the conversation.
- Feign radical domain-specific ignorance (in other words, claim to not even know the rudiments of what you're discussing).

Just Go with It!

After all that's been said, in most situations you have everything to gain and little to lose if you simply go with it. If you're fortunate enough to have someone attempt a belief-based intervention with you, it could be a remarkable opportunity to learn something about yourself and the methods used to help people become more humble about what they think they know. So, just go with it!

Conclusion

This chapter covered a range of strategies, skills, and techniques and offered advice for more seasoned conversationalists. Although not easy to categorize, many of the techniques in this chapter fall into the category of "how to engage with the close-minded" because they're best used when people won't budge from their confidence in a belief or because they emotionally cannot.

The techniques in this chapter are considered expert because they're difficult (Synthesis), or trying (Help Vent Steam), or require extreme patience (Probe the Limits). Some are difficult to do on the fly (Altercasting), whereas others (counter-intervention strategies) are difficult to practice because they require someone approaching you and attempting to conduct an intervention.

They are, however, not magic. Jedi mind tricks aren't necessary to excel at these techniques. Practice and patience are. It's like anything else, the more you practice the better you'll become. And the more you combine techniques from this book, the more effective you'll be.

seven

Master Level: Two Keys to Conversing with Ideologues

How to Move Unmovable People

#1—HOW TO CONVERSE WITH AN IDEOLOGUE
Switch to moral epistemology

#2—MORAL REFRAMING
Learn to speak moral dialects

> *One of the most pathetic—and dangerous—signs of our times is the growing number of individuals and groups who believe that no one can possibly disagree with them for any honest reason.*
>
> —*Thomas Sowell, Twitter, @ThomasSowell, July 30, 2018*

We define an ideologue as "one who is unwilling or unable to revise their (moral) beliefs." Trying to have a conversation with an ideologue almost never results in an actual conversation. It's someone speaking at you, usually by delivering messages.[1] This chapter teaches you how to understand and communicate with such people and offers strategies and techniques to intervene in their cognitions and instill doubt.

Here's the secret to success: understand how an ideologue's sense of morality relates to their personal identity. To do this, think of every conversation as being three conversations at once: about "What happened?" (facts); about feelings (emotions); and about identity (how each person sees themselves).[2]

If you're engaged in a moral conversation, your discussion is *always*—whether overtly or covertly—about identity issues.[3] When you're talking to an ideologue (or anyone else), it might appear that the conversation is about facts and ideas, but you're inevitably having a discussion about morality, and that, in turn, is inevitably a discussion about what it means to be a good or bad person. Decoding this connection is vital.

Morality and identity issues operate invisibly at the level of emotion rather than reason.[4] Literally.[5] Challenging these beliefs triggers the same brain responses as putting someone in physical danger.[6] Consequently, great care must be taken when engaging someone's morality and identity. If you want to have more effective conversations or interventions with people who are unwilling or unable to revise their beliefs, then you'll need to learn how to accomplish the following:

1. Engage someone's moral epistemology.
2. Become proficient at speaking other moral languages.

In what follows, we describe these skills and how you can develop them. In conjunction with other strategies in this book, they will enable you to engage more effectively with people who seem utterly unmovable, including religious hardliners, political extremists, and ideologues of all stripes.[7] Before beginning, however, expect frustration. Even when the best techniques are applied correctly, conversations with ideologues are extremely difficult. You'll need patience. When in doubt, go back to the basics: listen and learn. And, of course, know when to walk away.

Note: This chapter describes master-level skills. *We urge readers to gain proficiency with the material in the previous chapters before attempting to integrate them into conversations.* Additionally, much of the reasoning and source material behind the advice in this chapter is contained in extensive endnotes. We encourage engagement with that material to understand more accurately *how* and *why* moral conversations operate the way they do.

#1—How to Converse with an Ideologue

Ideologue, *noun*

[ahy-dee-uh-lawg, -log, id-ee-, ahy-dee-]

A person who zealously advocates an ideology.

Values, Values, Values

At the core of nearly all impossible conversations lies at least one person's inability to provide (realistic) disconfirmation criteria for beliefs or denial that any such criteria exist. This failure is usually accompanied by other features, such as redirection to their issues, everything being approached through their moral lenses, and all disagreement being interpreted to mean either there's something you're not understanding or that you're suffering from a moral failure.

You might, therefore, observe the following traits and behaviors: extreme sensitivity, hyper-defensiveness, overt righteousness, unwillingness to hear an opposing point of view, disproportionate levels of anger, sharp and unfair accusations, and demeaning or vilifying epithets.[8] There are many others, all of which involve some degree of hostility, self-righteousness, or entrenchment.[9] One telling sign of entrenchment is responding to substantive disagreement with weaponized moral language, for example, responding to "I'm not sure that conclusion follows" with something implying you are a morally bad person (such as, "You just don't care about dead children!").

When this happens, conversation—a discussion involving genuine give-and-take—seems impossible. It's close to impossible because the person with whom you're attempting to have a conversation is evangelizing, not conversing. Talking to a person with unshakable belief commitments is like playing chess with someone whose only piece is a hammer.[10] It's frustrating, infuriating, and possibly even physically endangering.[11]

Almost all such discussions appear to play out on the level of facts (or possibly name-calling or screaming).[12] That is, conversations with ideologues seem, on the surface, to be about issues, ideas, and evidence. But underneath they're about moral issues ultimately rooted in the ideologue's sense of identity, including their self-perception as a moral person and their sense of belonging to a community. If you have the right tools and sufficient patience, it is possible to have a conversation with such individuals, even if it's about an unhinged belief. Here's how: focus on moral epistemology. That is, change the subject from their beliefs to how they know their beliefs are true *and* how their beliefs contribute to their sense of personal identity.[13]

Speaking with an Ideologue: A Template

After someone has failed to provide disconfirmation criteria, if you wish to continue the conversation, we suggest the following template:

1. *Acknowledge* their intention and affirm their identity as a good, moral person—especially if you find their beliefs repugnant.[14]
2. *Change* the subject to underlying values.
3. *Invite* a deeper conversation about those underlying values (this begins the shift from beliefs to moral epistemology).
4. *Induce* doubt in their moral epistemology by helping them question the way they derive their moral beliefs.[15]
5. *Allow* the tether between the belief and the moral epistemology to sever on its own. (This will be accomplished after the conversation.)

Note that it's all about the process. Addressing moral epistemology is like addressing any other type of epistemology—figure out how someone knows what they think they know. Additionally, however, because moral beliefs operate in a far more complex milieu than most factual knowledge claims, you may have to delve into feeling questions such as, "Why do you *feel* that belief is more justified than competing beliefs?" and "Does the intense feeling that a belief is true make it more likely to be true?" Feeling questions can help you bridge a gap that exists within many conversations, unrecognized by the participants, who may wonder why they're failing to communicate. This gap lies between the facts that the conversation *seems* to be about (the number of gun deaths, immigration statistics, what happens on factory farms), on the surface, and the underlying issues that it is *really* about: issues of emotion, morality, or identity.

Plumbing moral epistemology can be especially difficult. When questioned about the foundations of moral beliefs, most people quickly develop an acute awareness of their lack of good reasons for believing as they do. This inspires discomfort and resistance. Yet the method of moral epistemological inquiry is identical to that of epistemological inquiry more generally: ask sincere questions about *how* your conversation partner came to moral conclusions, try to figure out whether their reasoning process supports those conclusions, and focus on targeted disconfirmation questions that relate to their sense of what it means to be a good person.

Breaking Down the Steps

Let's break down, in more detail, each of the steps in the template.

1. Acknowledge their intention and affirm their identity as a good, moral person[16]

Say, "It's clear to me that being a good person is important to you." This is important because ideologues tend to see themselves in one of two ways: virtuous moral pillars or desperate sinners seeking perfection/ redemption. In both cases, affirming either that they're a good person or that they have good intentions is crucial because it lowers their defensive posture and in some cases opens the door to moderating extreme beliefs.[17] It's also a vital preparatory step for the rest of the intervention.

You can *always* find something positive to say, even if the best you can do is to acknowledge (without accepting) their moral universe and recognize that they're adept at navigating within it. If you're struggling because someone's views are repulsive, acknowledge their good intentions, especially their intention to be a good person (recall Chapter 2, Intentions).[18] This is particularly important because it's part of a larger process to help your conversation partner question what being a "good person" means. Acknowledging that someone strives to be a good person does not mean he's increasing human well-being or ameliorating suffering—or even that he's succeeding at whatever he's attempting. This initial part of the conversation is about acknowledging values and good intentions, nothing more. You're just verbally recognizing that he values morality and that he's acting upon what *he believes* makes him good. There's no need, at this juncture, to ask questions about what makes a person a good person. Just briefly acknowledge and affirm that being a good person is important to him.

Many delicate conversations fail because nobody acknowledges that the other party is acting upon what they think is morally right. This is effortless to remedy: say, "It's clear to me that being a good person is important to you."

2. Change the subject to underlying values[19]

Say, "These beliefs seem really important to you. What are you basing them on?" If they're more educated, say, "What value informs these beliefs?" or "How did you derive those beliefs?"

If someone holds a belief tenaciously, it doesn't just "float out there" untethered to values. Contentious conversations hinge on beliefs that are almost always informed by particular values. For example, many people on both sides of the issue of immigration into the United States believe as they do because they think, "Good Americans hold this belief. I am a good American. I hold this belief." On a factual level, the conversation may indeed be about how many immigrants should be let into the country and what countries they should come from, but on a deeper level, the conversation is really based on, and informed by perceptions of, what values good

Americans should hold. Alternatively, maybe your conversation partner holds values that have nothing to do with being a good American and that instead rest on furthering "the greatest good for the greatest number of people." This would be your partner's underlying value.

One of the best ways to figure out what values inform a particular belief is simply to ask, "That position is based on what value?" The answer might not be immediately forthcoming, however, and you'll likely need to ask more questions (to ensure focus, be sure to orient the conversation around questions, as explained in Chapter 3). Here are additional questions to help you understand someone's underlying values:

1. "What values would have to change for your view to no longer be true?"

   ❏ In the case of immigration, possibly they're motivated by white ethnonationalism, the idea that most immigrants are nonwhite and that the United States should be a white country. Or perhaps the underlying value is rooted in a perceived necessity of cultural purity or having earned access to societal privileges but gets expressed as "Immigrants are changing our culture and stealing our jobs." To follow up, ask, "If those values changed would your conclusions also change?"

   ❏ Regarding assisted suicide, it may be that if someone does not believe assisted suicide should be an option it's because they believe there's a divine being that alone can determine the fate of human lives. So seeing human life as sacred and the province of a divine entity is the underlying value.

2. "What conditions would have to be different for your belief to be false?"

   ❏ This is a variant of a disconfirmation question. It's difficult and abstract, and you may have to ask follow-up questions to tease out underlying values. You can begin by giving empirical analogies. We noted our favorite from Carl Sagan in Chapter 5: "What conditions would have to be different for there to be no intelligent life elsewhere in the universe?" A simple "We could be the first" usually gets the point across.

By shifting the conversation to values that inform beliefs, you deny people access to their well-rehearsed defenses (which are usually just a form of circular reasoning, for example, "I believe it because it's in my holy book, and my holy book is true," or "White people are all racists, even those who deny it and self-identify as not racist").[20] Ideologues of all stripes have well-versed responses to defend their beliefs, but few and poor responses to defend the process that they use to arrive at their beliefs. (Many Christian apologists, for example, have extraordinarily sophisticated defenses of their conclusions, e.g., Jesus's resurrection from the dead, but flimsy defenses for leveraging faith as a process to arrive at those conclusions.[21])

Finally, don't worry about sounding "too philosophical." Most people love to talk about themselves and what they believe.

3. Invite a deeper conversation about the underlying values

Say, "I find that [what they articulated in the second stage, above] interesting. Let's explore those values." Your goal now is to help your conversation partner clearly articulate exactly what their values are, where they come from, how they know they're true, and how this relates to their sense of identity.

At this point, ask the following questions:

- I'd like to learn more about what you think makes someone a good person. How does someone know that acting in that way makes them good? What if they acted that way for a different reason?
- What attributes define good people? Is it how they think, act, or both?
- Do good people think about things in a certain way? (Notice how this question can help someone think about their epistemology without feeling they have to defend it.)

- How does [insert belief] relate to being a good person? What if a person believes that for a different reason? Are they still a good person?
- Which values motivate you to feel this way and believe that?
- Do you think you'd be a less moral person if you abandoned that belief? Why?
- Should someone who doesn't hold that belief be judged as less moral (than you)? Why? Could it be that they're just mistaken and not immoral? (This is an important question because it subtly suggests that someone apply the same standard to themselves.)
- How would you interpret an example of a person who you know is a good, moral person who does not hold that belief? Or one who holds the opposite of that belief?
- What if someone holds a similar conclusion but they arrived at it by different means? Would they be correct? For example, what if someone believes restricting firearm sales to felons is bad because they're a felon?

People assume their values are obvious, so you'll need to take your time in this stage.

Your goal is to invite your conversation partner to explain their moral epistemology by targeted identity-type questions. Each question can act as a micro-razor that has the potential to fray the tether between their belief and their reason for holding that belief, even if it takes time and later reflection to sever the connection.[22]

4. Induce doubt in their moral epistemology

Epistemology is the study of knowledge (remember Chapter 3, Focus on Epistemology). It deals with questions of how one knows what one claims to know. Moral epistemology is just epistemology applied to moral questions. That is, how does one know or come to know moral truths? You can also think about it like this: moral questions concern how we should act and what we should believe. Moral epistemology is the *process* we use to get answers to those questions.

Very few of us have given careful consideration to *how* we arrived at the answer to the question, "What should I value?" As Peter found when dealing with prison inmates and talking to hardline religious believers, and in thousands of conversations about morally contentious issues, few people have deeply considered the meanings and implications of morally relevant terms, like *justice, fairness, loyalty,* or *truth*. Our "guts" (more accurately, our moral intuitions), society, family, religion, culture, and so on, all offer the illusion that we've grasped timeless moral truths, how to uphold them, how to spot transgressors, and how to punish violators. Our belief-lives are trapped by feelings, culture, psychology, greater or lesser access to information, circumstances (including economic and social class), genetics, and the Zeitgeist. Rarely have we deeply pondered and scrutinized whether or not the *process* we use to come to moral knowledge can be relied upon to yield truth. *But we think we have.* We use our instincts to figure out whether someone has done a good or bad thing and whether this or that person is good or bad. Even though we have intense feelings about our moral conclusions, we're often only vaguely aware of the process that led us there.

Almost everyone has a brittle moral epistemology—this fragility is your main entry point in a belief intervention. It's the chink in our belief apparatus. It's where we're most vulnerable and it's *the* entryway into facilitating doubt and helping someone decrease the confidence in their beliefs. It's also the gateway to humility.[23]

5. Allow the tether between the moral epistemology and the moral conclusion to sever on its own.

In the end, you can let the conversation rest or conclude by revisiting the belief scale and asking how certain they are their belief is true. To help your conversation partner change her mind about a moral belief, make it your goal to sow doubts in the pathways that enable her to conclude she holds correct values. Think of these doubts as micro-razors (as described above) or as tiny cognitive wedges between their beliefs and the process they used to derive them.

Caution!

This process, even with all the details and caveats, remains easier said than done. There's no one correct way to go about it.

There will be deep emotional and identity undercurrents flowing through any conversation with an ideologue. It's easy to get caught in a conversational riptide and be pulled away from navigating the conversation toward moral epistemology. Engagements with ideologues require you to continuously recenter the discussion, either back to values questions that relate to identity or to efforts to learn why someone thinks as they do. Patience, calmness, and persistence are prerequisites for success.

Expect trouble. Placing wedges between someone's moral epistemology and the beliefs she has reached via that epistemology may cause "identity quakes."[24] An *identity quake* is the emotional reaction that follows from having one's core values disrupted. People may become defensive, lost, desperate, or angry. They may turn on you, deciding you're not to be trusted. You may even be dragged into your partner's identity quakes or lose her friendship. Over time, if her old sense of identity withers, she may grieve through feelings of denial, anger, depression, and guilt.[25]

Finally, be realistic. Expect these conversations to move people's moral attitudes only in tiny increments. Unless a catastrophic circumstance, such as the sudden death of a friend, forces an immediate seismic shift, moral attitudes tend to change glacially. That's especially true regarding attitudes connected to core concerns like right and wrong, purpose in life, community, family, identity, and death. If you succeed in instilling doubt, or in helping someone realize that the process they used to arrive at a belief cannot be relied upon to warrant their current degree of confidence, do not push.

Give people time to adjust, reconsider their positions, and modify their moral worldviews. When people *convince themselves* that the confidence they place in their beliefs is overinflated, they're more likely to revise their beliefs and those revisions are more likely to "stick" over time. Finally, remember to build Golden Bridges and praise your conversation partners for the courage to change their minds.

Summing Up: How to Converse with an Ideologue

It is possible to have productive conversations with (some) ideologues, zealots, extremists, and other morally entrenched individuals, but the process is difficult and requires patience, and there are no guarantees.[26] Success in producing doubt hinges upon affirming their sense of goodness, switching the conversation to values and identity, and then asking questions about their moral epistemology. This template offers another way to view the five-stage process above:

1. *Identify* that you're dealing with an ideologue.

    A good indicator is if they report 10 on a 1 to 10 belief scale, and they either state their beliefs have no disconfirmation criteria or offer wildly unrealistic criteria.

    ❑ Remember: The more extreme the confidence in a moral belief (especially 8 to 10 on the belief scale), the more difficult it is to give it a legitimate, rigorous justification. Even people who hold relatively moderate confidence levels in their moral beliefs (6 to 7 on the belief scale) are likely to have flimsy justifications that won't hold up to modest scrutiny.

2. *Acknowledge* their intention/motivation while affirming their identity as a good, moral person.

    Approaching conversation with an ideologue requires you to secure their self-worth before undermining overconfidence in their moral epistemology. Any technique that can reach an ideologue will, almost by definition, first have to secure their self-worth.

3. *Change* the subject to underlying values.

4. *Invite* a deeper conversation about the underlying values and do what you can to establish a shared sense of values (see Chapter 3:

Acknowledge Extremists, or appeal to the near-universal human values acknowledged above in step 2).

5. *Induce doubt* in their moral epistemology.

Ask targeted questions while integrating techniques from earlier chapters. These questions challenge the link between your conversation partner's belief and her sense of identity. The goal is often to lead them to see that there are other ways to enact their underlying values.

If your partner doesn't vaccinate her children, ask, "What qualities make someone a good mother?" This question shifts the conversation to more general moral terms and helps you avoid her likely well-rehearsed, fact-based message delivery service. After you've had this discussion, you can then bring the conversation to the role vaccination might play in discharging her sense of good parenting. This is an ideal segue to discuss moral epistemology—without ever using the word *epistemology,* of course. Also, remember to avoid facts.[27]

5a. If required: *Shift* to superordinate identities (discussed in Chapter 4).

When a conversation centers on race, gender, or any other divisive marker in identity politics, people can become defensive and tempers can flare. If you find the conversation getting heated or stuck, shift the focus to superordinate identity markers instead. Rather than dividing, these unify people. Superordinate identity markers go "up" and include commonalities among people, not down to identity features of certain groups (black skin, particular sex organs, etc.).

Crudely, "You're white (or Muslim) and I'm black (or Christian), but so what, because we're both Americans and both human beings." Notice how this statement moves the conversation toward common ground at the identity level. In question form, say: "Well, aren't we still both Americans? Aren't we both human?" Notice immediately that this was the tone and tenor of the majority of the

African American Civil Rights movement, which we still celebrate decades after its campaigns for racial equality.

6. *Sever* the tether between the conclusion and the moral epistemology, that is, how they arrived at the conclusions they base upon their values.

7. *Be patient* throughout.

8. *Build* Golden Bridges.

9. *Walk away* if you feel unsafe.[28]

Finally, you may need to figure out if *you're* the ideologue.[29] A good first step to consider whether you are thinking and behaving like an ideologue is to think of your cherished beliefs, ask yourself disconfirmation questions, and then write down the answers. Write them down because, to paraphrase physicist Richard Feynman, the easiest person to fool is yourself. Look at them in print. Show them to a friend who is not in your moral universe. Ask her if any of your answers seem wildly implausible. If she says "Yes," then that's an opportunity to reflect more deeply on your beliefs. If everyone you know is in your moral universe, it's time to expand your circle of friends.

If you can't generate disconfirmation responses, then be honest with yourself about whether the confidence you have in your beliefs is justified. Remember, *the more you want to hold the belief, the more difficult it will be to revise.* If you tend to think of everyone who disagrees with you as being morally deficient, or you find yourself describing them almost wholly in morally denigrating terms, chances are that *you* are the ideologue and need to conduct a series of interventions *on yourself.*

#2—Moral Reframing

The gap between your moral intuitions and your partner's can be partially filled by morally reframing conversations. This means recasting an idea or a claim in moral terms that are less likely to evoke a defensive posture and more likely to resonate with your conversation partner.[30] It can feel a bit like learning to speak another language. Allow us to explain.

On August 20, 2018, President Trump tweeted:

> It is outrageous that Poisonous Synthetic Heroin Fentanyl comes pouring into the U.S. Postal System from China. We can, and must, END THIS NOW! The Senate should pass the STOP ACT—and firmly STOP this poison from killing our children and destroying our country. No more delay!

His tweet was brought to moral psychologist Jonathan Haidt's attention by Conor Friedersdorf, a staff writer at *The Atlantic*. Haidt responded:

> Wow. This appeal hits the sanctity button (poison seeping in), loyalty (us vs them), authority (leaders must protect) and even care (kids). This is a rare 4-foundation appeal.

President Trump's tweet was, in other words, appealing to an unusually wide range of foundational moral values and accompanying moral intuitions.

Understanding Moral Intuitions

Think of moral intuitions as tendencies to lean toward certain (core) values—sanctity of life, freedom, safety, purity—rather than others. Our moral intuitions are formed *before* we try to figure out what's the right thing to do, what's not, and how we know our intuitions are justified (that is, moral epistemology). In politics, for example, liberals, conservatives, and libertarians often talk past one another by failing to understand each other's moral impulses.[31] Jonathan Haidt's research showed that this is because different groups have different moral intuitions.[32] His research is crucial to understanding how liberals who want to reach conservatives should make their points according to conservative values, and vice versa; the same goes for either side wishing to communicate with libertarians.[33]

As Douglas Stone and his colleagues note, "Reframing means taking the essence of what the other person says and 'translat[ing] it' into concepts that are more helpful."[34] Even before your conversation becomes stuck, you can reframe the issues in terms that resonate with the moral intuitions of the person across the divide. The type of moral reframing we advocate is rooted in Haidt's frameworks.

First, we'll give you a primer on the basics. Second, we'll offer a road map for moral reframing using Haidt's categories.

Moral Foundations

In their research to date, Haidt and his colleagues have identified six "moral foundations" (and the value they stand opposed to in each case):

- Care versus harm.
- Fairness versus cheating.
- Loyalty versus betrayal.
- Authority versus subversion.
- Sanctity versus degradation.
- Liberty versus oppression.[35]

Haidt describes these moral foundations as being equivalents to the different components of our sense of taste (sweet, sour, salty, bitter, savory), indicating that they're felt as closely and quickly as physical sensations, but applicable to our social universe.[36] Think of them as sensitivity to our underlying values. Conservatives tend to respond to all six moral foundations, with a particular propensity toward loyalty, authority, and sanctity and less of a leaning toward care. Liberals are most concerned with care and fairness, and then liberty, with the other three foundations almost absent (or presenting in remarkably different ways).[37] Libertarians are most concerned with a particular aspect of liberty, while they find the other five foundations less important.[38]

Effective conversations in the political arena are enhanced by keeping in mind these differences in moral foundations. Let's take the issue of gun control. Conservatives are sensitive to values that lead them to prioritize security (a kind of sanctity in society) and liberty. These values include the capacity to defend themselves against threats.[39] Liberals rarely talk about guns in terms of these values, focusing instead on statistics about harm.[40] A liberal saying, "I understand why you'd differ, but because people make mistakes, having such easy access to guns makes me feel less secure, and thus less free, not more," would do more to reach conservatives than quoting murder or accidental gun death statistics. A conservative hoping to reach liberals would do best to talk about the kinds of harms that are most effectively prevented by individual gun ownership.[41]

Nearly all political conversations are rooted in foundational values. This creates tremendous difficulty when your foundational values do not match those of your conversation partner. The ways you each frame issues, what you *feel* matters most, and even the language used will always be influenced by your respective foundational values. The result is that you and your partner are likely to talk past one another *even when you agree,* and common ground can be difficult to find. This makes conversations across moral divides difficult because the mismatch in values contributes to misunderstandings on moral and political issues. Worse, these disagreements are often felt emotionally, before you can think clearly, and they can be frustrating for both parties.[42]

Although it is difficult, one of the only ways to get around this problem is to make every effort to understand and speak on your conversation partner's terms—including her moral terms. We touched on this in Chapter 3 when discussing the disavowal of your own extremists, and now it's time to go further.[43] Maybe loyalty doesn't mean much to you, but if your partner is speaking from a position of conservatism, it will mean a lot to her. Thus, if you want to understand her position on kneeling in protest through the national anthem, you will need to understand the appeal to loyalty (to country) that she is making. If you cannot connect across that moral divide, then there's little chance you'll understand each other. The way to foster understanding is to tap into the relevant moral foundation and reframe the conversation *morally*. Doing so opens up new channels for effective communication.

Reframing

Moral reframing can be significantly improved by learning to speak other "moral dialects." You and your conversation partner may both speak English, but if he is an Orthodox Jew and you're a liberal hippie, you'll usually be speaking different moral dialects. Our language is rich in symbolism, and our moral intuitions are triggered by interaction with morally charged ideas. Thus, when you say a morally resonant word like *loyalty* or *security,* your conversation partner may hear something completely different from your intended meaning. A devout Muslim may hear the word *spiritual* with distinct moral resonances that others, say a hippie or an atheist, might not.

You can bridge seemingly impossible moral divides by learning to understand, appreciate, and speak other moral lingoes.[44] Like learning any new language, learning to speak conservativese or liberalese, or learning to understand and appreciate the rich symbolism in others' faith traditions, takes time, practice, and immersive interaction with native speakers. Here are some straightforward strategies and techniques for improving your speaking skill and understanding other moral languages:

- *Expose* yourself to other moral viewpoints and to *people* who hold opposing views.
  - ❏ Read materials from people with different moral outlooks, and spend time reflecting upon where those moral appeals lie and how they're achieved. This is easiest with material that deviates *slightly* from your own outlook in whichever direction you choose to explore.
  - ❏ Have real-time, face-to-face conversations, as opposed to engaging people in asynchronous, online environments.

In-person interactions offer an opportunity for immediate feedback, which is important because these engagements tend to be more "raw" and offer less time for reflection.

- ❏ Befriend people from different faith traditions or with no faith tradition. Listen to their moral dialects.
- ❏ Practice with friends who occupy a different moral space. (If all of your friends have identical moral beliefs, consider broadening your circle of friends.)

● *Home in* on particular words and terms.

- ❏ Ask your conversation partner why they've used particular words and not used other words. For example, if you hear someone use the word *equity,* ask them why they used *equity* and not *equality.* (See #2, below.) If someone uses the word *faith,* ask them why they didn't use *hope, trust,* or *confidence.*
- ❏ Remembering how your conversation partner is using particular words can help in future conversations with people who share similar convictions.

● *Listen* to your moral dialect like an outsider.

- ❏ Identify the way you use a word like *racist* and compare it to the way others use it. You may uncover a source of semantic disagreement or even an incommensurable worldview (that is, perspectives that are so different there's no basis to judge between them, such as the perspective of someone whose primary value is equity and that of a person whose primary value is liberty). Ask yourself what *you* mean by the word *racist* and what someone who vehemently disagrees means, and then think about what's causing the gap.

● *Read* the fundamentals of moral foundations theory and the science of moral intuitions. In particular, read and reflect on Jonathan Haidt's *The Righteous Mind: Why Good People Are Divided by Politics and Religion.*[45] Pay attention to understanding differences across moral divides.[46]

If possible, stay on the same identity page by speaking your partner's moral language. This applies to the obvious (if you're talking with a Catholic, call the communion wafer "the Host" and not "a cracker") and the subtle (if you're a liberal talking with a conservative, bring the conversation back to being American or patriotic). Conservatives' arguments can go a long way toward influencing liberals by reminding them of a commitment to minimizing harm and making things fair for as many people as possible.

How to Reframe a Conversation Morally

1. Use moral keywords.

   If you're talking to a conservative, invoke "leadership," "freedom," "family," "responsibility," and so on.[47] If you're talking to a liberal, appeal to "the disadvantaged," "the poor," "victims," "harm," and the like. If you bring up themes resonant with both sides, like "liberty," "decency," "morals," "equality," or "fairness," tailor your use according to how each side uses these words. That is, figure out how they're using the word "equality" and use it similarly.

2. Ask, "Can you think of a sentence in which the word X [e.g., "equity"] could be substituted for the word Y [e.g., "equality"] and the meaning of the sentence would not change?"

   If they say "No," respond, "Then why did you use X as opposed to Y?"

   If they say "Yes," ask them to tell you the sentence and try to figure out if it really is a perfect synonym.

The words people use trap them in a particular frame of mind. Asking the above question is a sort of disconfirmation question where the purpose is to help your conversation partner cast doubt on their word choice, and thus the moral infrastructure upon which they travel.

3. Interpret incommensurable moral disagreements as opportunities to learn a different moral language.[48]

If they have no disconfirmation criteria and they're 10 on the belief scale, then focus on how they're using certain words and on the tapestry of how those words come together to form their moral worldview. Remember, they're offering you a free lesson in how to speak a different moral language.

Conclusion

Seemingly impossible conversations typically have one thing in common: they're about *moral* beliefs rooted in one's sense of identity, but they play out on the level of facts (or assertions, name-calling, grandstanding, threats, etc.). That is, the discussion appears to be about issues (Muslim immigration), ideas (defending Western values, however these are understood,[49] from Muslim immigrants), and facts (numbers of immigrants from Islamic countries), but instead it's really about the type of person the entrenched individual perceives herself to be (I am a good person and good people believe this). The most difficult conversations, then, masquerade as discussions about something other than morality, but they are actually about what qualities, beliefs, attitudes, and behaviors individuals believe make them *good people* or *bad people* and why it is important to hold the right views among those.

Moral conversations are extremely difficult to navigate because moral beliefs are closely tied to issues of personal identity and community: that is, how one views oneself; what type of person one thinks one is; and how the participants in the conversation fit in with others in groups composed of members whose esteem they value. The added burdens of people thinking it's a virtue not to change their minds, while belonging to communities that reinforce their beliefs, make shifting their ideas in this area *nearly* impossible. (Colloquially, an unwillingness or inability to change one's mind is called "incorrigibility," philosophically it's termed "epistemic closure" or "doxastic closure," and in other domains like religion and pop morality it's known as "conviction."[50])

People often think moral issues are clear, with obvious answers, until their moral epistemology is challenged by targeted questions. At that point, the dizzying complexity can become overwhelming. When faced with this, individuals who are otherwise reasonable and well-meaning may shut off, hunker down, or claim offense. So, *take it slow*. Failure to appreciate this complexity contributes to widespread, unwarranted moral certainty, which prevents a culture from emerging in which we're capable of understanding different moral epistemologies. Most of these problems can be bypassed by using the techniques, strategies, and approaches described in this chapter.

eight

Conclusion

Y OU NOW HAVE THE TOOLS TO SPEAK YOUR MIND, UNDERSTAND, and be understood. You are empowered to navigate even the most difficult conversations. But you must use what you've learned. The techniques of the previous chapters will be worthless unless you practice. Along the way, expect failure and success. The successes will emerge because you've persisted.

Some of the techniques in this book will become your conversational bread and butter, and as you improve, we urge revisiting less-used sections and incorporating more techniques. Once you've grasped all the techniques, from beginner to master level, you will be equipped to rise confidently to conversational challenges. That said, there's no urgency. Start slowly. Build your repertoire, pay attention to what works and what doesn't, and keep practicing, keep talking, keep listening, and keep learning. Above all, take charge. There's no reason to cower, to be afraid to voice your opinion, or to fear disagreement. You know how to engage people with proven, evidence-based techniques. All that's left is for you to begin.

Acknowledgments

There are so, so many people to thank sincerely for making this book possible. Thanks go first to the researchers of *How to Have Impossible Conversations* for their hard work, attention to detail, and persistence. Their efforts solidified and enriched this book.

Thanks also go to Russell Blackford for his meticulous editing of the manuscript. Thanks are also due to Jane Dystel, Miriam Goderich, and Amy Bishop at Dystel, Goderich, and Bourret, LLC, and to Dan Ambrosio at Da Capo Press for being so persistent and helpful at moving this book from concept to developed manuscript to print. Their professionalism has been outstanding and they have been fantastic to work with. We'd also like to offer thanks to Douglas Stone, Bruce Patton, and Sheila Heen, authors of *Difficult Conversations*. Their thinking and concepts have directly informed our own, and their book is an indispensable contribution to this body of literature.

Furthermore, we offer our thanks to our families for their enduring patience. Thanks to CFI Portland and Dani Tofte for hosting the *Impossible Conversations* series. Thanks to Michael Shermer for his manuscript guidance. A heartfelt thank you to Marcie Hume for her conceptual guidance, Aubrey Ayash for his unwavering friendship, trust, and support, and Steve Gregg for his feedback. Thanks are also due to Bob Parker and Chris Matheson for conceptual guidance, and to Anthony Magnabosco and Helen

Pluckrose for constantly modeling patience and decency in their many conversations. Lastly, we offer our sincere thanks to all of the people who have been willing to have impossible conversations with us thus far and all who will be willing in the future.

Notes

one: When Conversations Seem Impossible

1. Regarding politics, many of our examples are from within an American political context. When we use the word *liberal,* readers outside of the United States should be aware that we are referring to left-wing political views with a history dating from the New Deal of the 1930s, which might be called "social democrat" or "progressive" in other contexts. We use the word *libertarian* to mean American-style political libertarianism, which places great emphasis on individual liberty and has something in common with what much of the rest of the world means by the term *liberal.*

two: The Seven Fundamentals of Good Conversations

1. For more on conversational goal management and strategic reasoning, see Mbarki, Bentahar, & Moulin, 2008; Waldron et al.,1990. Heinrichs, 2017 (esp. pp. 15–26), offers an accessible, less academic primer.

2. These are the essentials for a psychologically safe environment. See Edmondson, 2003; Edmondson & Roloff, 2008, pp. 187–188.

Writing in the context of productivity in work teams, Amy C. Edmondson defines a psychologically safe environment as one in which "no one will be punished or humiliated for errors, questions, or requests for help" (Edmondson, 2003, p. 267). In safe, trusting environments, people are "less likely to focus on self-protection" (Edmondson & Roloff, 2008, p. 188) and thus more likely to be genuine truth seekers focused on productive discussions. In the context of one-on-one conversations, the best way to create psychologically safe, trusting environments is by viewing the person with whom you're conversing as a partner, rather than as an adversary.

On the flip side, psychologically safe environments might be interpreted as those where some lines of criticism are not welcomed, so-called safe spaces, but this is an abuse of the term. Criticisms of our ideas are necessary for getting closer to truth. The crucial distinction is that criticism need not be punishing or humiliating, even if the recipient isn't fond of what is being said. There is a balance to be struck between securing sufficient psychological safety and providing an excessive and infantilizing form of safety, which can enable groupthink and delusion. This is the opposite of genuine truth-seeking.

Trust is central to psychologically safe environments. Absent trust, there is little hope for any productive discussion. However, viewing people as being on the same moral team is a dubious approach to securing trust. It functions as a kind of distrust-by-passing mechanism. That is, it allows you to trust someone even if you do not have good reasons for doing so. (This may be a substantial part of the reason why churches are so often sites of sexual abuse: too much trust is given too freely to someone viewed as being on the same moral team.)

As one can criticize and challenge another's ideas in an environment that does not violate trust, there is no reason to conflate psychologically safe environments with criticism-free "safe spaces."

3. Ekman, 2003, pp. 73–76. Note: We are aware of the controversy surrounding some of Ekman's findings, particularly regarding the connection between facial expression and emotion. See Lisa Feldman Barrett (2017), for example. We do not rely upon any of Ekman's scholarship that depends upon these particulars.

4. Habermas, 1985, pp. 22–27, 40, 122–145, 149–150; Stone, Patton, & Heen, 2010, pp. 37–38.

5. Cooperative goals, such as having a mutually engaging, thoughtful conversation, may be different from personal goals, like winning or making oneself appear intelligent.

6. Fisher, Ury, & Patton, 2011, pp. 163–168; Stone, Patton, & Heen, 2010, pp. 41–42, 52–53, 92–93, 244–257.

Certain kinds of disagreement are okay or even beneficial (task conflict, policy difference), while others are not (aggression, harsh language, threats of humiliation, especially in front of others). The latter are typical of call-out culture, shaming, and the like, which are present on both the political Left and the Right. (NB: In recent times, call-out culture may be more obvious on the Left than on the nonreligious Right, but it has frequently been a characteristic of the religious Right. Moreover, the Right is prone to "shut-out culture," which employs isolating behavior, that is, shunning, as opposed to admonitions.)

7. Friedersdorf, 2017.

8. Stone, Patton, & Heen, 2010, pp. 182–183.

9. Bennion, 1959, p. 23. (Though the provenance of this quotation is disputed, it is attributed to Aristotle in Bennion's *Religion and the Pursuit of Truth*.)

10. Stone, Patton, & Heen, 2010, pp. 166–167.

11. Habermas, 1985, pp. 22–27, 40, 122–145, 149–150.

12. An interesting passage by Amy C. Edmondson (2003, pp. 264–265) weaves together important themes emerging from the study of organizational teamwork:

"In this study, trust reduced the likelihood of relationship conflict in top management teams, such that task conflict (productive disagreement over the content of one's decisions and ideas that deepen cognitive understanding of the problem) was able to help the team produce better solutions. Termed 'creative abrasion' by Leonard-Barton (1995), task conflict thus may have to exist within a cushion of psychological safety to enable a learning climate of discussion, innovation, and productive group thinking. *Otherwise such conflict is destructive—characterized by aggression, harsh language, and the threat of humiliation in front of others* [emphasis added]. Similarly, Barsade and her colleagues (2001) found that *psychological safety moderates the effect of conflict on anger* [emphasis added]. Psychological safety allows groups to set high goals and work towards them through cycles of learning and collaboration."

Such themes of trust, psychological safety, and the potential for benefit from well-managed disagreement recur in the various papers collected in West, Tjosvold, and Smith (2003) and in the selection from them (including Edmondson's paper) contained in West, Tjosvold, and Smith (2005).

13. Stone, Patton, & Heen, 2010, pp. 145, 146, 156, 157, 206–208.

14. Stone, Patton, & Heen, 2010, pp. 131–146, 155–158, 177.

15. Using techniques from *A Manual for Creating Atheists* (Boghossian, 2013), Magnabosco interviews strangers about their deeply held beliefs. He films these engagements and posts them online. His videos can be found here: https://www.youtube.com/user/magnabosco210.

16. Boghossian, 2013.

17. Magnabosco, 2016a.

18. Fisher, Ury, & Patton, 2011; Phelps-Roper, 2017.

19. Grubb, 2010, p. 346; Kellin & McMurty, 2007.

20. Zunin & Zunin, 1972, pp. 6–9, 15.

21. Civility, 2015.

22. Lowndes, 2003.

23. Miller, 2005, p. 281.

24. For more detail on how to build rapport, see hostage negotiator Chris Voss's outstanding *Never Split the Difference: Negotiating As If Your Life Depended On It* (Voss & Raz, 2016, pp. 23–48).

25. The Danish television station TV2 created an advertisement, "All That We Share," that went viral. It pointedly illustrated how people have far more in common than they suspect (Zukar, 2017).

26. Stone, Patton, & Heen, 2010, pp. 139–140.

27. For a masterful application of this, watch Fred Rogers' (Mister Rogers) 1969 appearance before the United States Senate Subcommittee on Communications (BotJunkie, 2007).

28. Stone, Patton, & Heen, 2010, pp. 85–108, 163–184.

29. Stone, Patton, & Heen, 2010, pp. 207–208.

30. Stone, Patton, & Heen, 2010, pp. 25–43, 137–140, 196–197.

More accurately, delivering messages does not work in contentious conversations, especially across a moral divide. Delivering messages can work with people who already agree with you, but such speech is denigrated by calling it "preaching to the choir" for a reason.

Delivering messages across divides almost always fails. Failure is not necessarily caused by the content of the messages but by either the discrepancy in underlying assumptions or one's inability to speak another moral language. To help a conservative, for example, accept a liberal message (that contradicts the conservative's foundational values) is also to ask the conservative to question her conservative (moral) identity. That's a lot to ask, and it frequently results in the message being ignored. (This topic is developed at length in Chapter 7.) The conservative claims about "liberal media" for the last few decades, now echoed by liberals about right-wing media, provide an example of shooting the messenger and ignoring the message.

31. Lewin, 1998, pp. 115–116.

32. Lewin, 1947.

33. Lewin, 1947.

34. The advice against shooting the messenger is ancient, and so is the impulse it instructs against. Sophocles expressed it in the fifth century BCE in his tragic play *Antigone:* "No one loves the messenger who brings bad news" (Sophocles, trans. 1891, line 277). It was frequently an act of treason to kill the town crier, who spoke on behalf of a king or feudal lord (see "Top town crier . . . " 2010).

Sigmund Freud also famously gave an explanation for the impulse to shoot the messenger (Freud, 1936/1991, pp. 454–455). He wrote that it is a method of "fending off what is distressing or unbearable" and noted that it is a defensive response against feeling powerless. According to Freud, shooting the messenger not only distances someone from unwanted information but also acts as an overt display of power over the source of unwanted news.

Some modern corroboration of this view is available in the oncology literature, specifically pertaining to the ways patients receive the bad news when their doctor informs them they have cancer. In 1999, medical psychologist Melina Gattellari and her colleagues reported in *Annals of Oncology* that patient denial leads to misunderstanding and "shooting the messenger" (Gattellari et al., 1999). One solution, they argued, is to improve physicians' ability to communicate effectively.

For our purposes, if you play the role of messenger and deliver a deeply unwanted message, especially one that runs counter to someone's identity or sense of security, they will be tempted (hopefully only metaphorically) to shoot you. That is, to discount your message entirely and even become hostile to you and to whatever groups they perceive you as representing. For more, see Eric Horowitz's summary of literature about why messages backfire (Horowitz, 2013).

35. Plato, ca. 380 BCE/2006, 77c–78b.

36. The obvious exceptions to *everyone* having good intentions are psychopaths and sociopaths. These individuals do not take away from the thrust that most people with whom we will discuss politics *do* have good and often helpful intentions (Becker, 2015, esp. pp. 51–57; Neumann & Hare, 2008).

37. See Stone, Patton, & Heen, 2010, pp. 45–53. We tend to treat ourselves charitably (diminishing the negativity of our intentions and apologizing away our faults) and assume far worse of others. When discussing across a political divide, we're almost always also conversing across a *moral* divide. We have a tendency to think that those with different morals are *bad* people. It's then an effortless step from believing a person is a bad person to believing her intent is malicious.

38. Megan Phelps-Roper, who left the Westboro Baptist Church, makes this point in her TED talk (Phelps-Roper, 2017). Stone and his collaborators devote the entire third chapter of *Difficult Conversations* (Stone, Patton, & Heen, 2010) to the same point, with frequent reminders throughout the rest of the book. *It cannot be overstated that our assumptions about our partners' intentions are almost always worse than their true intentions.* Assuming worse intentions makes conversations less successful, profitable, and civil.

39. Stone, Patton, & Heen, 2010, pp. 46–48.

40. Doherty, Horowitz, & Dimock, 2014; Norton, 2002.

41. Intentions aren't everything when it comes to the moral valence of beliefs—consequences matter too, and thus so do truth and falsity of the beliefs. For example, having voted for John McCain over Barack Obama in 2008 because McCain is a Republican is clearly more morally acceptable than having done so because Obama is black. This remains the case even though the outcomes are the same and even if the intention behind the action remained hidden (see Harris, 2010). In this example, assume your partner voted for McCain because he thought McCain had a superior platform.

42. Stone, Patton, & Heen, 2010, pp. 51–52.

43. Stone, Patton, & Heen (2010, pp. 244–249) address the problem of a truly difficult conversation partner with bad intentions: "lying, bullying, or intentionally derailing the conversation to get what they want" (p. 244). The authors' advice is to avoid rewarding bad behavior and not escalate with tit-for-tat.

As an applicable aside, tit-for-tat is a highly successful game theoretic strategy (devised by Anatole Rapoport) for playing what is known as the Iterated Prisoner's Dilemma. In the Prisoner's Dilemma, each of two players can either cooperate or "defect" (such as confessing to a crime committed in concert with a fellow prisoner). To simplify slightly, there are three possible outcomes: if they cooperate, the players split some reward; if one defects and the other cooperates, the defector takes the entire reward; and if both defect, they both get nothing. Iterated Prisoner's Dilemma plays the game over and over, and the tit-for-tat strategy initially cooperates and then punishes any defection with a retaliatory defection in the next round. The strategy is susceptible to "defection loops" in which both players punish the previous defection with another, and the game unprofitably proceeds to its terminus with all defections.

If you have a partner with genuinely bad intentions (say, you're talking with a moral zealot who thinks your positions are fundamentally "evil," with an Internet troll, or with someone who is determined to "win" and wants to humiliate you in the process), assume that he is playing a defection-heavy or all-defection strategy and will punish your defections with further defections. Such a game has the result of rewarding him every time you attempt to forgive him and cooperate, although you'll never win. It is therefore better simply not to play such a game if it can be avoided.

Stone and his collaborators (Stone, Patton, & Heen, 2010) give positive advice for dealing with a genuinely bad actor if you must engage (or choose to try): change the subject and "seek to understand why they think their intentions and actions are justified" (p. 245). This gives you an opportunity to improve the conversation or persuade them to use a different tactic, or a clear reason to leave the conversation (as with Internet trolls and other bullies).

44. We're indebted to Sam Harris for this quotation.

45. Hess, 2017.

Many people, the present authors included, have been jaded by social media. We suffer from a quickness to dismiss people as trolls because we view dissent as trolling, or think others are ill-intentioned, or out of a tendency to think our positions are the only possible correct ones and no nuance is possible. On social media, it is extremely difficult to make reliable judgments about who is and is not a troll. For this reason—and others noted in later chapters—it is far better to engage someone about a contentious topic in person than it is over social media.

46. Boghossian, 2013.

47. Ekman points out that the emotional refractory period associated with frustration can often skew interpretations of others' intentions and may undermine belief revision (Ekman, 2003, pp. 39–40, 113, 120). This basic fact about frustration and anger may explain why someone who's angry seems less likely to revise their beliefs. Ekman notes that anger often triggers guilt, shame, and embarrassment for the person on the receiving end. This suggests that if a person is angry it decreases the likelihood they'll revise their belief because of a face-saving drive (p. 113). Anger enhances, not diminishes, belief entrenchment. As guilt, shame, and anger interact in the interpersonal milieu, the backfire effect is likely to come into play, leading someone who's angry to become even more committed to a belief. The face-saving drive is often a core component in triggering the backfire effect, in which attempts to change someone's mind backfire and lead them to reinforce their beliefs instead (Horowitz, 2013).

Finally, lack of a trusting environment makes it less likely that participants will seek to find the truth and more likely that they'll defend an idea even though they know it's incorrect (Ekman, 2003, pp. 38–39, 111, 115; Stone, Patton, & Heen, 2010, pp. 25–43). Ekman (2003) specifically notes that "anger calls forth anger" (p. 111). In the grip of anger, we enter a state of encapsulated thinking that distorts our views for the worse. Moreover, as anger arises from either offense or frustration (of our views, for example), it predisposes us to want to *win* rather than to converse. These features combine (see Boghossian, 2013, pp. 49–50, 70, 83–84) to entrench people in their views and thus drive a wedge between their views and people with whom they're arguing.

48. Hogarth & Einhorn, 1992.

49. Jost et al., 2003.

50. Johnson-Laird, Girotto, & Legrenzi, 2004; Schlottmann & Anderson, 1995.

51. Ekman, 2003, pp. 116, 144, 147. Ekman makes the point that anger often does irreparable damage to relationships. There are, however, more and less appropriate times and ways to navigate anger in conversations. Ekman writes, "Grievances must be considered, but not, I suggest, in the heat of anger" (p. 147). He also observes, "[Confrontational] remarks are an invitation for someone to say something mean-spirited, or act in an angry fashion, and that is not always in your interest or the interest of the angry person. Not that grievances or offenses should be ignored, but they may be more readily

dealt with once the moment of anger has passed" (p. 144). Stone, Patton, and Heen (2010) make the same point on pp. 125–126. For more, see Goulston, 2015, pp. 33–44.

52. These themes are developed in detail in Malhotra, 2016b.

53. Vlemincx et al., 2016, pp. 132–134.

three: Beginner Level: Nine Ways to Start Changing Minds

1. Stone, Patton, & Heen, 2010, pp. 166–167.

2. Ekman, 2003, pp. 111, 120.

3. In a paper that appears to be the origin of the term "illusion of explanatory depth," philosopher Robert Wilson and psychologist Frank Keil refer to it as "the shadows and the shallows of explanation" (Wilson & Keil, 1998).

4. Kolbert, 2017; for more, see TedX Talks, 2013.

People who suffer the most from the Unread Library Effect are the best candidates for the Dunning-Kruger effect (Kruger & Dunning, 1999). The Dunning-Kruger effect states that legitimate experts (no Unread Library Effect, because they've read much of the relevant library!) feel confident and people with very little or no understanding (extreme Unread Library Effect) are even more confident. People in between, who have some knowledge but who are not experts, dramatically lack confidence. They've realized and escaped the Unread Library Effect by having learned enough to know how much they don't know.

5. Rozenblit & Keil, 2002.

6. Rozenblit & Keil, 2002.

7. Fernbach et al., 2013.

Since extremism often goes hand in hand with entrenched beliefs, a moderating effect on political views may lead to more civil and productive political dialogue and more changed minds. Not only will civility and belief revision benefit from moderating extreme political views, but also the health of our entire body politic may improve for another reason. Extremists often accept the views of a relatively small number of deeply trusted leaders and believe them fervently. That is, extremists are gullible and easy to manipulate.

Many conservative extremists in the United States, for instance, spend enormous sums of money on guns and ammunition in response to a mere suggestion that a liberal politician might "take their guns," despite there being essentially no strong reason to believe any such thing will happen. Left-wing extremists will believe almost anything is anathema to their values (like eating tacos on Tuesdays) if it can be made to appear as revealing racist motivations or undertones. Extremists on both sides seem to throw money at snake-oil supplements and remedies sold by people perceived as moral leaders in their own moral tribes.

Extremists are also well-rehearsed in their leaders' talking points, deeply entrenched in their beliefs, and often literalists in their interpretations, and they vote in accordance with the dictates of their thought leaders. Moderating extreme political views can be expected to decrease gullibility and manipulability of the electorate, the benefits of which would reach into almost every corner of civic life.

8. Fernbach et al., 2013.

9. James Randi Educational Foundation, 2013.

10. Transcribed from video of an event featuring Damore at Portland State University (Freethinkers of PSU, 2018).

11. Devitt, 1994.

12. Boghossian, 2013.

13. For more here, see Haidt, 2012, esp. Chapter 7.

There's some complication with the fairness moral foundation. As Haidt explains, it is important to both liberals and conservatives, but in distinct ways. Liberals are concerned with fairness of opportunity, that is, with everyone getting a fair chance. Conservatives are concerned with fairness in terms of the justness of rewards, that is, they see people getting more than they have ostensibly earned as being particularly unfair. For conservatives, rewards to individuals should be in proportion to what they contribute. For liberals, everyone should have a fair chance to participate, and no one should have undue advantages that are inaccessible to others.

14. Overcoming this problem is difficult. It requires understanding each other's moral language (see Chapter 7), asking a lot of questions (some of which might be considered too personal), and patience. It is also a common problem across partisan divides. Research has shown people commonly misunderstand one another even over fundamental political terms, like *liberal, conservative, Democrat, Republican, progressive, libertarian, welfare, free,* and *liberty* (Devitt, 1994). It's better not to assume too much and instead to expect frustration at sorting out what seem like very basic understandings.

15. In his January 2017 podcast with Jordan Peterson, Sam Harris exhibits this technique with considerable skill when he and Peterson fundamentally disagree about the meaning behind the concept of truth (Harris, 2017).

16. Dennett, 2006, pp. 200–248.

17. People are extremely prone to believe incorrect conclusions based upon "the evidence" because of our susceptibility to two biases: confirmation bias and desirability bias (Tappin, van der Leer, & McKay, 2017). These two biases often lead us to look for, accept, and believe especially (or only) whichever evidence supports what we already believe (confirmation bias) or want to believe (desirability bias). In the example, Jon is primarily exhibiting desirability bias, which is very common with moral beliefs (Haidt, 2012).

18. Adapted from Boghossian, 2004, p. 213.

19. Voss & Raz, 2016, pp. 150–165.

20. Voss & Raz, 2016, pp. 150–165.

21. Stone, Patton, & Heen, 2010, p. 172.

22. Stone, Patton, & Heen, 2010, pp. 167–168.

23. In this sense, "No one cares how much you know until they know how much you care" refers ultimately to your capacity to signal virtue. In the moral sphere, it instructs that people are unlikely to care much about your opinion unless they can view you as a person who tends to have the right values, as determined from *their* perspective.

24. One of the more fascinating examples of the phenomenon of moral tribal entrenchment has been the rise of the New Atheism Movement over the past twelve to

fifteen years. The New Atheism Movement prided itself on being immune to the myriad problems associated with religious tribalism. In numerous ways, however, its supporters showed they were not immune after all (see Lindsay, 2015).

In the early years of the twenty-first century, Sam Harris, Richard Dawkins, and others argued that religious moderates bear some responsibility for religious extremism by propping up and normalizing religious beliefs and texts that are the seeds for some of the worst types of extremism, zealotry, and fundamentalism (Dawkins, 2006, p. 345; Harris, 2004, p. 20). As far as it went, this was intellectually justified. However, it sowed distrust of religious people among many atheists, particularly atheism activists, because "theists" were being seen, and caricatured, as a competing moral tribe (see Lindsay, 2015, pp. 57–59). The consequences have been serious for one of humanity's most pressing problems: breaking the grip of radical, fundamentalist interpretations of the Quran. Many atheism activists, rather than seeing liberal Muslims who wish to reform and liberalize mainstream Islamic thought as their natural and indispensable allies, fought against them because of their faith (Harris & Nawaz, 2015).

25. Explicitly acknowledging a point of moral agreement by disavowing extremists creates a point of *moral* agreement with your conversation partner, which is crucial common ground in conversations across divides. It also separates you from the moral tribe to which she fears you may have loyalties. This is no trivial point. In conversations where tribal loyalty is suspected, being willing to renounce the most extreme and belligerent members of your own side is a powerful "costly signal" because it carries the threat associated with betrayal of your group (Boghossian & Lindsay, 2016).

Costly signals are usually indicators that prove group commitment because they exact some price. They may involve expressing commitment to extreme and implausible dogmas of the group even at the risk of looking unhinged. However, costly signaling of the type we are describing works because you risk angering or alienating your own side to prove that you are committed to an open conversation. This will not only help your partner trust you more (since you've offered precious common ground) but also encourage her to see you as more reasonable and open-minded, and maybe even as committed to honest conversation. Furthermore, it will help her see you as an individual, not a member of a rival group, and thus she can treat you as someone who's unlikely to allow partisan blindness to circumscribe your conversation. For more here, see Thomson, 2011, pp. 80–81.

26. Stone and his collaborators explain how important it is to find common ground with conversation partners (Stone, Patton, & Heen, 2010, pp. 14–16). This observation meshes with the moral psychology research of Haidt, who has observed that "morality binds and blinds" (Haidt, 2012; this point is so important that Haidt uses the phrase extensively throughout the text and employs it to summarize the contents of roughly a third of his book *The Righteous Mind*). In addition to granting a point of (moral) agreement, which increases trust, acknowledging extremists situates you as morally opposed to the most frightening actors on your side, who reliably form the basis of any caricatures your partner might have. In conversations across highly contentious moral divides, the less your partner feels she can assume about your positions, the more room there is for productive communication.

27. Compromise is not guaranteed. For example, it is widely accepted that the American Civil War was fought because there could be no compromise over the institution of slavery. The issue had to be decided with no room for middle ground. In this case, we concur. Recognize the full reality here, however. The result of there being no possibility for compromise was *a terrible* war. Only a moral injustice so grave as to be *worse* than a bloody conflict can serve to make a war "just." (Philosophers analyze such issues as part of what they term "just war theory.") Whenever effective dialogue or compromise is possible, there is no good argument in favor of uncompromising extremism. The ends justify extreme means only in truly extraordinary circumstances—and no matter how strongly you feel about them, most circumstances aren't extraordinary.

28. Former Westboro Baptist Church member Megan Phelps-Roper notes that social media platforms (Twitter, in particular) were instrumental to enabling the conversations that led to her leaving her church. She extols the benefits of Twitter as a platform, especially the ability it provides to pause, set aside a conversation, and come back to it after having had time to calm down, think, investigate, and assimilate ideas. Face-to-face conversations do not comfortably provide this opportunity, as we feel under more pressure to respond immediately (Phelps-Roper, 2017).

29. Ekman, 2003.

30. The mirrored question mark (⸮), formerly referred to as a "percontation point" and sometimes called the "irony mark," is an example. It never gained widespread application.

31. These metaphors are credited to Chris Voss (Voss & Raz, 2016).

32. Horowitz, 2013; Nyhan, Reifler, & Ubel, 2013.

33. Multiple, independent lines of literature support this conclusion, for example, Horowitz (2013), Malhotra (2016b), Nyhan, Reifler, & Ubel (2013), and Stone, Patton, & Heen (2010, pp. 114–115). Our experience has also shown that attempting to conduct interventions in public forums, or where more than one person is present in face-to-face interactions, makes the intervention considerably more difficult. This is mostly because of taking pride in being right in front of others (and feeling shame, or "losing face," if shown to be wrong in front of others).

34. The public nature of social media posts ties them into a deep vein of research known as "commitment and consistency effects." These effects include a powerful bias that leads people to skew their thinking in ways that maintain consistency with their stated views and prior commitments. Making statements in public triggers a strong psychological impulse to remain consistent with one's stated views in front of any perceived audience, especially an audience whose esteem one values. In practical application, this means digging in one's heels under pressure and not changing one's mind. See Huczynski, 2004, p. 181; O'Reilly & Chatman, 1986; Vuori, 2013.

35. Phelps-Roper, 2017.

36. One of the most common patterns that plays out on social media is a venting loop. This occurs when a person posts something to vent their outrage or cognitive dissonance, then someone replies with an argument that triggers more outrage and cognitive dissonance that prompts another reply, which reciprocates back and forth (sometimes culminating in the termination of friendships or threats of violence). If you feel

compelled to offer information contrary to what another person posted, and that person responds by escalating the argument, leave the conversation there. Do not continue to engage them, especially on a public thread. In general, you want to engage with *people,* not with their cognitive dissonance.

37. There are convincing arguments that the toxicity of the current social environment may flow from our social media feeds perennially inducing the backfire effect, the seemingly paradoxical outcome when our existing convictions are actually strengthened by evidence that contradicts them. How does this happen? We scroll our feeds and repeatedly see outrageous posts (about some "other side") that galvanize us against those views by means of the backfire effect. Our advice: err on the side of prudence and don't use your personal Facebook page as a platform for religious or political topics. (See Barlett, 2017.)

38. When encountering information that's difficult to incorporate with preexisting beliefs, especially moral beliefs, people often feel uncomfortable. That discomfort—the mental stress caused by simultaneously holding contradictory beliefs—is called cognitive dissonance, and the brain goes to surprising lengths to resolve it. Social psychologist Leon Festinger's research, for example, demonstrates that we often seek to reduce our cognitive dissonance by attempting to rationalize preexisting beliefs, and on social media we do it for all to witness (Festinger, 1957).

Attempting to convince ourselves we're already right and recruiting like-minded peers who agree with us help us manage cognitive dissonance. By saying what we already believe, we hear it being said (or see it in writing) and thereby reinforce our beliefs. Alternatively, arguing against what's causing cognitive dissonance makes us feel better by affirming the reasons why we think it's incorrect (Festinger, 1957). For example, creationists have spent a great deal of time and ingenuity identifying alleged loopholes, shortcomings, or failures of evolutionary biology.

Recruiting like-minded peers who agree with us further reinforces our beliefs. The goal is to feel supported, and sometimes this behavior takes the form of "virtue signaling," which is publicly displaying our moral values and tribal commitments. It can be used to attract people who are already in agreement and enlist their support to elevate our status in the community formed around that belief (Campbell & Manning, 2018, pp. 48–58; Peters, 2015).

The point of rationalization (as a means to ease cognitive dissonance) is to *avoid* changing your mind (Jarcho, Berkman, & Lieberman, 2010, p. 1). Additionally, rationalizing publicly can drag other people into a similar state of cognitive dissonance and their own social media venting. This defines two of the most toxic patterns in social media conversation: viral outrage and rationalization loops (Kolbert, 2017).

A rationalization loop begins when you see something politically outrageous and rationalize it on social media. It develops when someone who doesn't agree with your position views your post and feels cognitive dissonance over what *you* wrote. Consequently, they rationalize their own dissonance. A rationalization loop occurs when their rationalization in response to your rationalizations triggers more of your rationalizing, and so on. Rationalization loops undermine civility and can develop into friendship-ending arguments.

39. See, for example, Anderson's "2016 Was the Year White Liberals Realized How Unjust, Racist, and Sexist America Is" (Anderson, 2016a). Of course, this issue is nuanced, and the Progressive Left has a point. Through exit polls, the Pew Research Center reported that many demographic gaps in the 2016 election were the most dramatic they'd been since 1980. The assumption that entire identity groups are to blame for these patterns, or that motivations are explicitly grounded in identity concerns, is, however, specious. Rather than following from a dispassionate view of the facts, it reflects a process of assigning blame. It also exemplifies a wider problem with thinking in terms of demographic identity groups (rather than thinking in terms of individuals). See Tyson & Maniam, 2016.

40. Tavernise, 2017.

41. Katie Rogers, writing for the *New York Times,* was able to summarize this problem the day after the election (Rogers, 2016). She cited an essay by L. V. Anderson, associate editor of the left-heavy online magazine *Slate,* published the same day and titled "White Women Sold Out the Sisterhood and the World by Voting for Trump" (Anderson, 2016b). Anderson and *Slate* appear to have maintained this line of blame through to the time of this writing.

The two sources referenced here are a minuscule sample of a staggering body of literature published since the 2016 election testifying to the same themes. Readers wishing to see how pervasive this attitude is should Google search terms such as "white women elect Trump."

42. Filipovic, 2016.

43. Stone, Patton, & Heen, 2010, pp. 60, 65.

44. Stone, Patton, & Heen, 2010, pp. 58–82.

45. Contribution is not the same as blaming the victim (Stone, Patton, & Heen, 2010, pp. 69–70). Contribution systems are the ways in which involved parties acted or did not act so as to contribute to the circumstances. Blame assumes somebody did something wrong. It's common to have done nothing blameworthy and still have contributed to a problem (Stone, Patton, & Heen, 2010, pp. 50–53, 120–121).

For example, admitting that there are violence issues unique to inner-city black communities is not blaming those communities for the systemic circumstances that lead to violence. Many problems are the results of vicious circles (problem A causes problem B, and problem B reinforces problem A, increasing and entrenching the issue), and acknowledging the full contribution system is one of the few ways to escape such traps. Many other problems have multiple causes (factors A, B, and C together cause problem D, but unless all of A, B, and C are present, D will not occur—for instance, a fire requires all of fuel, oxygen, and heat).

Misidentifying elements of the contribution system as illegitimate ("blaming the victim") makes these problems more difficult to solve. Aim for successful outcomes by doing away with blaming individuals or communities and instead focusing on the totality of contribution systems.

46. Stone, Patton, & Heen, 2010, pp. 60–64, 67.

47. The idea that partisanship has a poisonous effect on our body politic was articulated by John Stuart Mill in *On Liberty.* Mill (1859) wrote (in the only paragraph

containing the word *partisan* in the book): "Not the violent conflict between parts of the truth, but the quiet suppression of half of it, is the formidable evil: there is always hope when people are forced to listen to both sides; it is when they attend only to one that errors harden into prejudices, and truth itself ceases to have the effect of truth, by being exaggerated into falsehood" (p. 97).

48. Social psychologists like Henri Tajfel and John Turner have described this phenomenon of in-group elevation by out-group denigration in what is known as social identity theory (Tajfel, 2010). The general idea of social identity theory is that one's moral standing is tied to the moral standing of the groups with which one identifies. For example, if a conservative identifies as a conservative, every reason she has to view conservatives as good gives her a reason to believe that she must be good too, by association with the "good" group. This behavior is widely observed in politics and religion, and even among fans of rival athletes and sports teams. At its worst, this leads to an effect known as parochial altruism, in which the in-group is given more charity, kindness, and special treatment than it deserves, while out-groups are distrusted or even treated with undeserved hostility.

49. Stone, Patton, & Heen, 2010, pp. 200, 245.

50. Stone, Patton, & Heen, 2010, p. 76.

Because people often mistake identifying a contributory variable for blame, be careful when identifying a factor that contributes to a problem. Avoid saying things like, "Do you think drinking too much may have contributed to getting mugged at that dive bar?" This may be understood as blaming the victim of the mugging because muggings shouldn't happen. This reasoning, however, is fallacious. Saying X contributes to Y says nothing more than that X is a factor that makes Y more likely. Drinking "too much" may have been a variable that contributed to being targeted for a mugging. This does not mean that the victim is morally responsible for being mugged. In sensitive situations, it's safer to ask what factors of the overall situation may have contributed to the negative result.

51. Boghossian, 2006.

52. Phelps-Roper, 2017.

53. Horowitz, 2013.

54. Boghossian, 2013; Horowitz, 2013; Nyhan, Reifler, & Ubel, 2013.

55. Loftus, 2013.

56. Hubbard, 2007, p. 178.

This property generalizes from any sectarian group to any another (especially religions). Each finds the beliefs of the other to be, at best, unsupported and unlikely and, at worst, outlandish. See Loftus, 2013, for more.

57. Loftus, 2013.

58. This phrasing is borrowed from philosopher Walter Kaufmann's definition of faith: "intense, usually confident, belief that is not based on evidence sufficient to command assent from every reasonable person" (Kaufmann, 2015, p. 3).

59. Stone, Patton, and Heen (2010) advise not to worry about particular scripts or phrases so much as merely being present and authentic: "People 'read' not only your words and posture, but what's going on inside of you. If your 'stance' isn't genuine, the

words won't matter. What will be communicated almost invariably is whether you are genuinely curious, whether you genuinely care about the other person. If your intentions are false, no amount of careful wording or good posture will help. If your intentions are good, even clumsy language won't hinder you" (pp. 167–168).

60. Stone, Patton, & Heen, 2010, pp. 85–108, 163–184.

61. Stone, Patton, & Heen, 2010, pp. 163–184.

62. Given the Unread Library Effect, shifting to a learning frame can also be a secret weapon in instilling doubt while maintaining conversational civility, kindness, and rapport.

63. Johnson et al., 2018, p. 418.

64. See Edmondson, 2003, p. 257: "I have used the term 'psychological safety' (Edmondson 1999, 2002) to capture the degree to which people perceive their work environment as conducive to taking these interpersonal risks. In psychologically safe environments, people believe that if they make a mistake others will not penalize or think less of them for it. They also believe that others will not resent or penalize them for asking for help, information, or feedback. This belief fosters the confidence to take the risks described above and thereby to gain from the associated benefits of learning."

65. Edmondson, 2003, p. 256.

66. For more here, see the work of Amy C. Edmondson. She writes: "Leaders can create environments for learning by acting in ways that promote psychological safety. Autocratic behavior, inaccessibility, or a failure to acknowledge vulnerability all can contribute to team members' reluctance to incur the interpersonal risks of learning behavior" (Edmondson, 2003, p. 265).

67. Bradberry, n.d.

68. Bradberry, n.d.

69. TED, 2014.

70. Heinrichs, 2017, p. 64.

four: Intermediate Level: Seven Ways to Improve Your Interventions

1. Harvard Second Generation Study, 2015. See also Ware, 2012.

2. Lindsay, 2016; Ware, 2012.

3. Aristotle, trans. 1980, *The Nicomachean ethics* VII. 2 1156a4–5.

4. Political beliefs are largely moral beliefs. They can make or break relationships, though they're rarely a sufficient undergirding upon which to base strong friendships (Aristotle, trans. 1980, *The Nicomachean ethics* VII).

5. If you are tempted to believe the political affiliation of a loved one at your bedside would matter as you approach your death, we strongly encourage you to reassess your priorities. Reading the literature on hospice care (e.g., Ware, 2012) may prove life-changing.

6. Stone, Patton, & Heen, 2010, pp. 140–144, 153–154, 182–183.

7. Galef, 2017; Tavris & Aronson, 2008.

8. Horowitz, 2013.

9. A disagreement, especially regarding a moral issue, doesn't necessarily entail that someone committed a reasoning error. People have different starting points from

which subsequent beliefs can logically follow. For example, how developed a fetus must be before it's considered a person.

10. Research shows that there is a surge of dopamine associated with sticking to beliefs (Kolbert, 2017). This may partly explain why people are committed to proving their point even at the cost of friendships.

11. Chambers, 2009, pp. 147–148.

12. Ebenstein, 2013.

13. Fisher, Ury, & Patton, 2011, pp. 19–20, 200.

Additionally, Douglas Stone and his collaborators describe three "stories" we all have access to during any conversation: how you see it, how your partner sees it, and how an outsider would see it. They recommend this "third story," the outsider perspective, as the starting place for many difficult conversations. Their recommendation is to understand the gap between your position and your partner's in as much detail as possible before inviting their perspective. Only then, if circumstances permit, offer your own. See Stone, Patton, & Heen, 2010, pp. 147–162, and especially Loftus, 2013.

14. Stone, Patton, & Heen, 2010, pp. 137–138, 180–183.

15. Highlighting the importance of acknowledging feelings during conversations, Stone and his collaborators titled Chapter 5 of their book "Have Your Feelings (Or They Will Have You)" (see Stone, Patton, & Heen, 2010, pp. 85–108, 170–171, 188–189). Furthermore, Ekman has noted, "It is not useful simply to absorb another person's anger, or not to respond to it at all" (Ekman, 2003, p. 124).

16. The term "Golden Bridge" originated with Sun Tzu, a legendary Chinese military strategist. It was popularized by William Ury (1992).

Changing one's mind requires admitting a belief was in error. For many people, that feels humiliating. While the feeling of humiliation often arises from being perceived as stupid or immoral, holding a false belief does not make a person stupid or immoral. It makes that belief incorrect. Notice the move from people, being stupid or bad, to propositions, that is, to beliefs (Boghossian, 2002).

17. Malhotra, 2016a, 2016b.

18. Malhotra, 2016a.

19. Fisher, Ury, & Patton, 2011, pp. 18–19.

20. Horowitz, 2013.

21. Fisher, Ury, & Patton, 2011, p. 15; Horowitz, 2013.

22. Fisher, Ury, & Patton, 2011, pp. 16–17.

23. Malhotra, 2016a, 2016b.

24. Stone, Patton, & Heen, 2010, p. xxix.

25. Fisher, Ury, & Patton, 2011, p. 56.

26. Malhotra, 2016a, 2016b; Parsons & Zhang, 2014, p. 363; Stone, Patton, & Heen, 2010, pp. 125–126, 196–197.

There is a compelling case that Catholic confession is a kind of moral reset that works by being a Golden Bridge to "the fallen." However, it applies not to changing one's mind but rather to feeling like one once again belongs to the moral group. See Ariely, 2012.

27. Fisher, Ury, & Patton, 2011, pp. 23–24.

28. Mullins, 2002; Stone, Patton, & Heen, 2010, pp. 30–37.

29. Exodus 21:7–11, King James Version (KJV):

7 And if a man sell his daughter to be a maidservant, she shall not go out as the menservants do.

8 If she please not her master, who hath betrothed her to himself, then shall he let her be redeemed: to sell her unto a strange nation he shall have no power, seeing he hath dealt deceitfully with her.

9 And if he have betrothed her unto his son, he shall deal with her after the manner of daughters.

10 If he take him another wife; her food, her raiment, and her duty of marriage, shall he not diminish.

11 And if he do not these three unto her, then shall she go out free without money.

It is worth noting that Southern Baptists, the largest Protestant denomination in the United States, split from other Baptists over the issue of slavery because of Southern Baptist support of the institution.

30. Religious propositions are particularly difficult to overcome and the "reasons for doubt" approach may have limited utility in this domain. An oversimplified political example of the approach is, "I used to take a strong stand against illegal immigration until I found out that illegal immigrants commit fewer crimes than citizens and take jobs Americans aren't excited or willing to do."

31. Borowsky, 2011, p. 5.

32. Borowsky, 2011, p. 5.

33. The negotiator's tactics provided a form and degree of "interactional power and discursive control" that ultimately culminated in "the surrender of the hostage taker" (Borowsky, 2011, p. 16).

34. Borowsky, 2011, p. 5.

35. Fisher, Ury, & Patton, 2011, p. 23.

36. Fisher, Ury, & Patton, 2011, p. 47; Stone, Patton, & Heen, 2010, pp. 156–157, 174, 211–216.

37. Hostage negotiators often use the we-are-in-this-together perspective when speaking with hostage takers (Borowsky, 2011, p. 5; Taylor & Donohue, 2006).

38. Words even shape attitudes toward hospital patients and their treatment (Kelly & Westerhoff, 2010). A good example is calling someone an "addict" or "substance abuser" as opposed to someone with a "substance use disorder." Kelly and Westerhoff (2010) write: "Compared to those in the 'substance use disorder' condition, those in the 'substance abuser' condition agreed more with the notion that the character was personally culpable and that punitive measures should be taken. . . . Even among highly trained mental health professionals, exposure to these two commonly used terms evokes systematically different judgments. The commonly used 'substance abuser' term may perpetuate stigmatizing attitudes" (p. 202).

39. We can (and should) reframe issues in our conversations to keep them flowing. Stone, Patton, and Heen (2010) write, "Reframing works on all fronts; you can reframe anything the other person says to move toward a learning conversation." They add, "You'll need to be persistent, and you should expect to be constantly reframing the conversation to help keep it on a productive track" (pp. 204–205).

For a view on reframing during negotiations, see Ury, 1992.

40. Fisher, Ury, & Patton, 2011, pp. 23–24; Stone, Patton, & Heen, 2010, pp. 204–205.

41. See Gaertner et al., 1999.

42. In the martial arts of jiu jitsu and baguazhang, for example, going force-on-force is ill advised. Practitioners will be more successful when transforming or removing force and approaching from a better angle.

43. Ekman, 2003, p. 125.

44. Voss & Raz, 2016, pp. 96–112. This technique is discussed in the hostage negotiation literature noted in Chapter 6.

45. Voss & Raz, 2016, pp. 96–112.

46. Neiman, 2008.

47. The all-or-nothing mentality misses the relevant nuance in a conversation and operates as a half-true form of propaganda. It is destructive to effective conversations (Stone, Patton, & Heen, 2010, pp. 114–121).

48. Stone and his collaborators address the scenario when your partner cares a lot and you care a little. They suggest that when the circumstances are right just leaving the conversation as is may be the best strategy (Stone, Patton, & Heen, 2010, p. 246). They warn against caving in to emotional bullying, though, which is a perennial problem in political conversations: people who refuse to budge or discuss issues civilly often get their way by this means. Offering a broadly behaviorist take on the issue, they write, "As a long-term strategy for dealing with difficult behavior, it's not going to help. Giving in rewards bad behavior, and what gets rewarded gets repeated" (p. 242).

49. Stone, Patton, & Heen, 2010, pp. 39–40, 174–176.

50. This clever approach in application of scales is credited to sales persuasion expert Daniel H. Pink (Big Think, 2014).

51. To watch the application of this and other techniques, we highly recommend Anthony Magnabosco's Street Epistemology YouTube channel: https://www.youtube.com/user/magnabosco210 (accessed October 15, 2018).

52. Inviting your conversation partner to explain how to increase *your* level of confidence may expose their Unread Library Effect (Fernbach, 2013; Stone, Patton, & Heen [2010, p. 200] also advocates this kind of technique when conversations become stuck). For more on how the Unread Library Effect relates to metacognitive assessments and argumentative theories of reasoning, see Bromme, Thomm, & Ratermann (2016).

53. As mentioned previously, this surprisingly common problem comes from the Unread Library Effect. In the 2016 election, for example, people across the political aisle disliked the trade agreement known as the Trans-Pacific Partnership (TPP). The Right, following Donald Trump's economic nativism, rejected it for obvious reasons. The Left, following Bernie Sanders' antiglobalist populism, also rejected it, firmly enough so Democratic nominee Hillary Clinton had to change her stance from supporting it to rejecting it (which, in combination with her previous support, was electorally costly). Some people had strong enough feelings about the TPP to be single-issue voters.

One of the major criticisms of the deal was that it was too complicated for nonexperts to understand. And of course it was! The TPP is a major international trade agreement! Its detail and intricacy were conflated with a perceived lack of transparency, including determining its beneficiaries. Most voters, however, could not have had a truly informed opinion of the TPP. It is conceivable that the trade deal was so complicated that only a handful of experts in the world could have a legitimate claim of possessing an informed opinion. Nonetheless, it was considered a significant issue on both sides of the political aisle, and many people had far stronger opinions than could possibly be warranted by their claim to understanding it.

54. Nichols, 2017; TedX Talks, 2013; Wilson & Keil, 1998.

55. A version of this is used in hostage negotiations. For more here, see Grubb, 2010, p. 344, and Fisher, Ury, & Patton, 2011.

56. Many conversations devolve—smartphones in hand—into arguments ostensibly about facts. A discussion turning to weaponized, incompatible facts usually means the argument is not really about facts (e.g., how many people were killed by guns in a certain year, the number of people on welfare, the percentage of women and minority CEOs). Rather, it's about overlapping concepts of morality, identity, and ideology.

Experts at the Harvard Negotiation Project and elsewhere have pointed out that in such situations it's beneficial to switch gears, either addressing the identity issues directly or discussing what constitute fair and impartial standards (Fisher, Ury, & Patton, 2011, p. 47; Stone, Patton, & Heen, 2010, pp. 14–15, 126–127, 214). These issues can be addressed by asking, "Does it matter if the number of people killed by handguns was either double or half of the numbers we're disputing? If we found out that the number really was five times what we think it is, or one-tenth, would that change either one of our positions?"

Finally, attempting to figure out fair and impartial standards is a type of outsourcing. What sources one will or will not accept (e.g., Fox News or MSNBC) often speaks to one's moral identity.

57. Boghossian, 2013, p. 78.

This same question frequently emerges in the religion/atheism argument over what constitutes sufficient evidence to warrant belief in God and what sources should be consulted. Our experience teaches us that the question about what sources to trust should be kept abstract and divorced from specific topics. This is because people will bias what information they think is more or less trustworthy if they have a specific position to defend. When switching to a discussion about how one should trust evidence, a source, or an authority, it's best to discuss that topic either in the abstract, like an academic philosopher might, or with an entirely separate example. For instance, if you were having a conversation about something political, you might interrupt the flow and ask how someone determines whether a newspaper can be considered reliable. After there is some convergence upon standards for accepting evidence, sources, or authorities, then attempt to apply those standards to the specific case under contention.

58. Alternatively, your attempt at outsourcing may be met with hostility or incredulity. Your conversation partner may tell you that *every* information source is biased. Or, more conspiratorially, that it is controlled by some group, such as Illuminati, Jews, aliens, with an agenda. They may claim everything is fake news and everyone should distrust the entire "liberal media," "right-wing media," or "mainstream media" complex. In even more extreme instances, a person might not trust *any* media, including

"alternative" media (Ingram, 2017; Mitchell et al., 2014; Parker, 2016; Swift, 2016; Thompson, 2016). In these instances, your attempt at outsourcing has taught you something valuable about your conversation partner's epistemology—it's damaged. Consequently, you may have to rethink remaining in the conversation or switch entirely to learning about their epistemology, that is, focus the entire conversation on how they arrived at their beliefs.

59. Boghossian, 2013; Nichols, 2017.

60. Friedersdorf, 2017.

We strongly recommend the 2017 award-winning film about Daryl Davis, *Accidental Courtesy: Daryl Davis, Race & America,* and Davis's book *Klan-destine Relationships: A Black Man's Odyssey in the Ku Klux Klan* (Davis, 2011). Also highly recommended is Peabody and Emmy award-winning Deeyah Khan's documentary *White Right: Meeting the Enemy* (2017).

61. Steenburgh & Ahearne, 2012.

62. See Loftus, 2013.

63. Fisher, Ury, & Patton, 2011, p. 47.

64. Compare Kaufmann, 2015, p. 3: "Faith means intense, usually confident, belief that is not based on evidence sufficient to command assent from every reasonable person."

65. Stone, Patton, & Heen, 2010, p. 177.

five: Five Advanced Skills for Contentious Conversations

1. Boghossian, 2017.

2. Magnabosco, 2016a.

3. An important exception to keeping Rapoport's Rules is noted in Chapter 7. When speaking with an ideologue—someone who's unwilling or unable to change their beliefs—we suggest you *not* use Rapoport's Rules. Doing so may strengthen and calcify their confidence.

4. Dennett, 2013, p. 33.

5. Dennett, 2013, pp. 33–34.

6. Jennings & Greenberg, 2009; Trotter, 1995, p. 4.

7. Answers in Genesis, 2014.

8. Anomaly & Boutwell, 2017.

In the religious arena it could also be that the more counterevidence one is shown, the more one intensifies the original belief (Batson, 1975).

9. Tappin, van der Leer, & McKay, 2017.

10. Shermer, 2012.

11. Coyne, 2009; Masci, 2019.

12. People tend to care more about fitting in than about believing what's true. There's a common tendency for a person who disagrees with her ideological tribe to hide disagreement even if it is based upon the truth. This trait can create significant problems, notably on juries, as is illustrated vividly in the climactic courthouse scene of Harper Lee's novel *To Kill a Mockingbird*. It is also supported by legal research (see Lee, 1960; Waters & Hans, 2009). Finally, we highly recommend Timur Kuran's

important and underappreciated book *Private Truths, Public Lies: The Social Consequences of Preference Falsification* (Kuran, 1997). Kuran studies the mechanisms by which people come to misrepresent their own political preferences and their own knowledge.

13. For many adherents to literalist Christianity, the theory of evolution directly discredits the biblical story of Adam and Eve, thus Original Sin, and thus Jesus's Atonement. This fact presents an insurmountable moral-level roadblock for literalists to accept evolutionary theory. No amount of science will change these believers' minds until they can first be convinced that they'll attain salvation through faith in Jesus (thus eternal life) while embracing sound biology.

14. Flynn, Nyhan, & Reifler, 2017; Nyhan & Reifler, 2010.

15. Martí et al., 2018.

16. Borrowing from and enhancing Magnabosco, 2016b.

17. Cahill & Farley, 1995, pp. 77–79. On p. 96, they also note that in 1978 the Japan Buddhist Federation declared that ensoulment occurs at the moment of conception.

The point at which "ensoulment" occurs is a never-ending source of theological debate that has, at times, led many traditions, especially Christian ones, to adopt the view that it takes place at the moment of fertilization.

18. *Oxford English Dictionary,* entries: disconfirmation, disconfirm.

19. Boghossian, 2017.

20. This idea behind disconfirmation sometimes appears in the philosophical/epistemological literature either under the term *defeasible,* or in the philosophy of science literature as *falsifiable.* Although these two terms don't mean precisely the same thing, we use "disconfirmable" to capture the general essence of both.

Defeasibility differs from falsifiability in that the latter looks exclusively at empirical questions, that is, questions that can be tested. To demonstrate falsifiability, philosophers commonly use the famous example, "All swans are white," because the instance of just one nonwhite swan falsifies the hypothesis that all swans are white.

Moral beliefs, though not empirical, can be defeasible. (It should be noted that this statement is considered controversial among ethicists.) For example, near the beginning of Plato's *Republic* after "justice" is defined as "paying your debts," Socrates asks if it's just to give back a knife to a man from whom you've borrowed it if you think he'll commit murder with it (Plato, ca. 331/trans. 1992). In other words, Socrates' question points to the fact that "paying your debts" cannot always be just, so cannot provide a definition of justice, because there are instances when paying debts is a form of injustice. The point behind Socrates' question is to ask whether the condition that someone intended to commit murder was sufficient to undermine someone's belief that justice was "paying your debts."

21. Some theologians claim that "the self-authenticating witness of God's Spirit" (Craig, 2008, p. 46) is not defeasible. That is, it is self-justifying and there are no conditions under which it could be shown to be false.

22. Shklovskii & Sagan, 1966.

23. There is some evidence suggesting that the more disconfirmations of which one becomes aware, the more likely one will be to revise one's belief (Koriat, Lichtenstein,

& Fischhoff, 1980; Wynn & Wiggins, 2016, pp. 32–34). That is, beliefs could be made disconfirmable through presentation of counterexamples and evidence. However, this is somewhat misleading because the beliefs in question are descriptive facts about the world and lack an emotional and moral valence. Moreover, further research is needed to replicate the results of the Koriat, Lichtenstein, and Fischhoff study.

24. For more here, see Boghossian and Lindsay, "The Socratic Method, Defeasibility, and Doxastic Responsibility" (Boghossian & Lindsay, 2018). This article details how responsible belief formation relates to elements of Socratic questioning.

25. Philosophers recognize that when people form erroneous beliefs, it isn't always because they are using an ineffective epistemology; it can be because they are using an effective one with incomplete or incorrect information. A way to think about this is by remembering the adage "A stopped clock is right twice a day" (broken epistemologies sometimes accidentally find right answers). To this, we add a second point, " . . . but a clock that is functioning correctly, while set to the wrong time, is never right," meaning that a correctly functioning epistemology operating on incorrect or deficient information almost never gets to the truth (Lindsay, 2015). Overcoming this problem requires shifting to what is called a "doxastic" (belief-forming) frame to introduce new information that can then be incorporated into the existing and effective epistemology. The popular "What if I told you that . . . [some novel information]" meme is illustrative of this shift and how it operates (example: "What if I told you that both political parties are beholden to corporate interests?").

26. Ury, 1992, pp. 65–66. *Before* you ask "What if" questions, have your partner generate her own conditions. Though you may think particular "What if" questions will instill doubt, the person you're speaking to may not. Therefore, have them generate disconfirmability conditions before you suggest what they could be.

27. The division between an implausible disconfirmability condition and a *wildly* implausible disconfirmability condition is somewhat arbitrary. The plausibility of potential disconfirmability conditions exists on a spectrum. Implausible and wildly implausible are divided by a fuzzy boundary of whether or not most rational people would consider an implausible condition wildly implausible, and how much evidence it would require before accepting it. This characterization is pertinent because the most common reason why someone would provide a wildly implausible disconfirmation condition is because some other motivation (like personal identity or moral blindness) prevents them from considering more reasonable conditions.

There is a noteworthy exception. If you were to ask a particle physicist what could make him change his mind about the existence of the Higgs boson, you might hear a perfectly sincere and profoundly thoughtful response that seems (or is) wildly implausible, like, "Our entire conception of particle physics is wrong." The reason that any sincere answer would be wildly implausible is because the evidence consistent with the observation of the Higgs boson is so overwhelming that *only* a wildly implausible disconfirmation condition would justify modifying that knowledge claim. The majority of the beliefs you will encounter in everyday conversations will not be those of experts who are equipped with so strong a standard of evidence. (If you do find yourself in such a conversation, it's an opportunity to ask questions and learn.)

Finally, you'll have conversations with people who think their beliefs are held on the basis of impeccably high standards of evidence. They're often incorrect. Some standards of evidence require certain factors that take expertise to identify, namely, that the models they use are fully mature, powerful, and predictive and the methods by which they gather evidence are rigorous and reproducible (Stenger, Lindsay, & Boghossian, 2015). Many models that purport to give answers to seemingly every question are immature (e.g., theology), and many claims of evidence for those models are not rigorous or reproducible (e.g., they might rely upon testimony or revelation).

28. We're reminded of Sam Harris's pointed questions, "If someone doesn't value evidence, what evidence are you going to provide to prove that they should value it? If someone doesn't value logic, what logical argument could you provide to show the importance of logic?" (TubeCactus, 2011).

29. Dennett, 2006, pp. 200–248.

30. Nyhan & Reifler, 2010.

31. Harrington, 2013.

32. Boghossian, 2012, pp. 715–718.

33. Boghossian, 2013, pp. 59–62.

34. Boghossian, 2013, pp. 60–61; FFRF, 2013.

Also worth noting is what researcher Tappin and associates term "desirability bias" (Tappin, van der Leer, & McKay, 2017). That is, individuals "update" their beliefs if evidence comports with *desired* outcomes. In the case of the alleged bones of Christ, desire for the bones to be *anyone* else's would cause an individual to overestimate evidence that is consistent with that conclusion.

35. ABC News, 2004.

36. Longsine & Boghossian, 2012; Swinburne, 1990, 1997, 2001, 2005.

37. Chapple & Thompson, 2014.

38. Ury, 1992, pp. 66–67.

39. There is a famous evangelical tract that manipulates the Ten Commandments and the general association they have with morality (Comfort, 2006, pp. 291–293). It runs roughly like this:

Pastor: What do you call someone who tells lies?
Victim: A liar.
Pastor: Have you ever told a lie, any lie?
Victim: Yes. . . .
Pastor: What does that make you?
Victim: A . . . liar.
Pastor: [Repeats the same pattern with other violations, like petty theft or cursing, before continuing] Do you know what the Bible says about liars, thieves, and people who curse in vain? It says they're sinners who will be damned to hell. You said you're a liar, a thief, and a person who curses. Do you want to go to hell like the Bible says you will?
Victim: No. . . .
Pastor: Well, here's the good news. You don't have to. Did you know that if you accept Jesus into your heart, as your personal Lord and Savior, he will save you from

your sins, and you'll have eternal life with him in Heaven? [And here begins the indoctrination, after having manipulated the victim into believing himself a moral failure.]

40. Boghossian, 2017; Stone, Patton, & Heen, 2010, p. 213.

41. Leonard & Yorton, 2015, pp. 21–22.

42. Leonard & Yorton, 2015; Stone, Patton, & Heen, 2010, pp. 39–40.

43. When two points of view apparently conflict, that may not imply they are *contradictory*. Contradictory points of view cannot be reconciled, but seemingly conflicting accounts can be reconciled when the reason for conflict arises from each person having a different perspective. I can think the soup is "too hot" while you think it's "just right" if our perspective on the appropriate temperature of soup disagrees. More pertinently, I could tell you that nuclear power is a great way to generate clean electricity from a perspective comparing it to fossil fuels and you could reply that because nuclear waste is dangerous it isn't a good way to generate clean electricity. In this case we might acknowledge that nuclear waste is very dangerous, *and* it is clean relative to our alternatives because nuclear waste represents a different kind of "dirty" problem than do fossil fuels, which can create substantial amounts of air pollution.

44. Ury, 1992, p. 51.

45. Voss & Raz, 2016, pp. 150–165.

46. Ury, 1992, p. 51. NB: Although Ury used the word *opponent* in *Getting Past No,* we recommend you use *partner* instead when thinking about engaging in conversation. Despite his use of the word *opponent* throughout the book, Ury acknowledges the value of seeing conversations, including the negotiations upon which he particularly focuses, as collaborative partnerships (e.g., p. 84).

47. Ury, 1992, p. 51.

48. Stone, Patton, & Heen, 2010, pp. 194–195, 205.

49. Ekman, 2003, p. 111: "One of the most dangerous features of anger is that anger calls forth anger, and the cycle can rapidly escalate. It takes a near-saintly character not to respond angrily to another person's anger, especially when that person's anger seems unjustified and self-righteous."

50. Ekman, 2003, pp. 115, 120.

51. Quoted in Eve Starr's "Inside TV" column in the *Greensboro (NC) Record* (Starr, 1954). NB: This quotation is widely attributed to the satirist Ambrose Bierce among many others; its true origins are unclear.

52. Pause to consider how angry computers make you when they aren't acting the way you think they should. Perhaps you've struggled with a word processor that will not enumerate your endnotes properly and spent far too long trying to fix this (as has the author immediately before typing this note). You may have become angry because you felt the "stupid [expletive omitted] thing" should operate in a way that it currently isn't. Perhaps because computers are so effective at doing what they do, it often feels like the computer *should* work, even when you can't make it work. This leads to a kind of frustration (or wrath) that evokes a unique appreciation for the existence of the rather obscure word *defenestrate*. There is a reason for this that comes up in conversations as well. Paul Ekman points out that even infants respond with anger when presented with physical interference. In fact, developmental psychologists note that physical

interference is the "most effective situation for calling forth anger in infants" (Ekman, 2003, p. 110).

Adding your beliefs about your conversation partner's intentions can change the degree of frustration in your conversations. If you assume benign or helpful intentions behind your partner's words and positions, you can decrease your frustration. This also works if you can convince yourself that your partner's most frustrating behaviors are *unintentionally* frustrating. On the other hand, your frustration level will increase if you think your partner is acting neglectfully (of your feelings, say) or in a deliberately provocative or offensive fashion. Feelings of obstruction are common in conversations across moral or political divides. Often, political conversations evoke anger when it feels like "the other side" is supporting policies that would obstruct life, liberty, or pursuit of happiness.

53. Ekman, 2003, p. 125.

54. Once anger enters into conversations it creates a struggle not to meet anger with anger, which can result in saying "unforgivable things" (Ekman, 2003, p. 115). Ekman notes something that we should all be mindful of: anger frequently damages relationships "momentarily and sometimes permanently" and "often brings about angry retaliation" (p. 120). We would add that it also leads to belief entrenchment and a certain desperation to defend beliefs at all costs. This desperation rises proportionally with the level of anger. For these reasons, Ekman notes, "we are usually better off when we don't act on our anger," and "an angry person should consider, and often does not, whether what is making him or her angry can be best dealt with by expressing anger." He concludes by underscoring what's obvious but worth stating: "the remedy will be easier to achieve if the grievance is dealt with after anger has subsided" (p. 120).

55. See Ury, 1992, pp. 27–29. Also, this fact, and the two noted below, follow from Ekman, 2003:

"Emotions can prevent us from having access to all that we know, to information that would be at our fingertips were we not emotional but that during the emotion is inaccessible to us. When we are gripped by an inappropriate emotion, we interpret what is happening in a way that fits with how we are feeling and ignore our knowledge that doesn't fit.

"Emotions change how we see the world and how we interpret the actions of others. We do not seek to challenge why we are feeling a particular emotion; instead, we seek to confirm it. We evaluate what is happening in a way that is consistent with the emotion we are feeling, thus justifying and maintaining the emotion." (Ekman, 2003, pp. 38–39)

Ekman likens this to Fodor's notion of information encapsulation by a worldview. Generally, Fodor's view is that information that contradicts a worldview cannot be accessed or incorporated as readily as information that supports it (Fodor, 1983). (This is similar to what philosophers refer to as the Coherence Theory of Truth.) Ekman's take is that emotions hijack our cognitions into a temporary emotion-driven worldview. This worldview encapsulates information in ways that seek to confirm or justify the emotion, particularly anger, disgust, and fear. Ekman does not speculate that these particular emotions carry this trait so strongly, but the embarrassment of feeling them might play some role.

56. Ekman, 2003, pp. 38–39, 65; Fodor, 1983.

57. Ekman, 2003, pp. 38–39, 65; Fodor, 1983.

58. Ekman, 2003, pp. 38–39, 65; Fodor, 1983.

59. The emotional refractory period associated with anger can lead to rumination, or "stewing." This tends to maintain or even increase anger. Brad Bushman, professor of communication and psychology at the Ohio State University, shows that attempting to vent while angry often induces rumination rather than helping discharge anger (Bushman, 2002). Rumination can be overcome by a number of means, including taking a time-out to relax or meditate (Jain et al., 2007) and even taking long walks, in natural settings if possible (Bratman et al., 2015).

60. Ekman (2003) writes: "It is important to remember that emotional signals do not tell us their source. We may know someone is angry without knowing exactly why. It could be anger at us, anger directed inward at his or her self, or anger about something the person just remembered that has nothing to do with us" (p. 56). This theme is echoed by Douglas Stone and his collaborators when they advise to assume that we don't know our partners' background stories or intentions (Stone, Patton, & Heen, 2010, pp. 30–37, 46–53). One practical consequence of this is that if you're conversing with someone and they become upset, you may not have said anything wrong or inappropriate.

61. Ury, 1992, pp. 17, 32–33.

62. Voss & Raz, 2016, p. 204.

63. Ury, 1992, pp. 27–29, quotation on p. 29.

64. Ury, 1992, p. 108 (among others); Voss & Raz, 2016, pp. 29–31, 47.

65. Ury, 1992, pp. 37–39.

66. Ury, 1992, p. 43.

67. Voss & Raz, 2016, p. 44.

68. Ekman, 2003, pp. 133–135.

69. Ury, 1992, pp. 27–28.

We tend to feel our moral reactions and then rationalize them. Consequently, when we feel righteous anger we have a tendency to justify that anger to ourselves and thus maintain or escalate it (Haidt, 2012, p. 76). If you're strong-willed, this creates an exception to our general rule about avoiding contentious conversations via social media. Though we still urge private discussion, electronic communication can allow you to take time to calm down and reflect before you reply. This can make conversations possible that are almost impossible to keep amicable in person.

70. Ekman and others note that life background "scripts" (essentially, unresolved feelings related to negative or traumatic events in one's past) can intensify anger triggers or prolong their effects. Becoming aware of these triggers (or overcoming them) ahead of time may help you avoid anger (Ekman, 2003, pp. 38–51). Furthermore, *Difficult Conversations* (Stone, Patton, & Heen, 2010, pp. 34–36) notes that we often fail to know (or we make unrealistic assumptions about) our conversation partners' background experiences and worldviews. That is, because your conversation partners are usually not aware of your triggers it places the onus on you to try to defuse them beforehand.

71. James was once treated to a construction foreman telling him that he liked bringing teenagers to difficult job sites to earn a little money and educate them on why

they should go to college. He would make them do hard physical labor in the heat and humidity of deep summer in the Tennessee Valley. Then, he'd lecture them. He told James that his script ran roughly like this: "So, I used to ask them after a few days of killing them out in this sun and heat and humidity, 'Do you think you want to go to school or keep working like a n****r out in this heat your whole life?' but you can't say that anymore, so I ask them instead, 'Do you want to go to school or keep working like a Mexican out here?'"

By the man's clear sense of pride in having (sort of) removed the n-word from his vocabulary, it was easy to tell that he didn't think he was saying something offensive so much as being plain and earnest. After he made his point, James said, "Saying 'working like a Mexican' isn't really acceptable either." Crucially, *James didn't do this before he acknowledged that he understood the foreman's point* and proceeded through that part of the conversation. The foreman acknowledged his explanation and told James he'd try to say, "bustin' your ass," in the future. James could have interrupted him from the start and immediately "called out" his language, but he might not have had as much success in bringing the issue to the foreman's awareness. If he'd interrupted and told the foreman his language was "not cool," or, far worse, put him on the identity-level defensive by insinuating that he was a racist or calling him a racist outright, it's unclear whether or not the man's behavior would have changed accordingly.

72. Parrott, 2001, p. 343.

73. Dittmann, 2003, p. 52.

74. Stone, Patton, & Heen, 2010, pp. 208–210.

75. Ury, 1992, p. 76; Voss & Raz, 2016, pp. 56, 62.

76. Denson, DeWall, & Finkel, 2012; Ekman, 2003, pp. 39, 54, 115, 120.

77. Ekman, 2003, pp. 39, 54, 115, 120; Lerner & Tiedens, 2006.

78. Quote in Fisher, Ury, & Patton, 2011, p. 16.

We advise that you do this by practicing "manual empathy." This will help you figure out "what it is like to be a beetle," as Fisher and his collaborators put it (p. 16). It is similar to, but a bit more involved than, what Chris Voss calls "tactical empathy" and cites as being indispensable to effective negotiations in high-stakes situations (Voss & Raz, 2016, pp. 51–54). Manual empathy takes tactical empathy a step further by drawing your imagination fully into the relevant emotional experience of your conversation partner. To do manual empathy, you have to imagine yourself feeling like your partner is likely to feel *until you can feel it yourself,* then ask yourself how you'd like the situation to proceed. This provides you a clearer choice for how you will actually proceed.

79. Voss & Raz, 2016, esp. pp.140–161.

80. Voss & Raz, 2016, esp. pp.140–161.

81. Ekman writes a warning for what to expect if provocations lead to your partner becoming angry: "Suppose someone is furious about having been insulted in public. During his or her fury it will not be easy to consider whether what was said was actually meant as an insult. Past knowledge about the person and about the nature of insults will be only selectively available; only that part of the knowledge that supports the fury will be remembered, not that which would contradict it. If the insulting person explains or apologizes, the furious person may not immediately incorporate this information (the

fact of an apology) in his behavior" (Ekman, 2003, p. 39). If you don't know your partner well, you may be running a bigger risk than you suspect. As Ekman notes, "Those individuals who generally have faster and stronger emotional responses will have a much harder time cooling off a hot trigger" (p. 48).

82. Ekman, 2003, p. 118: "I believe that nearly everyone can prevent acting or speaking when angry, even when enraged." By waiting until your anger has subsided before responding to an email or text, you will, at the least, be able to choose a more careful way to express what you want to say. In accordance with Ekman's advice (pp. 54, 115, 120), you will also be more likely to avoid making unfair assumptions about your partner's intentions and motivations and less likely to say things you may later regret. That is, you'll have a greater opportunity to maintain and further a productive civil dialogue if you let your anger subside before replying.

83. Chapman, 2015, p. 192.

84. Chapman, 2015, p. 192.

85. Voss & Raz, 2016, esp. pp. 49–73.

86. Kubany et al., 1992, pp. 505–516.

87. Voss & Raz, 2016, esp. pp. 26–48.

88. Rogers, 1975; Voss & Raz, 2016, esp. pp. 51–73.

89. Ekman is abundantly clear on this point. He writes, "It is not useful simply to absorb another person's anger, or not respond to it at all. The offending person needs to learn that what he or she has done has displeased us if we want the person to stop doing it" (Ekman, 2003, p. 124). This meshes rather well with points in *Difficult Conversations* about how feelings, if not dealt with, don't go away but keep begging for attention (Stone, Patton, & Heen, 2010, pp. 86–90). Absorbing another's anger is likely to breed resentment, which is its own feeling that then needs to be handled (Stone, Patton, & Heen, 2010, pp. 89–90).

six: Six Expert Skills to Engage the Close-Minded

1. John Stuart Mill would probably encourage this approach.

2. The dialectic originated with ancient Greek philosophers. The term *dialektike* was used to describe discussions between two or more people seeking to discover truth through reasoned arguments. Much of Socrates' conversation can be viewed through this lens: a systematized process of asking questions to arrive at the truth (Boghossian, 2002, 2003). In fact, the history of Western intellectual thought could also be viewed as an attempt to use reason to understand reality and reconcile competing claims.

3. See Fichte, 1794–1795/1970; Hegel, 2010. For a concise summary, consult Maybee, 2016.

4. Singer, 1983.

5. Haidt, 2012.

6. Kaplan, Gimbel, & Harris, 2016; Pascual, Rodrigues, & Gallardo-Pujol, 2013.

7. Ekman, 2003, pp. 133–135.

8. Lindsay, 2015.

9. Boghossian, 2002.

10. Cohen et al., 2007; Correll, Spencer, & Zanna, 2004; Horowitz, 2013.

11. Goulston, 2015, pp. 145, 188, 194.

12. Stone, Patton, & Heen, 2010, pp. 89–90.

In *On Anger,* the Roman philosopher Seneca famously quipped that anger is the foe, or (depending on the translation) the enemy, of reason (Seneca, ca. 45 CE/trans. 1995, p. 21). He went on to remark as follows:

"Mankind was begotten for mutual assistance, anger for mutual destruction. The one would flock together with his fellows, the other would break away. The one seeks to help, the other to harm; the one would succour even those unknown to him, the other would fly at even those who are dearest. Man will go so far as to sacrifice himself for the good of another; anger will plunge into danger, if it can draw the other down." (Seneca, ca. 45 CE/trans. 1995, p. 23)

He wrote that it is easier to banish passions such as anger than to try to govern them. In essence, anger is too powerful and stubborn to be governed. In this passage, he explained poignantly just how emotions such as anger are the foe of reason:

"Moreover, reason itself, entrusted with the reins, is only powerful so long as it remains isolated from the affections. Mixed and contaminated with them, it cannot contain what it could previously have dislodged. Once the intellect has been stirred up and shaken out, it becomes the servant of the force which impels it." (Seneca, ca. 45 CE/trans. 1995, p. 25)

13. Stone, Patton, & Heen, 2010, pp. 97–98.

14. Stone, Patton, & Heen, 2010, pp. 97–99.

15. Stone, Patton, & Heen, 2010, pp. 91–94.

16. Stone, Patton, & Heen, 2010, pp. 94–97, 102–105.

17. Goulston, 2015, p. 105.

18. Spitzer & Volk, 1971.

19. Weinstein & Deutschberger, 1963.

There is conflicting evidence on the efficacy of altercasting. For a more skeptical view, see Turner et al., 2010. It should also be noted that altercasting is frequently used by sales staff and con men (Pratkanis, 2000, esp. pp. 201–203).

20. We recommend that altercasting be employed only in the sorts of ways advocated here. Specifically, conversational interventions should make use of altercasting only to instill doubt, take favored solutions off the table, advance civility, and help people become less confident and more humble about their beliefs.

21. As noted in Chapter 2, where we described Kurt Lewin's World War II sweetbread study, self-generated ideas can be far more powerful than delivered messages. This effect is even more pronounced when commitment to social roles becomes involved. Lewin documented group-generated solutions having *more than twelve times* greater effectiveness at persuading people to change their behaviors as compared to people being instructed with the same information (Lewin, 1947). Lewin's study did not separate between the impacts of social commitment and self-generation of solutions, but for the present purposes this is less important.

22. Some notable hostage negotiation techniques that can be effectively applied to conversations come from the evidence-based approaches of SAFE (Substantive Demands, Attunement, Face Frames, Emotional Distress), BCSM (Behavioral Change Stairway Model), and REACCT (Recognition, Engagement, Assessment, Contracting,

Controlling, and Transferring) (McMains & Mullins, 2014). These established methods all use defusing techniques that are effective at de-escalating tense situations wherein lives are literally on the line. We recommend consulting the sources cited throughout this section for more information on hostage negotiation techniques and their applications.

23. McMains & Mullins, 2014, p. 134.

24. Our discussion of this concept generally follows that of Chapter 3 in McMains and Mullins (2014).

25. McMains & Mullins, 2014, p. 134.

26. Again, see McMains & Mullins, 2014, Chapter 3.

27. McMains & Mullins, 2014, p. 135.

28. McMains & Mullins, 2014, p. 135.

29. Hammer, 2007; *Hostage Negotiation,* 1987, p. 12.

30. *Hostage Negotiation,* 1987, p. 14.

31. *Hostage Negotiation,* 1987, p. 14.

32. *Hostage Negotiation,* 1987, p. 14.

33. *Hostage Negotiation,* 1987, p. 14.

34. This intervention is experimental in that it is backed only by our inferences from the literature and our own experience. It is not found directly in the peer-reviewed scholarship that we've consulted.

35. Dennett, 2013, p. 33.

36. Boghossian, 2004.

37. Boghossian, 2013.

38. For a prominent example of a plea to doubt your doubts, see Uchtdorf, 2013.

39. If someone does this to you, either they don't know what they're doing in terms of a belief/epistemological intervention or they have some other motive, such as recording you and trying to elicit a confession or admission.

40. This stance is called "true for." People making this argument (if it can be called that) are claiming something is true for them and not true for you. For why this fails, see Swoyer, 1982. If it is used, seasoned interventionists can easily get around it with the following counter-counter-technique (derived, with gratitude, from Anthony Magnabosco). If someone says something is true for them, ask to borrow one of their possessions, such as their water bottle, sunglasses, phone, or keys. Then claim that you believe "Possession means ownership is true for me, so it is true for me that this is mine now." When they object, you can immediately *ask* them (do not tell), "Why can things be true for you, but not true for me?" or "When does 'true for me' work and when doesn't it?"

seven: Master Level: Two Keys to Conversing with Ideologues

1. Rather than being immoral, ideologues tend to suffer from being hyper-moral (Pinker, 2008). One might think of the verbally abusive preaching of early American Calvinists, like the infamous Jonathan Edwards and his diatribe posing as sermon, "Sinners in the Hands of an Angry God."

2. This is a primary theme in the book *Difficult Conversations* (the idea is introduced in Stone, Patton, & Heen, 2010, pp. 7–8, and developed throughout the following

chapters). In moral conversations, feelings usually flare up and identity is the underlying issue generating emotion.

Identity conversations are about who the participants believe themselves to be. Conversations between spouses often go awry because they're arguing over what it means for each to be a good spouse, even while the argument seems to be about who takes the trash out and when. The antivaccination public argument seems to be about medical science but is really about what it means to be a good parent. Many religious arguments are about what it means to be a good person, where "good person" is itself interpreted differently by each participant, often defined by their respective religions' moral principles (Lindsay, 2015, pp. 106–114).

Identity is complicated. The most important thing to recognize is that identity is a tapestry of beliefs about the self, many of which are moral beliefs. Indeed, some of our core identity beliefs, to which we're most sensitive, are moral beliefs. Suppose you call someone a racist or identify something they said as racist. You are hoping the person will acknowledge being called out, recognize the truth in your accusation (supposing it is true), feel morally ashamed, and change their view. This almost never happens. Someone who has been accused of racism will almost never respond along the lines of, "Yeah, my bad—that was racist and I shouldn't have said it." Instead, people argue that they are not racist, and in order to reject your accusation and vindicate themselves in their own minds they might subsequently adhere more tightly to, or come to adopt, genuinely racist views.

If you call out your conversational partner for racism, you might hope that he'll feel like a bad person and change his mind. Psychologically, however, he will find it much easier to employ denial, rejection, or counterarguments, all of which ultimately lead to further belief entrenchment. Alternatively, the person you accused might just become angry and lash out. This identity-based mechanism is exactly what we've discussed earlier regarding the backfire effect. (Remember, the backfire effect causes people to double down when presented with evidence that conflicts with their beliefs. (See Trevors et al., 2016.) There are better ways of changing minds than attempting to shame someone with a stigmatizing label, and we've already covered many of those in detail (see also Horowitz, 2013).

3. Douglas Stone, Bruce Patton, and Sheila Heen (2010) recommend excellent techniques for dealing with identity issues in difficult conversations. Primarily, they advocate spending time recognizing your own identity issues that come up in conversations and asking yourself what's at stake if you change your mind. Much of this work should be done outside the context of the conversations themselves. It can be dealt with only in times of introspection and self-interrogation.

You should also be aware of, and anticipate, the identity issues likely to be faced by your conversation partners. Depending on the context of the discussion, you might even want to make identity issues explicit by asking about them. Say, "This topic seems really personal for you. Can you tell me what makes it that way?" Additional techniques for dealing with identity-level issues in moral conversations are presented throughout *Difficult Conversations* (see especially Stone, Patton, & Heen, 2010, pp. 111–128).

4. Our "guts" make moral decisions for us. Consequently, we grossly underestimate the difficulty of providing reasons for why we believe what we believe. There's an evolutionary explanation for this: it's quick. For more, see Joshua Greene's *Moral Tribes* (2013) and Daniel Kahneman's iconic *Thinking, Fast and Slow* (2011). Even more detail can be found in the less accessible, but highly informative *Judgment under Uncertainty: Heuristics and Biases* (1982), edited by Daniel Kahneman, Paul Slovic, and Amos Tversky, with contributions by the editors and other authors. Decision-making speed is crucial in fluid physical and social environments where questions must be answered urgently. Should I run into the burning house and save my dog? Our guts are less than good, however, for getting the answers right. Because we need to make snap moral judgments in many situations, we've evolved to make our moral decisions *before* we can think them through, not after (Greene, 2013, pp. 105–146; Shermer, 2012, esp. p. 6).

In short, moral reasoning comes after moral intuitions; in other words, we develop *reasons for* our moral feelings as opposed to *reasoning to* moral conclusions. For example, we have a moral feeling or intuition that something (anal sex, perhaps, or eating horse meat) is disgusting and then we generate reasons for *why* it's disgusting. This is called a "post hoc rationalization" and it's ubiquitous. Everyone does it. Think about it like this: our moral decisions are made before we're aware of them and then our rational mind kicks in like a defense attorney, making a case for why our gut felt as it did (Haidt, 2012, pp. 48–50).

You may feel, or even think, you've carefully considered your moral positions, but overwhelming evidence shows otherwise. The moment a morally charged idea enters your mind—say, whether teenagers' parents should support their children's choices to be sexually active—you have already leaned one way or another. Your moral intuition will come first, and then you'll think of reasons to justify it.

It's not hard to see how all this makes conversations more difficult. Moral conversations take place in an environment where people know far less about topics than they think they do, intensely *feel* the truth of their beliefs, hold their beliefs with self-righteous tenacity, have a sense that those beliefs should be obvious to everyone, and don't clearly understand why they are reacting as they are to potentially disrupting information. At the same time, they are psychologically primed to argue on behalf of beliefs formed intuitively, prior to any careful consideration.

5. Haidt notes that we engage in *psychosocial valuation* (that is, evaluating ourselves and others socially and psychologically) along three primary dimensions. The first of these is nearness of kin. The second is reputation or social standing. The third Haidt defines more nebulously as "divinity," and he devotes a great deal of discussion to it in *The Happiness Hypothesis*. By "divinity," he means a sense of moral goodness as felt within the moral framework, community, and culture in which one operates (Haidt, 2006, pp. 181–213; Lindsay, 2015, pp. 84–85).

Our moral intuitions do not seem to be merely precognitive (from the Latin meaning "before" and "acquiring knowledge") but are also directly tied to our limbic systems. That is, we respond to our moral intuitions emotionally before we have a chance to think about them. The plainest evidence supporting this claim is that physical disgust (such as we'd experience from getting too near a decomposing animal) and moral disgust (such as we'd experience from hearing about a heinous crime) evoke the same physical reaction and arise in largely the same physiological way (Cohen et al., 2009, pp. 963–976).

The blurriness of the line between moral and physical disgust is also evident in occasionally finding the foods of other cultures disgusting, regardless of how they taste or whether they are wholesome. If you're from the United States, eating cats and dogs is a good example.

Other reasons to believe our moral intuitions evoke profoundly emotional reactions are fairly obvious: moral outrage (anger induced from seeing something morally disagreeable) arises quickly, and this is one of the most persistent features of the human condition. It's the source of many, many problems that, it's fair to say, wouldn't be problems for *Star Trek*'s hyperrational Vulcans.

6. Kaplan, Gimbel, & Harris, 2016.

7. Deep moral beliefs can change. There are, for example, many examples of former religious hardliners who escaped their ideologies. See Aspen Institute, 2015; Phelps-Roper, 2017; Shelton, 2016.

8. The accusations and epithets are likely to have overtones suggesting you're a bad or worthless person—think "racist," "bigot," "trash," "shill," "cuck," the whole range of epithets that dehumanize people by portraying them as vermin and other despised animals, and, of course, "piece of shit," the timeless dehumanizing insult that plays most directly upon our disgust module. You might be accused, without any reasonable justification, of hating entire demographics, wanting bad things to happen, or hating society.

9. For example, the accusations and epithets mentioned in the previous note might be accompanied by attempts to shame you in place of offering arguments, attempts to talk over you, and insistence that beliefs opposed to yours are too obvious to need explaining or justifying. You might even be told in so many words to be silent and listen.

10. There is a well-known analogy known as "pigeon chess" ("Pigeon chess," 2016) that speaks to contentious conversations. The phrase originated to describe conversations with creationists. Scott Weitzenhoffer, in a famous comment published on amazon.com, wrote, "Debating creationists on the topic of evolution is rather like trying to play chess with a pigeon—it knocks the pieces over, craps on the board, and flies back to its flock to claim victory" (Weitzenhoffer, 2005). This idea analogizes outward.

Discussing matters with an ideologue can feel like attempting to play chess with someone who's swinging a hammer and smashing the board. The assumption of pigeon chess is that the other player has no clue how the game (the scientific investigation of life's diversity) is played. Likewise, an ideologue is a single-minded zealot whose only tool is her moral certainty.

11. Whitney & Taylor, 2017.

Attempting conversations with an ideologue can be dangerous, not only emotionally but also sometimes physically (Michel, 2017).

12. Beck, 2017; Haidt, 2012, pp. 161–166; Haidt, 2016; Stone, Patton, & Heen, 2010, pp. 25–43; Willer, 2016.

13. Focusing on moral epistemology is similar to focusing on epistemology more generally. The method is nearly identical, though the content is often more nuanced and complex: be curious; ask a lot of genuine, targeted questions; and focus on *how* your partner came to know what she thinks she knows.

Explorations of moral epistemology, however, are more difficult for two reasons. First, morality is complicated. It deals with guesses about how best to maximize human flourishing, a subject we hardly know how to define, much less how to optimize across so many individual opinions and cultures with so many competing interests. There are also scholars who disagree with the notion that morality is tied to flourishing, and thus we have the problem of different and even conflicting moral starting points.

Second, morality has a personal dimension. Much of what constitutes our personal identity and place in our communities is tied directly to our sense of morality—assertions about what make actions good or not-so-good. Matters of identity don't change easily, especially when revising one's beliefs requires admitting that one's actions might have been not-so-good. Worse, not only is individual identity tied up in morality, so is communal identity. We're interested in being "good people" for ourselves, but we're also *very* interested in being perceived as good people by others. (This idea has roots in antiquity. Plato depicts it in Book I of the *Republic,* through the character of Thrasymachus, though the view is then developed, but not endorsed, by Plato's brothers, Glaucon and Adeimantus, in Book II. The concept revolves around seeming versus being just. Socrates also notably argues against the view in *Gorgias.*) Communal and cultural norms inform us as to what "good" and "bad" mean. More complex still, norms change over time. In fact, cultures are broadly defined by their moral outlooks together with sets of practices and traditions.

Engaging one's moral epistemology can be difficult. Morality is desperately complex, but it's also immediate, personal, and tied to our senses of self and fitting in to our communities. It is thus easy to understand how someone who has never deeply reflected on their moral epistemology could be flummoxed by basic, targeted questions.

14. Cohen et al., 2007; Cohen, 2012.

15. For this step, in particular, we suggest relying heavily on other techniques that are explained throughout this book. Specifically, ask questions and listen, especially if you find certain views repellent or unfathomable. We particularly recommend using techniques that expose the Unread Library Effect and using outsider perspectives.

Reasoning to a moral conclusion is extraordinarily complicated, and even when it is accomplished, it may not override the emotional architecture underneath it for a long time, if ever. People tend to overestimate their ability to reason morally because of their tendency to think (trust) that moral intuitions lead them to the truth.

16. Cohen et al., 2007; Cohen, 2012.

17. Horowitz, 2013.

18. In many cases, "being a good person" may mean being a good *particular kind of* person. For example, it is likely that many people with strict dietary beliefs view themselves as *healthy* or *health-conscious* people. Antivaccine believers are likely to identify as good and caring parents. People who want to punch others they perceive as Nazis view themselves as righteous protectors of the oppressed. Antigovernment

militia types are likely to see themselves as virtuous defenders of some principle like liberty. When you can, tailor your acknowledgments accordingly to achieve maximum effect.

19. You can minimize the opportunities for a zealous partner to rehearse moral conclusions they've developed in defense of their position. Switch the question to over-arching values *as soon as possible* to turn a sermon back into a conversation.

20. Fisher, Ury, & Patton, 2011, pp. 23–30; Trepagnier, 2017.

21. An example of the tendency to have weak justifications for articles of faith like the Resurrection can be found in E. P. Sanders' *The Historical Figure of Jesus* (1993). Sanders presents a scrupulously cautious, minimalist, and skeptical assessment of what we could potentially conclude about Jesus as a historical figure, based on what little was written about him in antiquity. For example, he finds little that is historically useful in the Gospel of John, which he portrays as a theological manifesto strewn with some historical nuggets. But his scholarly scruples desert him when he reaches the topic of the Resurrection. In effect, he says that he doesn't know how, but *somehow* the Resur-rection just happened. For anyone even slightly skeptical about Christianity's claims, seeing this giant epistemological leap by Sanders is likely to undermine the credibility of an otherwise masterful work on an important topic. For an interesting take on why this happens, see Thomson & Aukofer, 2011.

22. You can also think about this process as follows: because moral reasoning is exceedingly complicated, and moral epistemologies are notoriously brittle, you are in-viting your conversation partner to explore the Unread Library with regard to their own moral attitudes. See Fernbach et al., 2013; Rozenblit & Keil, 2002.

23. Recognizing that we rarely have good reasons for our moral beliefs should lead us to cultivate something often lacking in conversations: moral humility. That is, we should enter into moral conversations not absolutely certain of our starting principles and willing to recognize that we've probably not been as thoughtful and rigorous about how we arrived at our moral beliefs as we normally assume we've been. Unfortunately, this is obvious only to those few who have earnestly reflected on their moral beliefs, have considered the possible weaknesses in their own moral epistemologies, understand something of the complexity involved in moral reasoning, and know how to generate defeasibility criteria.

We cannot rely upon other people to be morally humble, nor can we force them. We can model moral humility in our conversations, but, to paraphrase Socrates, a person doesn't want what he doesn't think he lacks. If you don't think you lack moral humility, why try to obtain it?

24. The phrase "identity quake" is from Stone, Patton, & Heen, 2010, p. 113.

25. Patton, 1998.

26. Of note, not all ideologues will be open to conversation. For a variety of rea-sons, they might be too entrenched in their beliefs. This book is designed to help you understand what to do to have effective conversations, but if a person absolutely refuses to be a conversation partner, you cannot force discussion upon them. You'll need to walk away or resort to other methods to reach such people. (For specifics on how to deconvert jihadis, where this is possible, see Peter's INR5 talk in Säde, 2015.)

27. If you're looking for a more detailed explanation of this counterintuitive phenomenon, we recommend the papers in Section 1 of *Return to Reason: The Science of Thought,* published by *Scientific American* and edited by Lisa Pallotroni (2018). This easy-to-read e-book is packed with useful information to understand why human beings think the way we do.

28. If you're trying to talk with an ideologue, you discover he's actually "crazy," and you absolutely cannot walk away, we recommend Mark Goulston's techniques in *Talking to "Crazy": How to Deal with the Irrational and Impossible People in Your Life* (2015). We borrow the term "crazy" from Goulston, a psychiatrist and hostage negotiations trainer. Although "crazy" is considered an antiquated and vulgar term for people who suffer from mental health issues, Goulston uses it to mean people who are extremely upset and/or irrational. For more about when to walk away, see Chapter 4 of his insightful book.

29. Friedersdorf, 2017; Goulston, 2015, pp. 43–74.

30. Stone, Patton, & Heen, 2010, pp. 202–206.

31. Graham, Nosek, & Haidt, 2012.

Jonathan Haidt makes the case that religions and politics are similar in terms of moral psychology. In a 2017 City Lab interview for *The Atlantic,* he noted, "The psychology of politics is really the psychology of religion, understanding national elections is not about what's the most efficient policy. It really is the psychology that we evolve to be religious; we evolve to do intergroup conflict; we evolve to make things sacred and encircle around them" (Florida, 2017).

32. Moral foundations theory lays out these differences in considerable detail. Graham, Nosek, & Haidt, 2012; Haidt, 2012; Iyer et al., 2012. The reader is reminded that the terms *liberal, conservative,* and *libertarian* are used here in the US political context.

33. Khazan, 2017.

The French mathematician and philosopher Blaise Pascal (1670/1958) noted this some 350 years ago, writing in his *Pensées,* 9:

"When we wish to correct with advantage, and to show another that he errs, we must notice from what side he views the matter, for on that side it is usually true, and admit that truth to him, but reveal to him the side on which it is false. He is satisfied with that, for he sees that he was not mistaken, and that he only failed to see all sides. Now, no one is offended at not seeing everything; but one does not like to be mistaken, and that perhaps arises from the fact that man naturally cannot see everything, and that naturally he cannot err in the side he looks at, since the perceptions of our senses are always true." (p. 4)

34. Stone, Patton, & Heen, 2010, p. 202.

35. Haidt, 2012, pp. 180–216.

36. Haidt, 2012, p. 315.

37. Some liberal values present atypically. It's plausible that liberals are not lacking other foundations so much as that they have a radically different understanding of them. Some of Haidt's argument about liberal morals depends upon the case that Western liberal societies are "WEIRD." That is, Western, educated, industrialized, rich, and democratic. According to Haidt (2012), these societies have apparently lost touch

with at least one aspect of human psychosocial valuation (that is, how we evaluate the subjective worth of ourselves and others). The missing element is what he calls "divinity," and his contention is roughly that WEIRD societies seem not only insensitive to but also directly questioning of such moral foundations as sanctity, authority, and loyalty (Haidt, 2012). There are reasons to suspect, however, that contemporary WEIRD societies merely interpret these foundations differently. For example, individuals from some demographics use "coolness" (of a certain kind) as an individualistic stand-in for sanctity. The nearly ubiquitous phrase "Not cool!" for a cultural transgression of certain magnitudes provides one window into this phenomenon. In WEIRD societies, we police and reinforce our sense of cultural "divinity" in such terms.

Authority and loyalty may also be understood in certain nontraditional phrasings. That being so, it appears that themes of authority and loyalty are morally salient for left-wing radicals despite not taking their usual form. The groups formed by left-wing radicals are often very small and committed to being subversive to external authority. This makes them relatively unstable, so they are prone to schismatic factionalizing. Nonetheless, they often generate intense loyalty to causes. This is directed more toward ideas and ideals than to people, and it rests in the authority of moral arguments that group members find persuasive (compare Graham, Nosek, & Haidt, 2012).

Consider, too, the "sanctity" moral foundation (sometimes referred to as the "purity foundation"). There is certainly an impulse to moral purity on the radical Left, but it manifests primarily as ideological purity. See, for example, almost every battle (and there are many) that rages within the feminist Left over what constitutes the right kind of feminist (for more, see Ferguson, 2010).

38. Iyer et al., 2012.

39. Graham, Nosek, & Haidt, 2012; Haidt, 2012, pp. 180–216; Iyer et al., 2012.

40. Graham, Nosek, & Haidt, 2012; Haidt, 2012; Iyer et al., 2012.

41. Conservatives and libertarians are currently winning the gun control debate in the United States. Because of conservatives' success at delivering the message that individual gun ownership prevents certain kinds of harms—perhaps more effectively than any other means—and liberals' failure to articulate their case in terms that are morally resonant with conservatives, the conservative arguments have so far proved decisive. Liberals may be correct that the costs of individual gun ownership outweigh the benefits (in terms of harm), but this case falls flat in the American electorate because the deeper issues that resonate with conservatives and libertarians—especially the freedom to protect oneself—have no clear answer from the liberal side of the argument.

42. Haidt, 2012.

43. Your conversation partner, if entrenched in her moral views, may perceive you as an ideologue (even if you aren't) if your beliefs are not congruent with hers. Even a modestly entrenched conservative is likely to expect that anyone willing to identify themselves as a liberal is probably a left-wing ideologue, or at least sympathetic to radical leftist views. Similarly, many more devout religious people assume that almost every atheist is angry and likely to start sniping at, or arguing against, their religion.

Ideologues make the news (or gossip columns) and become the poster examples that one moral group uses to "understand" other moral groups. For example, far more Americans know about Islamist extremism and terrorism than they do about the Islamic faith, and they'll associate what they know about Islam with anyone identifying as a Muslim. (Test this claim by asking someone who associates Islam with terrorism by asking them the difference between Sunni and Shia Islam. Chances are, they won't know the difference.) This problem is exacerbated by a habit of "nutpicking" by the media and people using social media (Drum, 2006). *Nutpicking* means cherry-picking examples of fringe behavior in an attempt to characterize a group by its worst examples.

This leads to an assumption of extremism that can create difficulties in conversations. These are assumptions your partner makes about you, but if you are an ideologue yourself, the assumptions go both ways. First, your partner will assume you espouse more extreme views than you do. Second, your partner will often be more familiar with extreme views that caricature your side than they will be with more nuanced views. Thus, many Americans know little more about Islam than its association with Islamist terrorism; many conservatives would be surprised to find out most liberals are neither socialists nor communists; and many liberals would be surprised to discover that most conservatives are not racists and have no sympathy for any kind of white supremacism. Third, your partner may be defensive about being perceived as an ideologue on his side.

Even when neither participant in a conversation is an ideologue, the assumption of extremism often arises in a way that creates much of the same difficulties as dealing with an actual ideologue. It is worth the effort to mitigate these problems. (One technique for doing this has already been discussed: disavow your own tribe's ideologues.)

44. For more, see Heinrichs, 2017, pp. 220–228.

45. Haidt, 2012.

46. For more, see Graham, Nosek, & Haidt, 2012; Greene, 2013; Haidt, 2012; and Iyer et al., 2012.

47. Khazan, 2017; Lakoff, 2010; Pascal, 1670/1958.

48. Stone, Patton, & Heen, 2010, p. 146.

49. It is often unclear what is meant when people claim to be defending Western values against Islam. Are they referring to religious and moral values that they associate with Christianity (and perhaps also Judaism), or do they mean Enlightenment values such as individual liberty, freedom of speech, secular government, and due process of law for those accused of crimes? In fact, they may not be clear in their own minds on exactly what values they are trying to defend. Commitment to a specifiable set of values is likely not what's really motivating them.

50. Boghossian, 2013.

Bibliography

ABC News. (2004, February 10). *Six in 10 take Bible stories literally, but don't blame Jews for death of Jesus* [PDF file]. Retrieved from https://abcnews.go.com/images/pdf/947a1ViewsoftheBible.pdf.

Altercasting. (n.d.). In *Oxford Reference*. Retrieved from http://www.oxfordreference.com/view/10.1093/oi/authority.20110803095405945.

Anderson, L. V. (2016a, December 29). 2016 was the year white liberals realized how unjust, racist, and sexist America is. *Slate*. Retrieved from http://www.slate.com/blogs/xx_factor/2016/12/29/_2016_was_the_year_white_liberals_learned_about_disillusionment.html.

Anderson, L. V. (2016b, November 9). White women sold out the sisterhood and the world by voting for Trump. *Slate*. Retrieved from http://www.slate.com/blogs/xx_factor/2016/11/09/white_women_sold_out_the_sisterhood_and_the_world_by_voting_for_trump.html.

Anomaly, J., & Boutwell, B. (2017, April 25). Why citing a scientific study does not finish an argument. *Quillette*. Retrieved from http://quillette.com/2017/04/25/citing-scientific-study-not-finish-argument/.

Answers in Genesis. (2014, February). *Bill Nye debates Ken Ham—HD (Official)* [Video File]. Retrieved from https://www.youtube.com/watch?v=z6kgvhG3AkI.

Aristotle. (1980). *The Nicomachean ethics*. Oxford, England: Oxford University Press. (Original work published third century BCE).

Aspen Institute. (2015, July 4). *Radical: My journey out of Islamist extremism* [Video File]. Retrieved from https://www.youtube.com/watch?v=Jlf7W_z3b8U.

Barlett, J. (2017, July 16). The backfire effect—why people don't listen on social media. *iNews*. Retrieved from https://inews.co.uk/opinion/comment/backfire-effect-people-dont-listen-social-media/.

Barrett, L. F. (2017). *How emotions are made: The secret life of the brain*. Boston, MA: Houghton Mifflin Harcourt.

Batson, C. D. (1975). Rational processing or rationalization? The effect of disconfirming information on a stated religious belief. *Journal of Personality and Social Psychology, 32*(1), 176–184.

221

Beck, J. (2017, March 13). This article won't change your mind: The facts on why facts alone can't fight false beliefs. *The Atlantic*. Retrieved from https://www.theatlantic.com/science/archive/2017/03/this-article-wont-change-your-mind/519093/.

Becker, S. (2015). *The inner world of the psychopath: A definitive primer on the psychopathic personality*. North Charleston, SC: CreateSpace.

Bennion, L. L. (1959). *Religion and the pursuit of truth*. Salt Lake City, UT: Deseret Book Company.

Big Think. (2014, May 21). *How to persuade others with the right questions: Jedi mind tricks from Daniel H. Pink* [Video File]. Retrieved from https://www.youtube.com/watch?v=WAL7Pz1i1jU.

Boghossian, P. (2002). Socratic pedagogy, race and power. *Education Policy Analysis Archives, 10*(3). Retrieved from http://epaa.asu.edu/ojs/article/view/282.

Boghossian, P. (2003). How Socratic pedagogy works. *Informal Logic: Teaching Supplement, 23*(2), 17–25.

Boghossian, P. (2004). *Socratic pedagogy, critical thinking, moral reasoning and inmate education: An exploratory study* (Doctoral dissertation, Portland State University). Retrieved from https://philpapers.org/rec/BOGSPC-2.

Boghossian, P. (2006). Socratic pedagogy, critical thinking, and inmate education. *Journal of Correctional Education, 57*(1), 42–63.

Boghossian, P. (2012). Socratic pedagogy: Perplexity, humiliation, shame and a broken egg. *Educational Philosophy and Theory, 44*(7), 710–720.

Boghossian, P. (2013). *A manual for creating atheists*. Durham, NC: Pitchstone Publishing.

Boghossian, P. (2017). What would it take to change your mind? *Skeptic, 22*(1). Retrieved from https://www.skeptic.com/reading_room/what-evidence-would-it-take-to-change-your-mind/.

Boghossian, P., & Lindsay, J. (2016). The appeal of ISIS: Trust, costly signaling, and forming moral teams. *Skeptic, 21*(2), 54–56. Retrieved from https://www.skeptic.com/reading_room/the-appeal-of-isis-islamism-trust-and-costly-signaling/.

Boghossian, P., & Lindsay, J. (2018). The Socratic method, defeasibility, and doxastic responsibility. *Educational Philosophy and Theory, 50*(3), 244–253.

Borowsky, J. P. (2011). Responding to threats: A case study of power and influence in a hostage negotiation event. *Journal of Police Crisis Negotiations, 11*(1), 1–19.

BotJunkie. (2007, June 29). *Mister Rogers defending PBS to the US Senate* [Video File]. Retrieved from https://www.youtube.com/watch?v=yXEuEUQIP3Q.

Bradberry, T. (n.d.). 9 things that make you unlikable. *Forbes*. Retrieved from http://www3.forbes.com/leadership/9-things-that-make-you-unlikable/.

Bratman, G. N., Hamilton, J. P., Hahn, K. S., Daily, G. C., & Gross, J. J. (2015). Nature experience reduces rumination and subgenual prefrontal cortex activation. *Proceedings of the National Academy of Sciences, 112*(28), 8567–8572.

Bromme, R., Thomm, E., & Ratermann, K. (2016). Who knows? Explaining impacts on the assessment of our own knowledge and of the knowledge of experts. *Zeitschrift für Pädagogische Psychologie, 30*(2–3), 97–108.

Bushman, B. J. (2002). Does venting anger feed or extinguish the flame? Catharsis, rumination, distraction, anger, and aggressive responding. *Personality and Social Psychology Bulletin, 28*(6), 724–731.

Cahill, L. S., & Farley, M. A. (1995). *Embodiment, morality, and medicine.* Dordrecht, the Netherlands: Springer.

Campbell, B., & Manning, J. (2018). *The rise of victimhood culture: Microaggressions, safe spaces, and the new culture wars.* Cham, Switzerland: Palgrave Macmillan.

Chambers, A. (2009). *Eats with sinners: Reaching hungry people like Jesus did.* Cincinnati, OH: Standard Publishing.

Chapman, G. (2015). *Anger: Taming a powerful emotion.* Chicago, IL: Moody Publishers.

Chapple, I., & Thompson, M. (2014, January 23). Hassan Rouhani: Iran will continue nuclear program for peaceful purposes. CNN. Retrieved from http://www.cnn.com/2014/01/23/world/europe/davos-rouhani-peaceful-nuclear-program/index.html.

Cohen, A. B., Keltner, D., Oveis, C., & Horberg, E. J. (2009). Disgust and the moralization of purity. *Journal of Personality and Social Psychology, 97*(6), 963–976.

Cohen, G. L. (2012). Identity, belief, and bias. In J. Hanson (Ed.), *Ideology, psychology, and law* (pp. 385–404). Oxford, England: Oxford University Press.

Cohen, G. L., Sherman, D. K., Bastardi, A., Hsu, L., McGoey, M., & Ross, L. (2007). Bridging the partisan divide: Self-affirmation reduces ideological closed-mindedness and inflexibility in negotiation. *Journal of Personality and Social Psychology, 93*(3), 415–430.

Comfort, R. (2012). *The way of the master.* Orlando, FL: Bridge-Logos.

Correll, J., Spencer, S. J., & Zanna, M. P. (2004). An affirmed self and an open mind: Self-affirmation and sensitivity to argument strength. *Journal of Experimental Social Psychology, 40*(3), 350–356.

Coyne, J. A. (2009). *Why evolution is true.* New York, NY: Penguin.

Craig, W. L. (1994). *Reasonable faith: Christian truth and apologetics.* Wheaton, IL: Crossway Books.

Craig, W. L. (2008). *Reasonable faith: Christian faith and apologetics.* 3rd ed. Wheaton, IL: Crossway Books.

Davis, D. (2011). *Klan-destine relationships: A black man's odyssey in the Ku Klux Klan.* Far Hills, NJ: New Horizon Press.

Dawkins, R. (2006). *The God delusion.* New York, NY: Houghton Mifflin.

Dennett, D. C. (2006). *Breaking the spell: Religion as a natural phenomenon.* New York, NY: Viking Penguin.

Dennett, D. C. (2013). *Intuition pumps and other tools for thinking.* New York, NY: W. W. Norton.

Denson, T. F., DeWall, C. N., & Finkel, E. J. (2012). Self-control and aggression. *Current Directions in Psychological Science, 21*(1), 20–25.

Devitt, M. (1994). The methodology of naturalistic semantics. *Journal of Philosophy, 91*(10), 545–572.

Dittmann, M. (2003). Anger across the gender divide. *Monitor on Psychology, 34*(3), 52.

Doherty, C., Horowitz, J. M., & Dimock, M. (2014, January 23). Most see inequality growing, but partisans differ over solutions. Pew Research Center. Retrieved from http://www.people-press.org/2014/01/23/most-see-inequality-growing -but-partisans-differ-over-solutions/.

Drum, K. (2006, August 11). Nutpicking. *Washington Monthly*. Retrieved from https:// washingtonmonthly.com/2006/08/11/nutpicking/.

Duggan, M. (2001). More guns, more crime. *Journal of Political Economy, 109*(5), 1086–1114.

Ebenstein, D. (2013). *I hear you: Repair communication breakdowns, negotiate successfully, and build consensus . . . in three simple steps.* New York, NY: AMACOM.

Edmondson, A. C. (2003). Managing the risk of learning: Psychological safety in work teams. In M. A. West, D. Tjosvold, & K. G. Smith (Eds.), *International handbook of organizational teamwork and cooperative working* (pp. 255–275). Chichester, England: Wiley.

Edmondson, A. C., & Roloff, K. S. (2008). Overcoming barriers to collaboration: Psychological safety and learning in diverse teams. In E. Salas, G. F. Goodwin, & C. S. Burke (Eds.), *Team effectiveness in complex organizations: Cross-disciplinary perspectives and approaches* (pp. 183–208). New York, NY: Routledge.

Ekman, P. (2003). *Emotions revealed: Understanding faces and feelings.* London, England: Weidenfeld & Nicolson.

Ferguson, M. L. (2010). Choice feminism and the fear of politics. *Perspectives on Politics, 8*(1), 247–253.

Fernbach, P., Rogers, T., Fox, C. R., & Sloman, S. A. (2013). Political extremism is supported by an illusion of understanding. *Psychological Science, 24*(6), 939–946.

Festinger, L. (1957). *A theory of cognitive dissonance.* Stanford, CA: Stanford University Press.

FFRF. (2013, January 17). *Peter Boghossian—2012 National Convention* [Video File]. Retrieved from https://www.youtube.com/watch?v=9ARwO9jNyjA.

Fichte, J. G. (1970). *The science of knowledge: With the first and second introductions.* Trans. P. Heath & J. Lachs. Cambridge, England: Cambridge University Press. (Original work published 1794–1795)

Filipovic, J. (2016, November 8). The revenge of the white man. *Time*. Retrieved from http://time.com/4566304/donald-trump-revenge-of-the-white-man/.

Fisher, R., Ury, W. L., & Patton, B. (2011). *Getting to yes: Negotiating agreement without giving in.* New York, NY: Penguin.

Florida, R. (2017, April 26). If cities ruled the world. Citylab. Retrieved from https:// www.citylab.com/equity/2017/04/the-need-to-empower-cities/521904/.

Flynn, D., Nyhan, B., & Reifler, J. (2017). The nature and origins of misperceptions: Understanding false and unsupported beliefs about politics. *Political Psychology, 38*, 127–150.

Fodor, J. A. (1983). *The modularity of mind: An essay on faculty psychology.* Cambridge, MA: MIT Press.

Freethinkers of PSU. (2018, February 25). *James Damore at Portland State (2/17/18)* [Video File]. Retrieved from https://www.youtube.com/watch?v=VCrQ3EU8_PM.

Freud, S. (1991). *On metapsychology: The theory of psychoanalysis: "Beyond the pleasure principle," "The ego and the id," and other works.* Edited by A. Richards, translated by J. Strachey. Harmondsworth, England: Penguin. (Original work published 1936)

Friedersdorf, C. (2017, February 13). "Every racist I know voted for Donald Trump." *The Atlantic.* Retrieved from https://www.theatlantic.com/politics/archive/2017/02/every-racist-i-know-voted-for-donald-trump/516420/.

Gaertner, S. L., Dovidio, J. F., Nier, J. A., Ward, C. M., & Banker, B. S. (1999). Across cultural divides: The value of a superordinate identity. In D. A. Prentice & D. T. Miller (Eds.), *Cultural divides: Understanding and overcoming group conflict* (pp. 173–212). New York, NY: Russell Sage Foundation.

Galef, J. (2017, March 9). Why you think you're right, even when you're wrong. *Ideas.Ted.Com.* Retrieved from http://ideas.ted.com/why-you-think-youre-right-even-when-youre-wrong/?utm_campaign=social&utm_medium=referral&utm_source=facebook.com&utm_content=ideas-blog&utm_term=social-science.

Gattellari, M., Butow, P. N., Tattersall, M. H. N., Dunn, S. M., & MacLeod, C. A. (1999). Misunderstanding in cancer patients: Why shoot the messenger? *Annals of Oncology, 10*(1), 39–46.

Goulston, M. (2015). *Talking to "crazy": How to deal with the irrational and impossible people in your life.* New York, NY: AMACOM.

Graham, J., Nosek, B. A., & Haidt, J. (2012). The moral stereotypes of liberals and conservatives: Exaggeration of differences across the political spectrum. *PloS One, 7*(12), e50092.

Greene, J. (2013). *Moral tribes: Emotion, reason, and the gap between us and them.* New York, NY: Penguin.

Grubb, A. (2010). Modern day hostage (crisis) negotiation: The evolution of an art form within the policing arena. *Aggression and Violent Behavior, 15*(5), 341–348.

Habermas, J. (1985). *The theory of communicative action.* Vol. 2. Translated by J. Habermas & T. McCarthy. Boston, MA: Beacon Press.

Haidt, J. (2006). *The happiness hypothesis: Finding modern truth in ancient wisdom.* New York, NY: Basic Books.

Haidt, J. (2012). *The righteous mind: Why good people are divided by politics and religion.* New York, NY: Pantheon.

Haidt, J. (2016, November). *Can a divided America heal?* [Video file]. Retrieved from https://www.ted.com/talks/jonathan_haidt_can_a_divided_america_heal?autoplay=true.

Hammer, M. R. (2007). *Saving lives: The S.A.F.E. model for resolving hostage and crisis incidents.* Santa Barbara, CA: Praeger.

Harrington, N. (2013). Irrational beliefs and socio-political extremism. *Journal of Rational-Emotive & Cognitive-Behavior Therapy, 31*(3), 167–178.

Harris, S. (2004). *The end of faith: Religion, terror, and the future of reason.* New York, NY: W. W. Norton.

Harris, S. (2010). *The moral landscape: How science can determine human values.* New York, NY: Free Press.

Harris, S. (2017, January 27). #62—What is true? A conversation with Jordan B. Peterson [Podcast]. Retrieved from https://www.samharris.org/podcast/item /what-is-true.

Harris, S., & Nawaz, M. (2015). *Islam and the future of tolerance: A dialogue.* Cambridge, MA: Harvard University Press.

Harvard Second Generation Study. (2015). Study of adult development. Massachusetts General Hospital and Harvard Medical School. Retrieved from http://www .adultdevelopmentstudy.org/grantandglueckstudy.

Hegel, G. W. (2010). *The science of logic.* Translated by G. D. Giovanni. New York, NY: Cambridge University Press. (Original work published in three volumes 1812–1816)

Heinrichs, J. (2017). *Thank you for arguing: What Aristotle, Lincoln, and Homer Simpson can teach us about the art of persuasion.* New York, NY: Three Rivers Press.

Hess, A. (2017, February 28). How the trolls stole Washington. *New York Times Magazine.* Retrieved from https://www.nytimes.com/2017/02/28/magazine/how-the -trolls-stole-washington.html?_r=0.

Hogarth, R. M., & Einhorn, H. J. (1992). Order effects in belief updating: The belief-adjustment model. *Cognitive Psychology, 24*(1), 1–55.

Horowitz, E. (2013, August 23). Want to win a political debate? Try making a weaker argument. *Pacific Standard.* Retrieved from https://psmag.com/want-to-win-a -political-debate-try-making-a-weaker-argument-446f21de17a1#.42pi40gwr.

Hostage Negotiation: A Matter of Life and Death. (1987). Darby, PA: Diane Publishing Co.

Hubbard, L. R. (2007). *Scientology: The fundamentals of thought.* Commerce, CA: Bridge Publications.

Huczynski, A. (2004). *Influencing within organizations.* London, England: Routledge.

Ingram, M. (2017, February 1). Most Trump supporters don't trust the media anymore. *Fortune.* Retrieved from http://fortune.com/2017/02/01/trump-voters-media -trust/.

Iyer, R., Koleva, S., Graham, J., Ditto, P., & Haidt, J. (2012). Understanding libertarian morality: The psychological dispositions of self-identified libertarians. *PloS One, 7*(8), e42366.

Jain, S., Shapiro, S. L., Swanick, S., Roesch, S. C., Mills, P. J., Bell, I., & Schwartz, G. E. (2007). A randomized controlled trial of mindfulness meditation versus relaxation training: Effects on distress, positive states of mind, rumination, and distraction. *Annals of Behavioral Medicine, 33*(1), 11–21.

James Randi Educational Foundation. (2013, October 25). *Peter Boghossian— authenticity—TAM 2013* [Video File]. Retrieved from https://www.youtube.com /watch?v=OGaj4j_az98&t=3s.

Jarcho, J. M., Berkman, E. T., & Lieberman, M. D. (2010). The neural basis of rationalization: Cognitive dissonance reduction during decision-making. *Social Cognitive and Affective Neuroscience, 6*(4), 460–467.

Jennings, P. A., & Greenberg, M. T. (2009). The prosocial classroom: Teacher social and emotional competence in relation to student and classroom outcomes. *Review of Educational Research, 79*(1), 491–525.

Johnson, K. E., Thompson, J., Hall, J. A., & Meyer, C. (2018). Crisis (hostage) negotiators weigh in: The skills, behaviors, and qualities that characterize an expert crisis negotiator. *Police Practice and Research, 19*(5), 472–489.

Johnson-Laird, P. N., Girotto, V., & Legrenzi, P. (2004). Reasoning from inconsistency to consistency. *Psychological Review, 111*(3), 640–661.

Jones, D. A. (2004). Why Americans don't trust the media: A preliminary analysis. *Harvard International Journal of Press/Politics, 9*(2), 60–75.

Jost, J. T., Glaser, J., Kruglanski, A. W., & Sulloway, F. J. (2003). Political conservatism as motivated social cognition. *Psychological Bulletin, 129*(3), 339–375.

Kahneman, D. (2011). *Thinking, fast and slow.* New York, NY: Farrar, Straus & Giroux.

Kahneman, D., Slovic, P., & Tversky, A. (Eds.). (1982). *Judgment under uncertainty: Heuristics and biases.* Cambridge, England: Cambridge University Press.

Kaplan, J. T., Gimbel, S. I., & Harris, S. (2016, December 23). Neural correlates of maintaining one's political beliefs in the face of counterevidence. *Scientific Reports, 6,* art. no. 39589. Retrieved from https://www.nature.com/articles/srep39589.

Kaufmann, W. A. (2015). *The faith of a heretic.* 2nd ed. Princeton, NJ: Princeton University Press.

Kellin, B., & McMurtry, C. (2007). STEPS—structured tactical engagement process: A model for crisis negotiation. *Journal of Police Crisis Negotiations, 7*(2), 29–51.

Kelly, J. F., & Westerhoff, C. M. (2010). Does it matter how we refer to individuals with substance-related conditions? A randomized study of two commonly used terms. *International Journal of Drug Policy, 21*(3), 202–207.

Khazan, O. (2017, February 1). The simple psychological trick to political persuasion. *The Atlantic.* Retrieved from https://www.theatlantic.com/science/archive/2017/02/the-simple-psychological-trick-to-political-persuasion/515181/?utm_source=twb.

Killias, M. (1993). International correlations between gun ownership and rates of homicide and suicide. *CMAJ: Canadian Medical Association Journal, 148*(10), 1721–1725.

Kolbert, E. (2017, February 27). Why facts don't change our minds. *The New Yorker.* Retrieved from http://www.newyorker.com/magazine/2017/02/27/why-facts-dont-change-our-minds.

Koriat, A., Lichtenstein, S., & Fischhoff, B. (1980). Reasons for confidence. *Journal of Experimental Psychology: Human Learning and Memory, 6*(2), 107–118.

Kruger, J., & Dunning, D. (1999). Unskilled and unaware of it: How difficulties in recognizing one's own incompetence lead to inflated self-assessments. *Journal of Personality and Social Psychology, 77*(6), 1121–1134.

Kubany, E. S., Muraoka, M. Y., Bauer, G. B., & Richard, D. C. (1992). Verbalized anger and accusatory "you" messages as cues for anger and antagonism among adolescents. *Adolescence, 27*(107), 505–516.

Kuran, T. (1997). *Private truths, public lies: The social consequences of preference falsification.* Cambridge, MA: Harvard University Press.

Lakoff, G. (2010). *Moral politics: How liberals and conservatives think.* Chicago, IL: University of Chicago Press.

Lee, H. (1960). *To kill a mockingbird.* Philadelphia, PA: J. B. Lippincott.

Leonard, K., & Yorton, T. (2015). *Yes, and: How improvisation reverses "no, but" thinking and improves creativity and collaboration—lessons from the second city.* New York, NY: HarperCollins.

Lerner, J. S., & Tiedens, L. Z. (2006). Portrait of the angry decision maker: How appraisal tendencies shape anger's influence on cognition. *Journal of Behavioral Decision Making, 19*(2), 115–137.

Lewin, K. (1947). Group decision and social change. In T. Newcomb & E. Hartley (Eds.), *Readings in social psychology* (pp. 197–211). New York, NY: Holt, Rinehart & Winston.

Lewin, M. A. (1998). Kurt Lewin: His psychology and a daughter's recollections. In G. A. Kimble & M. Wertheimer (Eds.), *Portraits of pioneers in psychology* (Vol. III, pp. 105–120). Washington, DC: American Psychological Association.

Lindsay, J. (2015). *Everybody is wrong about god.* Durham, NC: Pitchstone Publishing.

Lindsay, J. (2016). *Life in light of death.* Durham, NC: Pitchstone Publishing.

Loftus, J. (2013). *The outsider test for faith: How to know which religion is true.* Amherst, NY: Prometheus Books.

Longsine, G., & Boghossian, P. (2012, September 27). Indignation is not righteous. *Skeptical Inquirer.* Retrieved from https://www.csicop.org/specialarticles/show/indignation_is_not_righteous.

Lowndes, L. (2003). *How to talk to anyone: 92 little tricks for big success in relationships.* New York, NY: McGraw-Hill.

Lukianoff, G., & Haidt, J. (2018). *The coddling of the American mind: How good intentions and bad ideas are setting up a generation for failure.* New York, NY: Penguin.

Magnabosco, A. (2016a, April 21). *Street Epistemology: Kari | Examining cardinal beliefs* [Video File]. Retrieved from https://www.youtube.com/watch?v=JnF6MenyiEQ.

Magnabosco, A. (2016b, December). *Street Epistemology quick-clip: Sam | Weighing the soul* [Video File]. Retrieved from https://www.youtube.com/watch?v=5IgZSYaazFc&feature=youtu.be.

Malhotra, D. (2016a, October 14). How to build an exit ramp for Trump supporters. *Harvard Business Review.* Retrieved from https://hbr.org/2016/10/how-to-build-an-exit-ramp-for-trump-supporters.

Malhotra, D. (2016b). *Negotiating the impossible: How to break deadlocks and resolve ugly conflicts (without money or muscle).* Oakland, CA: Berrett-Koehler.

Martí, L., Mollica, F., Piantadosi, S., & Kidd, C. (2018). Certainty is primarily determined by past performance during concept learning. *Open Mind, 2*(1), 47–60. https://doi.org/10.1162/opmi_a_00017

Masci, D. (2019, February 11). For Darwin Day, 6 facts about the evolution debate. *Fact Tank.* Pew Research Center. Accessed February 10, 2017. Retrieved from http://www.pewresearch.org/fact-tank/2017/02/10/darwin-day/.

Maybee, J. E. (2016, Winter). Hegel's dialectics. In *Stanford encyclopedia of philosophy*. Retrieved from https://plato.stanford.edu/entries/hegel-dialectics/.

Mbarki, M., Bentahar, J., & Moulin, B. (2008). A formal framework of conversational goals based on strategic reasoning. In *International conference on industrial, engineering and other applications of applied intelligent systems* (pp. 835–844). Berlin, Germany: Springer.

McMains, M., & Mullins, W. C. (2014). *Crisis negotiations: Managing critical incidents and hostage situations in law enforcement and corrections*. 5th ed. New York, NY: Routledge.

Michel, C. (2017, June 30). How liberal Portland became America's most politically violent city. *Politico*. Retrieved from http://www.politico.com/magazine/story/2017/06/30/how-liberal-portland-became-americas-most-politically-violent-city-215322.

Mill, J. S. (1859). *On liberty*. London, England: Longman, Roberts & Green.

Miller, L. (2005). Hostage negotiation: Psychological principles and practices. *International Journal of Emergency Mental Health, 7*(4), 277–298.

Mitchell, A., Matsa, K. E., Gottfried, J., & Kiley, J. (2014, October 21). Political polarization and media habits. Pew Research Center. Retrieved from http://www.journalism.org/2014/10/21/political-polarization-media-habits/.

Mullins, W. C. (2002). Advanced communication techniques for hostage negotiators. *Journal of Police Crisis Negotiations, 2*(1), 63–81.

Neiman, M. (2008). Motorcycle helmet laws: The facts, what can be done to jump-start helmet use, and ways to cap damages. *Journal of Health Care Law & Policy, 11*, 215–248.

Neumann, C. S., & Hare, R. D. (2008). Psychopathic traits in a large community sample: Links to violence, alcohol use, and intelligence. *Journal of Consulting and Clinical Psychology, 76*(5), 893–899.

Nichols, T. (2017). *The death of expertise: The campaign against established knowledge and why it matters*. New York, NY: Oxford University Press.

Norton, S. W. (2002). Economic growth and poverty: In search of trickle-down. *Cato Journal, 22*(2), 263–275.

Nyhan, B., & Reifler, J. (2010). When corrections fail: The persistence of political misperceptions. *Political Behavior, 32*(2), 303–330.

Nyhan, B., & Reifler, J. (2018, May 6). The roles of information deficits and identity threat in the prevalence of misperceptions. *Journal of Elections, Public Opinion and Parties*. Advance online publication. https://doi.org/10.1080/17457289.2018.1465061.

Nyhan, B., Reifler, J., & Ubel, P. A. (2013). The hazards of correcting myths about health care reform. *Medical Care, 51*(2), 127–132.

O'Reilly, C. A., & Chatman, J. (1986). Organizational commitment and psychological attachment: The effects of compliance, identification, and internalization on prosocial behavior. *Journal of Applied Psychology, 71*(3), 492–499.

Pallatroni, L. (Ed.). (2018). *Return to reason: The science of thought*. New York, NY: Scientific American Ebooks.

Parker, K. (2016, November 20). Fake news, media distrust and the threat to democracy. *Denver Post*. Retrieved from http://www.denverpost.com/2016/11/20/fake-news-media-distrust-and-the-threat-to-democracy/.

Parrott, W. G. (2001). *Emotions in social psychology: Essential readings*. New York, NY: Psychology Press.

Parsons, R. D., & Zhang, N. (2014). *Counseling theory: Guiding reflective practice*. Los Angeles, CA: SAGE Publications.

Pascal, B. (1958). *Pascal's pensées*. New York, NY: E. P. Dutton. Retrieved from https://www.gutenberg.org/files/18269/18269-h/18269-h.htm. (Original work published 1670)

Pascual, L., Rodrigues, P., & Gallardo-Pujol, D. (2013, September). How does morality work in the brain? A functional and structural perspective of moral behavior. *Frontiers in Integrative Neuroscience, 7*, art. no. 65. Retrieved from https://www.frontiersin.org/articles/10.3389/fnint.2013.00065/full.

Patton, B. M. (1998). Difficult conversations. *Dispute Resolution Magazine, 5*(4), 25–29.

Peters, M. (2015, December 24). Virtue signaling and other inane platitudes. *Boston Globe*. Retrieved from https://www.bostonglobe.com/ideas/2015/12/24/virtue-signaling-and-other-inane-platitudes/YrJRcvxYMofMcCfgORUcFO/story.html.

Phelps-Roper, M. (2017, February). *I grew up in the Westboro Baptist Church. Here's why I left* [Video File]. Retrieved from http://www.ted.com/talks/megan_phelps_roper_i_grew_up_in_the_westboro_baptist_church_here_s_why_i_left.

Pigeon chess. (2016, December 27). *RationalWiki*. Retrieved from http://rationalwiki.org/wiki/Pigeon_chess.

Pinker, S. (2008, January 13). The moral instinct. *New York Times Magazine*. Retrieved from http://www.nytimes.com/2008/01/13/magazine/13Psychology-t.html.

Plato. (1992). *Republic*. Translated by G. M. A. Grube. Indianapolis, IN: Hackett. (Original work published ca. 380 BCE)

Plato. (2006). *Plato's Meno*. Edited by D. Scott. Cambridge, England: Cambridge University Press. (Original work published ca. 380 BCE)

Pratkanis, A. R. (2000). Altercasting as an influence tactic. In D. J. Terry & M. A. Hogg (Eds.), *Attitudes, behaviour, and social context: The role of norms and group membership* (pp. 201–226). New York, NY: Psychology Press.

Rogers, C. R. (1975). Empathetic: An underappreciated way of being. *The Counseling Psychologist, 5*(2), 2–10.

Rogers, K. (2016, November 9). White women helped elect Donald Trump. *New York Times*. Retrieved from https://www.nytimes.com/2016/12/01/us/politics/white-women-helped-elect-donald-trump.html.

Rozenblit, L., & Keil, F. (2002). The misunderstood limits of folk science: An illusion of explanatory depth. *Cognitive Science, 26*(5), 521–562.

The RSA. (2012, August 15). *The truth about dishonesty—Dan Ariely* [Video File]. Retrieved from https://www.youtube.com/watch?v=ZGGxguJsirI.

Säde, R. (2015, October 6). *Peter Boghossian—Imagine No Religion 5, Islamism and doubt* [Video File]. Retrieved from https://www.youtube.com/watch?v =_I5-SUdBpaQ.

Sanders, E. P. (1993). *The historical figure of Jesus*. New York, NY: Penguin.

Schlottmann, A., & Anderson, N. H. (1995). Belief revision in children: Serial judgment in social cognition and decision-making domains. *Journal of Experimental Psychology: Learning, Memory, and Cognition, 21*(5), 1349–1364.

Seneca, L. A. (1995). *On anger*. In J. M. Cooper & J. F. Procopé (Eds.), *Seneca: Moral and political essays* (pp. 17–116). Cambridge, England: Cambridge Press. (Original work published 1st century CE)

Shelton, C. (2016, April). *Me, my mom and Scientology* [Video File]. Retrieved from https://www.youtube.com/playlist?list=PLGrPM1Pg2h713UyF8wjTT4L3tVqId 7KKW.

Shermer, M. (2012). *The believing brain: From ghosts and gods to politics and conspiracies—how we construct beliefs and reinforce them as truths*. New York, NY: St. Martin's Press.

Shklovskiĭ, I., & Sagan, C. (1966). *Intelligent life in the universe*. San Francisco, CA: Holden-Day.

Singer, P. (1983). *Hegel*. Oxford, England: Oxford University Press.

Sophocles. (trans. 1891). *The Antigone of Sophocles*. Edited with introduction and notes by Sir Richard Jebb. Cambridge, England: Cambridge University Press. (At the Perseus Project)

Spitzer, S. P., & Volk, B. A. (1971). Altercasting the difficult. *American Journal of Nursing, 71*(4), 732–738.

Starr, E. (1954, November 3). Groucho Marx quotation. In Inside TV [column]. *Greensboro (NC) Record.*

Steenburgh, T., & Ahearne, M. (2012, July–August). Motivating salespeople: What really works. *Harvard Business Review.* Retrieved from https://hbr.org/2012/07 /motivating-salespeople-what-really-works.

Stenger, V., Lindsay, J., & Boghossian, P. (2015, May 8). Physicists are philosophers, too. *Scientific American.* Retrieved from: https://www.scientificamerican.com /article/physicists-are-philosophers-too/.

Stone, D., Patton, B., & Heen, S. (2010). *Difficult conversations: How to discuss what matters most*. New York, NY: Penguin.

Swift, A. (2016, September 14). Americans' trust in mass media sinks to new low. Gallup. Retrieved from http://www.gallup.com/poll/195542/americans-trust-mass -media-sinks-new-low.aspx.

Swinburne, R. (1990). The limits of explanation: The limits of explanation [*sic*]. *Royal Institute of Philosophy Supplements, 27,* 177–193.

Swinburne, R. (1997). *Simplicity as evidence of truth*. Milwaukee, WI: Marquette University Press.

Swinburne, R. (2001). *Epistemic justification*. Oxford, England: Oxford University Press.

Swinburne, R. (2005). *Faith and reason.* Oxford, England: Oxford University Press.

Swoyer, C. (1982). True for. In M. Krausz & J. W. Meiland (Eds.), *Relativism: Cognitive and moral* (pp. 84–108). Notre Dame, IN: Notre Dame University Press.

Tajfel, H. (Ed.). (2010). *Social identity and intergroup relations* (European Studies in Social Psychology). 7th ed. Cambridge, England: Cambridge University Press.

Tappin, B. M., van der Leer, L., & McKay, R. T. (2017). The heart trumps the head: Desirability bias in political belief revision. *Journal of Experimental Psychology: General, 146*(8), 1143–1149.

Tavernise, S. (2017, February 18). Are liberals helping Trump? *New York Times.* Retrieved from https://www.nytimes.com/2017/02/18/opinion/sunday/are-liberals-helping-trump.html.

Tavris, C., & Aronson, E. (2008). *Mistakes were made (but not by me): Why we justify foolish beliefs, bad decisions, and hurtful acts.* Boston, MA: Houghton Mifflin Harcourt.

Taylor, P. J., & Donohue, W. (2006). Hostage negotiation opens up. In K. Schneider & C. Honeyman (Eds.), *The negotiator's fieldbook: The desk reference for the experienced negotiator* (pp. 667–674). Washington, DC: American Bar Association.

TED. (2014, June 27). *How to speak so that people want to listen | Julian Treasure* [Video File]. June. Retrieved from https://www.youtube.com/watch?v=eIho2S0ZahI.

TedX Talks. (2013, November 14). *The illusion of understanding: Phil Fernbach at TEDxGoldenGatePark* [Video file]. Retrieved from https://www.youtube.com/watch?v=2SlbsnaSNNM.

Thompson, D. (2016, September 16). Why do Americans distrust the media? *The Atlantic.* Retrieved from https://www.theatlantic.com/business/archive/2016/09/why-do-americans-distrust-the-media/500252/.

Thomson, J. A., & Aukofer, C. (2011). *Why we believe in God(s): A concise guide to the science of faith.* Durham, NC: Pitchstone Publishing.

Top town crier to be crowned as Hebden Bridge hits 500. (2010, August 20). *BBC News.* Retrieved from http://news.bbc.co.uk/local/bradford/hi/people_and_places/arts_and_culture/newsid_8931000/8931369.stm.

Trepagnier, B. (2017). *Silent racism: How well-meaning white people perpetuate the racial divide.* New York, NY: Routledge.

Trevors, G. J., Muis, K. R., Pekrun, R., Sinatra, G. M., & Winne, P. H. (2016). Identity and epistemic emotions during knowledge revision: A potential account for the backfire effect. *Discourse Processes, 53*(5–6), 339–370.

Trotter, C. (1995). *The supervision of offenders—what works? A study undertaken in community based corrections, Victoria: First & second reports to the Australian Criminology Research Council, 1995.* Melbourne, Australia: Social Work Department, Monash University.

TubeCactus. (2011, June 4). *That's soulless!—What evidence or logical argument can you provide?* [Video File]. Extract from Is the Foundation of Morality Natural or Supernatural? debate, William Lane Craig vs. Sam Harris, University of Notre Dame, Notre Dame, Indiana. Retrieved from https://www.youtube.com/watch?v=pk7jHJRSzhM&t=1m10s.

Turner, M. M., Banas, J. A., Rains, S. A., Jang, S., Moore, J. L., & Morrison, D. (2010). The effects of altercasting and counterattitudinal behavior on compliance: A lost letter technique investigation. *Communication Reports, 23*(1), 1–13.

2Civility. (2015). *Skill practice: Inquire, paraphrase, acknowledge* [Unpublished manuscript]. Illinois Supreme Court Commission on Professionalism.

Tyson, A., & Maniam, S. (2016). Behind Trump's victory: Divisions by race, gender, education. Pew Research Center. Retrieved from http://www.pewresearch.org/fact-tank/2016/11/09/behind-trumps-victory-divisions-by-race-gender-education/.

Uchtdorf, D. F. (2013, October). Come, join with us. Presentation at The Church of Jesus Christ of Latter-Day Saints, General Conference. Retrieved from https://www.lds.org/general-conference/2013/10/come-join-with-us?lang=eng.

Ury, W. (1992). *Getting past no: Negotiating with difficult people.* London, England: Random Century.

Vlemincx, E., Van Diest, I., & Van den Bergh, O. (2016). A sigh of relief or a sigh to relieve: The psychological and physiological relief effect of deep breaths. *Physiology & Behavior, 165,* 127–135.

Voss, C., & Raz, T. (2016). *Never split the difference: Negotiating as if your life depended on it.* New York, NY: HarperCollins.

Vuori, T. (2013). How closed groups can drift away from reality: The story of a knocked-out Kiai master. *International Journal of Society Systems Science, 5*(2), 192–206.

Waldron, V. R., Cegala, D. J., Sharkey, W. F., & Teboul, B. (1990). Cognitive and tactical dimensions of conversational goal management. *Journal of Language and Social Psychology, 9*(1–2), 101–118.

Ware, B. (2012). *The top five regrets of the dying: A life transformed by the dearly departing.* Carlsbad, CA: Hay House.

Waters, N. L., & Hans, V. P. (2009, September 1). A jury of one: Opinion formation, conformity, and dissent on juries. Cornell Law Faculty Publications. Retrieved from http://scholarship.law.cornell.edu/cgi/viewcontent.cgi?article=1113&context=lsrp_papers.

Weinstein, E., & Deutschberger, P. (1963). Some dimensions of altercasting. *Sociometry, 26*(4), 454–466.

Weitzenhoffer, S. D. (2005, March 16). Problem with debating creationists [review of *Evolution vs. creationism: An introduction* by Eugenie C. Scott]. Retrieved from https://www.amazon.com/review/R2367M3BJ05M82.

Wells, S. (2015). Hostage negotiation and communication skills in a terrorist environment. In J. Pearse (Ed.), *Investigating terrorism: Current political, legal and psychological issues* (pp. 144–166). Chichester, England: Wiley-Blackwell.

West, M. A., Tjosvold, D., & Smith, K. G. (Eds.). (2003). *International handbook of organizational teamwork and cooperative working.* Chichester, England: Wiley.

West, M. A., Tjosvold, D., & Smith, K. G. (Eds.). (2005). *The essentials of teamworking: International perspectives.* Chichester, England: Wiley.

Whitney, E., & Taylor, J. (2017, May 24). On eve of election, Montana GOP candidate charged with assault on reporter. *NPR.* Retrieved from http://www

.npr.org/2017/05/24/529862697/republican-s-altercation-with-reporter-shakes-up -montana-race-on-eve-of-voting.

Willer, R. (2016, September). *How to have better political conversations* [Video File]. TED. Retrieved from https://www.ted.com/talks/robb_willer_how_to _have_better_political_conversations.

Wilson, R. A., & Keil, F. (1998). The shadows and shallows of explanation. *Minds and Machines, 8*(1), 137–159.

Wynn, C. M., & Wiggins, A. W. (2016). *Quantum leaps in the wrong direction: Where real science ends . . . and pseudoscience begins*. New York, NY: Oxford University Press.

Zukar. (2017, February 1). *All that we share—ZUKAR Translations EN, FR, NL, PO, GE* [Video File]. Retrieved from https://www.youtube.com/watch?v=i1AjvFjVXUg.

Zunin, L. M., & Zunin, N. (1972). *Contact: The first four minutes*. New York, NY: Ballantine Books.

Index

talking points, 61
template for speaking with an
ideologue, 160–161,
168–170
thanking conversation partner for
conversation, 31
that, using, 81
theology, implausible
disconfirmation conditions and,
111–112
thinking
learning how people think,
65–66
using scales to help partner
reverse their, 88
thought experiment, 142
Time magazine, 55
tribalism, extremism fostering,
47–48
triggers
anger, 96, 127–128
negative emotion, 96
trolls, blocking, 28
Trump, Donald
blame for election of,
54–55
conversation about media bias
against, 104–105, 109
identifying contributions in
election of, 56–57
tweets appealing to foundational
moral values, 171
trust
balkanization of, 147
building rapport and, 16–17
sharing values and, 46–47
truth, finding in conversation, 11
truths of logic and mathematics are
not disconfirmable, 106
Twitter, 52, 54, 171

understanding
letting friends be wrong and
one's own, 75
listening and, 19–20
shifting from winning to, 12–13
universe, conversation about genesis
of, 64–65
Unread Library Effect fallacy,
36–38, 39, 89
altercasting and, 142
venting and, 138
Ury, William, 121–122, 126
us, using, 81

vaccine deniers, belief and, 101,
169
values
conversing with an ideologue
and, 159–160
conversing with an ideologue and
changing subject to, 162–164,
168
conversing with an ideologue and
inviting deeper conversation
about, 164–165, 168–169
sharing, 46–47
Veggie Tales (television program),
73
venting, 132, 135–139
helping someone vent,
138–139
vignettes, conversation
on affirmative action, 1–3
on belief in God, 14–16, 97
on belief women should be
stoned for adultery, 35–36
on bias in media, 104–105
on intervention to change sport
fan's team preference, 28–30
on meaning of justice, 58–59